T0319828

ARCHITECTS OF AUSTERITY

ARCHITECTS OF AUSTERITY

International Finance and
the Politics of Growth

Aaron Major

Stanford University Press
Stanford, California

Stanford University Press
Stanford, California

Library of Congress Cataloging-in-Publication Data

Major, Aaron, author.
  Architects of austerity: international finance and the politics of growth/ Aaron Major.
    pages cm
  Includes bibliographical references and index.
  ISBN 978-0-8047-8834-2 (cloth: alk. paper)
1. Economic policy. 2. International finance. 3. Economic development—Government policy. 4. Government spending policy. 5. Neoliberalism. 6. Economic history—1945– I. Title.
  HD87.M26 2014
  332'.042—dc23

                                        2013042054

ISBN 978-0-8047-9073-4 (electronic)

Typeset by Thompson Type in 10/14 Minion

Contents

Illustrations

Acknowledgments

THIS BOOK HAS BEEN A LONG TIME COMING. MANY PEOPLE HAVE helped along the way, and those who shaped the early versions of this project are no less important than those who have helped see this book to completion. The John F. Kennedy Library Foundation and the Lyndon Baines Johnson Library Foundation both provided research grants that allowed me to spend time poring through their archival materials. I also received a grant from the Research Foundation of the State University of New York that allowed me to travel to visit the archives of the OECD in Paris. The staff and archivists at the Kennedy and Johnson Presidential Libraries, the OECD archives, and the archives of the Federal Reserve Bank of New York gave invaluable research assistance. My colleagues Richard Lachmann and Beth Popp-Berman were very generous with their time, reading and commenting on multiple versions of multiple chapters. Fred Block and Monica Prasad were generous enough to read a first draft of the full manuscript and helped me to see what this book was really about. Stephen Hellman gave great feedback on an early draft of the chapter on Italy, and Steven Major helped separate the wheat from the chaff in the concluding chapter. Aaron Passell, Noah McClain, and Monika Krause have long been sounding boards for my ideas about, and frustrations with, this project. Manuscripts do not become books without the assistance and enthusiasm of editors, and Margo Fleming has given both in spades. Finally, Rebekah has unfailingly given me her best even when I have been at my worst.

1 Crisis, Austerity, and the Neoliberal Turn

POLITICS IN THE POSTFINANCIAL CRISIS WORLD IS DEFINED BY the struggle over austerity. Like a tidal wave that follows an earthquake, financial collapse in U.S. credit markets in the fall of 2008 quickly spread to Western Europe, toppling economies that, once the dust settled, were revealed to also have been built on their own shaky financial footings. Even as the causes of the crisis are still being sorted out, government officials have faced a clear and distinct choice about how to move forward. On the one hand, they could walk the path carved by historical experience by trying to jump-start the stalled economic engine through the kind of strong fiscal measures that their predecessors had taken when faced with the Great Depression nearly a century ago. On the other hand, they could continue to walk the path of neoliberalism by restoring order and balance in credit markets and government finances in the hopes that market forces would work their magic. With few exceptions they chose the second path, simultaneously back-stopping credit markets with emergency credit to the banking system and, even more dramatically, forcing state ledgers back into balance through harsh austerity measures.

First to stride down the path of austerity was the Papandreou government in Greece, which, despite having been elected on a left-wing and antineoliberal platform in 2009, called for €500 million in cuts to public spending, reduced holiday pay for pensioners and civil servants, and increased taxes on consumption in the spring of 2010. Later that year Prime Minister Brian

Cowan unveiled the National Recovery Plan for Ireland built on €10 billion in cuts to public spending, a 12 percent reduction in the minimum wage, reductions in public sector pay, and increased taxes on consumer goods. Over the course of the year the governments of Portugal, France, Spain, and Romania proposed similar measures.

In the United States, 2010 saw the rise of the political star of the Tea Party, a far-right political movement whose primary purpose is to shrink the size of the federal debt through massive cuts in public spending and social services. Yet, even though this particular movement can be written off as extremist, there is no denying that the commitment to austerity has seeped so deeply into the American political mainstream that politicians no longer debate whether budgets need to be balanced but only how to do it: raise taxes or reduce spending.

When governments announce the need for austerity measures, they couch them in the language of "shared sacrifice." Everyone needs to tighten his or her belt; politics must give way to sound economic principles. According to the proponents of austerity, these policies are the rational response, indeed the only reasonable response, that, however painful they may be, can repair a broken economy. Yet, despite the ubiquity of this narrative it takes only a moment's critical reflection to see that austerity, like the broader neoliberalization of the economy of which it is a part, is neither neutral nor natural. Beneath the universalist language of shared sacrifice lies a deeply political project.[1] In the eyes of the proponents of austerity, if government debt is too high it is because irresponsible politicians have used the national treasury to cater to every whim and desire of a caterwauling public—handing out unrealistic pensions, being too generous with health care, and letting public sector workers take home bloated paychecks. If the financial system has become nothing more than a flimsy house of cards, it is because consumers have failed to learn to live within their means and are too obsessed with big homes, fancy cars, and a continuous display of conspicuous consumption. To be sure, those who champion austerity will also level some blame for the nation's financial woes on lax banking regulation and overzealous financial speculators. But, at its core, the push for austerity is grounded in the belief that the reason that we all got into this mess and cannot pull ourselves out of it is because irresponsible, profligate governments, workers, and consumers have gotten in the way of the kind of healthy, sustained economic growth that comes only from robust private investment in a context of monetary and price stability. If governments overspend they threaten the economy with ruinous inflation, and if they dare to tax corporations they stifle the business owner's will to invest. If workers and consumers push for a greater share of the economic pie, they threaten corporate profitability and competitiveness in the global economy.

While frustrating for those who would prefer that a different path be taken, the strength of the movement for austerity may seem unsurprising; just further confirmation of the continuing power of neoliberal social forces to shape policy agendas. Yet, when looked at in historical perspective, the fact that neoliberalism and its austere approach to crisis management have been so resilient in the face of the global economic collapse of 2008 is very puzzling. Crises tend to break up existing political coalitions and shake core understandings about the workings of the economy.[2] Or at least they did in the past. Classical liberalism and its laissez-faire ethos gave way to Keynesianism in the face of the global depression of the 1920s and 1930s. For decades the Keynesian principle that activist state intervention in the economy and a more equitable distribution of economic rewards was the surest way to sustained prosperity dominated both the field of professional economics and the halls of economic policy making but then fell victim to the global crisis of capitalism of the 1970s. Knocked from its high perch, Keynesianism was replaced by a new incarnation of economic liberalism, what scholars now generally recognize as a "neoliberal" turn in economic thinking and economic policy making. Like the economic paradigms that came before it, neoliberal doctrine has spread from its foundational centers and become truly global.

So although the proponents of austerity claim that their approach to economic management is simply common sense, it is in fact a fairly recent common sense or, to be more precise, the rebirth of an old common sense once discredited nearly a century ago. History shows that there is nothing natural or necessary about austerity. It is but one of several possible means of dealing with an economic crisis. Why, then, have the politics and policies of austerity proven so resilient in the face of crisis?

In this book, I address this question by drawing a historical arc from the era of the classical liberal era of the nineteenth-century gold standard to the politics of neoliberal austerity of the early twenty-first century. As already suggested, although economic liberalism has always had its adherents, it has not always been dominant. Rather, from the beginning of the First World War through the Bretton Woods era the proponents of economic liberalism struggled against the forces of "embedded liberalism"—the belief that economic policy need not be subsumed to the abstract, universal "laws" of the market but rather needs to be attuned to the cultural and political particularities of each national context.

Within this larger story I conduct a detailed empirical investigation of the politics of growth in the 1960s, a critical turning point when nascent efforts to liberalize the global economy provoked an ongoing debate between policy makers across North America and Western Europe over the question of international economic cooperation in an increasingly interdependent global economy and, in doing so, raised larger questions about whether global capitalism would be defined by classical liberalism or embedded liberalism.

The core argument of this book is that the rise, consolidation, and resiliency of neoliberalism and its economics of austerity are tied to international institutional configurations that increase the influence of financial interests over national economic governments. Specifically, I show that the rise and consolidation of austerity as a dominant economic policy paradigm can be traced to what I am calling the transnationalization of monetary authority. By this I mean the increasing cohesion of state financial officials—central bankers and finance ministers—in transnational and intergovernmental institutions and the increased centrality of these institutions in the regulation of the international financial system.

Beginning in the early 1960s, central banks took on more and more of the responsibility of managing an international monetary system that had outgrown the institutional arrangements put in place at Bretton Woods in 1944. National governments saddled with substantial balance of payments deficits and facing speculative attacks against their currencies grew increasingly dependent on financing arranged through central banks who have long clung to the core tenets of classical liberalism: currency stability, fiscal balance, and economic restraint. It was from this position of having acquired significant international monetary power that state monetary authorities were able to coerce social democratic governments back onto the path of austerity.

These transformations in the institutions of international monetary management that took place in the 1960s were only the beginning of what would ultimately become a deeper consolidation of a transnational monetary authority in the post–Bretton Woods era. After the collapse of Bretton Woods in the 1970s, the management of an increasingly crisis-prone global economy was consolidated in the international forums of monetary cooperation: the Bank for International Settlements, the International Monetary Fund (IMF), the meetings of the Group of Ten, and, in the 1990s, the European Central Bank. In the era of classical liberalism, individual financial institutions were strong, but true international cooperation was elusive. In the neoliberal era, the monetary authorities are cohesive and coordinated as organizational histories and national allegiances have given way to a shared understanding of the state's proper role in the economy. The strength and resiliency of neoliberalism and its policies of austerity derive from this international institutional architecture that has elevated the transnational monetary authority to the heights of global economic management.

This book builds on scholarship on the rise, diffusion, and resiliency of neoliberalism in two ways. First, while many scholars have already discussed the role that collapse of Bretton Woods played in the emergence of neoliberalism, much of this research focuses on the way in which the collapse of Bretton Woods unleashed private transnational capital to wreak havoc on a deregulated global economy, opening space for free market ideas.[3] I take a different tack, arguing that the resilience of austerity is rooted in the public, or quasi-public, institutions and organizations that have been center stage in the process of reregulating the post–Bretton Woods international monetary system under a "new international financial architecture." While this term is most often used to describe the vast and expanding system of international organizations regulating global finance, I argue that three aspects in particular have been critical for the institutionalization of neoliberalism and austerity as dominant economic policy paradigms: the widespread diffusion of inflation-targeting regimes, which brings with it increased policy-making autonomy for central banks; the adoption of market-based capital regulation through reserve requirements; and the consolidation of monetary authorities' role as lender of last resort during times of global financial crisis.

Second, in addition to offering new insight into the contemporary politics of austerity, the transnationalization of monetary authority is very much part of the story of the financialization of modern capitalism or the growing weight of financial activity and financial-sector profits in the process of capital accumulation. Krippner's recent account of the financialization of the U.S. economy shows how domestic politics, specifically the way in which state elites "stumbled on" finance as a solution to the deep economic crises of the 1970s and 1980s, laid the political and economic groundwork for the thorough financialization of economic activity that took hold in the 1990s and 2000s.[4] While not denying the importance of these domestic factors, this book links these domestic developments to international institutional transformations that have supported and legitimated domestic processes of financialization.

Historical Lessons, Historical Antecedents: From Social Democracy to Austerity in the 1960s

This book addresses the global politics of the present through a historical investigation of the relationship between international monetary power and national economic policy making in North America and Western Europe in the late postwar period. In the first decade following the end of the Second World War, most North American and Western European countries pursued a moderate-to-conservative path to economic growth. In Western Europe, center-right political parties held off the socialists' and communists' demands for higher wages, nationalization of industry, and high levels of public spending. Instead, center-right governments channeled economic resources into private and public capital investment with the goal of becoming competitive in international export markets. Similarly, in the United States the Eisenhower administration followed a very moderate program of countercyclical Keynesianism, maintaining a very slow, but stable, rate of economic growth while keeping a watchful eye for any signs of price inflation that could not only hurt the trade balance but, even more importantly, weaken the international value of the dollar, the currency on which the postwar international monetary system rested.

By the early 1960s it appeared that this era of economic conservatism was coming to a close as liberal and social democratic political parties returned to power. Such was the case in three countries that form the core of this book's empirical analysis: the United States, the United Kingdom, and Italy. In the first two cases, liberal parties—the Democrats in 1961 in the United States and Labour in 1964 in the United Kingdom—returned to the head of government after having been out of power for close to a decade. In Italy the ruling party, the Christian Democratic Party, remained in power but drastically shifted its political strategy in 1962 by trying to forge for the first time in the postwar period a center-left governing coalition with the socialists.

Despite a domestic political climate conducive to left-wing economic policies, in all three cases social democratic projects were never fully realized or were quickly abandoned, replaced instead with policies that restricted, or even reduced, the share of national income going to workers and consumers. In the United States, the Kennedy growth agenda took the form of "commercial Keynesianism," which was based primarily on supporting private investment through tax cuts for private corporations and the wealthy and which, in turn, required keeping government spending—particularly government social spending—in check. In the United Kingdom and Italy austerity measures were more direct and, because they came directly on the heels of real social democratic policy reforms, felt more harsh: Budgets were cut, access to consumer credit was sharply restricted, and wages were placed under control.

These sudden breaks with social democracy and the turn to austerity are the historical puzzles that drive the analysis in this book. As in other cases when governments have abandoned national growth experiments for market-friendly austerity measures, the pressure to do so in each case came from international political and economic forces. Specifically, when the United States, the United Kingdom, and Italy abandoned their growth experiments, they did so while facing massive balance of payments deficits that were generating financial market speculation against their currency. For many scholars of international political economy, this fact points to a rather simple explanation for the shift from social democracy to austerity: Facing a severe balance of payments deficit, national governments did what they necessarily had to do, constricting domestic economic growth to restore the balance of trade and reduce the outflow of foreign investment capital.

Yet it is precisely the obviousness of austerity as the appropriate policy response to a severe balance of payments deficit in these cases that demands critical investigation. Only in retrospect do the policy responses of state officials to a payments crisis, or any other crisis for that matter, appear obvious. Observing policy makers when these decisions were actually made, or at least observing them through the records of their decisions that they left behind, it becomes immediately clear that the causes, severity, and solutions to payments crises were clouded in uncertainty and deeply contested.

Today, researchers and policy officials are used to having immediate access to accurate data on a whole range of economic phenomenon. This was not the case in the 1960s. National accounting, let alone balance of payments accounting, was still new. Countries varied widely in how they defined, and calculated, their individual balance of payments positions.[5] Moreover, even if these technical problems could have been solved and agreement could have been reached that a balance of payments deficit had become so severe as to warrant some kind of compensating domestic policy response, the questions of how to respond, and which policy instruments to use, were open to a wide range of views and interpretations. The balance of payments measures the economic transactions of a national economy with the rest of the world. It includes typical economic transactions like trade in goods and services, foreign direct investment, and financial investment. It also includes transactions such as military spending, foreign aid, and even the spending of tourists traveling overseas. To have a balance of payments surplus means that you export more than you import, you attract more capital and investment then you send out, you are host to a foreign military base, or perhaps you attract more foreign tourists. As such, the balance of payments is an index measure of a broad range of economic activities, each of which is determined by its own set of complex factors. Trade imbalances, for example, could arise from divergent exchange rates, divergent cost structures, or divergent regulatory policies. An imbalance, in other words, does not prescribe an obvious policy response.

What makes the cases of the American, British, and Italian turns to austerity so striking, when viewed side-by-side, is that despite all of these ways in which payments deficits lend themselves to a variety of possible policy responses, despite the fact that the underlying causes behind each country's payments deficit were different, and despite the fact that each was trying to manage its payments deficit while simultaneously grappling with domestic economic and political issues that were quite different in each case, the specific content of each response is nearly identical.

The question that needs to be answered, therefore, is: Why was austerity selected as the common policy response to a balance of payments crisis in each of these three cases? The answer lies with the weakening of the international institutions formed at Bretton Woods and the increasing international monetary power of the international financial community that resulted. Although the United States, the United Kingdom, and Italy all arrived at their payments deficits through different means, by the early 1960s resolving payments deficits, or at least papering over them to prevent a speculative run against their currencies, increasingly came to depend on the active cooperation of foreign central banks and other monetary authorities.

In the 1960s the Bretton Woods settlement came under severe stress. The governments in North America and Western Europe worked together to slowly but surely dismantle restrictions against transnational capital movements, resulting in a significant increase in short-term, cross-border capital transactions that overwhelmed the existing mechanisms of balance of payments financing. The critical consequence of this change in the global economic landscape was the creation of new mechanisms of balance of payments financing that elevated national monetary authorities into the heights of the international monetary system.

One of the central arguments of this book is that it was not payments deficits per se that triggered a turn to austerity but rather the evolving mechanisms of balance of payments financing that made warding off currency speculation dependent on the cooperation and confidence of private international investors and public financial authorities. These shifting structures of dependency provided the mechanism through which foreign central banks and other international financial organizations could significantly influence the direction of other governments' national economic agendas. The policy ideas of the international financial community—policies of austerity—were selected into national policy-making processes not because they were technically superior but because they were given real, material weight by the changing distribution of international monetary power.

The prevailing accounts of the rise of neoliberalism and its global diffusion have yet to appreciate these important transformations in the institutional mechanisms of balance of payments financing, the effect that they had on restructuring relationships of financial dependency, and the way in which this empowered state monetary authorities to push for a return to a classically liberal understanding of the relationship between international economic stability and national economic growth. Investigating economic policy making during the critical decade of the 1960s thus provides analytical leverage on the broader question of how, and when, international monetary power shapes the course of national economic policy making.

Austerity and Neoliberalism

The concept of neoliberalism is most often used to describe an interrelated bundle of ideas and policies that mark a fundamental shift in modern democratic societies in the state's relationship to the economy and to its citizens. Neoliberalism is grounded in neoclassical economic theory, specifically neoclassical theory's belief in the technical and moral superiority of free markets over state direction of the economy. The growing weight of this market-centered ideological framework manifests as a transformation in state policies that, in general, have tried to undo the social-democratic Keynesian compromises of the postwar era through a process of marketization—lifting regulations on economic activity, privatizing state-owned enterprises, and subjecting more and more of the social world to the discipline of market competition.[6]

As many scholars have pointed out, however, the ideological purity of neo-liberal discourse is frequently muddied when put into practice. For one, the core tenets of neoliberalism are applied very inconsistently. Policy makers and policy experts who espouse neoliberalism's free-market ideology are loathe to spend public funds on social welfare protections for the poor but easily fund the expansion of militaries, police forces, and prisons.[7] They laud the market's wisdom in choosing economic winners and losers except, as recent experience shows, when market failures threaten large corporations. The disconnect between ideology and practice bespeaks a fundamental tension that underlies the resurgence of economic liberalism as the dominant paradigm framing policy discussions.

As Karl Polanyi famously argued, economic liberalism is premised on a utopian fiction, one that believes that markets can successfully organize society when, in reality, markets tend toward disorganization and social disruption. Because of this, Polanyi argues, periods of history when market fundamentalism reigned supreme have also been those that generated new forms of protection against the market.[8] Contemporary scholars have built on Polanyi's insight to draw attention to the "neoliberal dilemma" that comes with the return of economic liberal ideology. The crux of this dilemma is that those who believe in the supremacy of free markets have had to find ways to be interventionists when markets fail while at the same time appearing to give full sway to the free market.[9] It is through the repeated resolution of this dilemma that policy making takes on a distinctly neoliberal form. The outcomes may not be purely free market but are shaped by the pervasiveness of market ideology.

While drawing attention to the neoliberal dilemma helps to make sense of the contradictions between the purity of market ideology and the reality of policy outcomes over the last thirty years, by itself it does not explain why the resolution of the neoliberal dilemma falls so frequently on the shoulders of society's least advantaged. It does not, in other words, explain the distributional patterns of neoliberalism. To understand the distributional patterns of actually existing neoliberalism we need to recognize that economic liberalism is more than just a free-market ideology; it is an ideology that couples market stability to economic austerity.

As Mark Blyth has recently pointed out, austerity is premised on a particular understanding of market failure, namely that markets fail when private business confidence is low. If business owners are not confident about the future, then they will not invest, and if they do not invest, then factories remain idle and workers sit unhired. What drains business owners of their confidence in the economy? According to the economic liberals, classic or neo, confidence is lost when governments overspend and "crowd out" private investment or when workers demand too much and cut too deeply into profits. Restoring confidence requires austerity, a specific kind of economic deflation that targets these threats to confidence.[10]

It would be a mistake, however, to see austerity as simply the concrete policy measures that state officials derive from the broader tenets of free market ideology. Austerity has its roots in specific economic interests, not just in a specific set of ideas. More than any other segment of the broader business community, those whose fortunes are tied to financial investments have the most to lose from not only the monetary and debt crises that follow economic depression but also the price inflation that typically accompanies a booming economy. In times of crisis the threat to finance is obvious as assets plummet in value or disappear altogether. In times of boom, the threat to finance is subtler as price inflation erodes the real value of old debts and thus reduces anticipated rates of return.

The history of austerity thus runs deeper than the history of a particular idea. It is the history of the rise, fall, and reemergence of finance. In the era of classical liberalism, nations lurched through periods of growth and forced deflation as central banks opened and closed the valves of credit according to the needs of international monetary stability. In the postwar era, many national governments relegated their financial institutions to a secondary, subservient role as a new commitment to growth competed with the old orthodoxy. In the neoliberal era, finance is resurgent.[11] Although the images of Ronald Reagan and Margaret Thatcher will perhaps forever be associated with the turn to neoliberalism, it was the deregulation of global capital markets and the elevation of state monetary authorities to the heights of the management of international capitalism that were critical for restoring and preserving finance's capacity to push national governments back onto the straight and narrow of austerity.

Explaining the Global Spread of Neoliberalism

It is not enough to document a correlation between eras of finance and eras of austerity. To be convincing this account needs mechanisms, clear channels through which the interests of finance are able to influence decision making about economic policy. A significant body of scholarship has emerged that tries to understand the domestic-level political, economic, and cultural factors determine if, when, and how countries make the neoliberal turn.[12] This is an important, and lively, scholarly discussion, and there can be no doubt that domestic factors matter for understanding contemporary political developments in very important ways. But neoliberalism has now become a truly global phenomenon as more and more countries, particularly through the 1980s and 1990s, have fallen under the sway of economic liberalism and its politics of austerity. To link the turn to neoliberalism to the resurgence of finance, it is necessary to show how the international financial community has been able to effect the global diffusion of its ideas and interests.

Recognizing neoliberalism's global context presents a real challenge for social scientists, and that is to locate where, in the complex fabric of globalization, the ideas and practices that make up neoliberalism are located and, even more difficult, to identify the mechanisms through which the global overwhelms the national. A useful starting point is a recent review of the social science scholarship on the international diffusion of neoliberal policies conducted by Beth Simmons, Frank Dobbin, and Geoffrey Garrett. They identify three major mechanisms that scholars see as driving processes of international policy diffusion: economic competition, ideological emulation, and coercion.[13]

Competition and Economic Liberalism
Economic competition is now, more than ever, global in scale. Strong national industries in poor countries may suddenly look very weak when forced to compete with the industrial giants of the rich countries; investment capital, critical for growth, is now in the hands of foreign investors who, quite literally, have a whole world of opportunities before them. Faced with such pressures, the story goes, national governments entered into a "race to the bottom," pushing through neoliberal reforms in an effort to remain competitive in the new global environment.[14]

This is an elegant and very plausible story that seems to go a long way toward explaining the neoliberal turn in the 1970s and 1980s, as these were the decades when accelerating levels of foreign trade and foreign investment brought more and more industries, and more and more countries, into direct economic competition. However, while no one denies the reality of accelerating economic globalization, it is not at all clear that the effects of these structural changes necessarily point toward shrinking states and freer markets. Indeed, just as the globalization debate was beginning in the late 1970s, political scientist David Cameron gave an alternative narrative about the consequences of global competition for national economic and social welfare policy making.

Cameron's very counterintuitive argument was that economic globalization would not weaken the national state, but rather it would strengthen it. This, he hypothesized, would happen as domestic social forces demanded that their national governments protect them from global market forces. Cameron tested this theory on a fairly small set of Western countries, and his research painted a much more complex picture than either the "race to the bottom" or his own theory suggested. Cameron could find no direct relationship between a country's openness to the global economy and the size of the national government. Too many domestic institutional variables—including the composition of national industry and the structure of labor organizations—mediated the effects of global economic forces.[15]

This debate about the effects of global economic competition has sparked a whole generation of scholarship seeking to tease out the finer points of the economic globalization story. Cameron's study, after all, was limited to a small number of relatively advanced OECD countries over the period from 1960 to 1975 when, many would argue, the forces of economic globalization had yet to be fully unleashed. And yet, after more than thirty years of work, with studies incorporating data from over a hundred countries across decades of time, Cameron's general finding remains largely intact. By themselves, global economic forces have an ambiguous and sometimes contradictory effect on the size, composition, and practices of national governments. Economic globalization does not necessarily strengthen the welfare state, but neither does it eviscerate it.[16]

Emulation in the World Polity

Given the empirical limitations of macrostructural arguments about the impact of economic globalization on national states, other scholars have turned their focus to the policy-making process itself and the way in which policy makers come to understand complex economic phenomena and devise concrete policy responses. A few decades ago, political scientist Hugh Heclo raised an important point about the policy-making process. He noted that state officials are elected or appointed to positions that force them to confront a wide range of economic, political, and social problems, and yet they often do not have the technical training or expertise needed to make sense of these problems, let alone craft feasible policy solutions to them. Policy making is thus conducted under conditions of deep uncertainty: Before policy can be crafted, policy makers must first come to some understanding as to the nature and origins of whatever problem or crisis they are trying to contend with and then develop a cause-and-effect understanding of how it might be solved by different policy options.[17]

Building on this critical insight, many scholars are now arguing that social scientists need to pay attention to the technical ideas and normative frameworks that provide concrete solutions to esoteric, and complex, economic problems. As Mark Blyth wryly observed, the global economy does not come with an instruction sheet.[18] What matters from a policy-making standpoint are not flows of goods and capital per se but rather the way in which ideas and norms construct particular understandings of economic dynamics and their consequences. It is not enough for economic growth to slow, for debts to accumulate, for trade balances to shift into the red; the near-infinite arrays of data that one can use to describe economic processes must be interpreted, given meaning, and constructed as the result of some causal force.[19] Scholars who focus on the social construction of economic phenomena thus understand neoliberalism as resulting from a transformation in the basic ideas and principles that guide policy makers' understandings of the causes of economic growth and decline and the appropriate policy response to each.

By focusing on ideas, researchers have turned attention back to the policy makers themselves and the process of policy making in a complex and uncertain environment. At the same time, however, few people would deny that ideas matter in the policy-making process. The challenge is to be able to explain why some ideas "win out" and become the road maps that policy makers use to navigate complex economic problems, while also explaining why competing ideas fail to gain traction in the policy-making process.

The International Diffusion of Ideas

This question becomes all the more difficult to answer given that, while policy making itself takes place within national political institutions, the construction of frameworks and ideas about the economy increasingly takes place at the international level. Technical ideas—whether they are ideas about the costs and benefits of atomic power, the state of global warming, or the appropriate fiscal policy tools to combat a recession—are generated by experts, and expertise is increasingly housed within what Peter Haas has called transnational "epistemic communities." These communities of experts can give weight to particular policy ideas by imbuing them with a sense of global, expert opinion. Drawing on this concept, John Ikenberry has argued that the postwar international economic settlements took the form that they did because the ideas of the American and British economists who handled the negotiations were able to draw on the growing global legitimacy of Keynesian economic principles.[20]

Ideas can also be spread by powerful international organizations. In the case of the neoliberal turn of the 1980s, scholars generally recognize that the International Monetary Fund was a powerful force pushing economic liberalism, both in its efforts to get countries to adopt more market-friendly economic policies and in its efforts to show that countries are better off if they remove restrictions on cross-border capital movements across the globe.[21]

According to one prominent strand of research in the sociology of international policy diffusion, the ideas that take hold within epistemic communities and international organizations spread globally because these communities and organizations are part of a larger "world polity."[22] Since the end of the Second World War, international social interaction has become increasingly formalized into transnational networks of governmental and nongovernmental organizations and increasingly dense ties between these organizations and national governments. These processes provide the institutional context within which national governments attempt to cooperate and coordinate their activities. This context is defined, in part, by sets of internationally shared norms, principles, and values that assert a "logic of appropriateness" on state officials, situating them within roles and expectations that support some policies and practices while delegitimizing others. Understood in this way, governments do not act simply on some internally generated national interest but rather within a circumscribed realm of acceptable behaviors that helps states define and understand their own interests and shapes the way that governments understand their position in a broader international community. The formal organization of the world polity thus institutionalizes a set of cultural pressures on national governments that leads to the diffusion of those ideas and frameworks seen as legitimate by this densely interconnected global community.[23]

While this is a powerful explanation of the diffusion of neoliberalism, the world polity framework has some significant limitations. For one, it does really answer the question of how some economic ideas come to prominence and others do not as much as it refocuses scholarly attention on global, as opposed to national, processes. For example, scholars now generally recognize that the International Monetary Fund has been a powerful force for diffusing the idea that countries are better off if they remove restrictions on cross-border capital movements across the globe. But how did this idea come to be so entrenched within the IMF? Jeffrey Chwieroth shows that during the 1980s and 1990s there was real debate between those who advocated for a gradual turn to liberalization and those who pushed for a "big bang"—that is, rapid and thorough removal of capital controls. By the mid-1990s the big-bang approach had eclipsed the gradualist position.

Why? In his discussion of the battle of ideas between the gradualists and the big-bangers, Chwieroth leaves us with no explanation as to how it was that the big-bang advocates pulled this off. Rather, he shows both sides using similar ideational strategies—engaging in normative entrepreneurship, selectively using data, and framing interpretations of economic conditions—but, apparently, with greater or lesser degrees of success.[24]

In addition, world polity theory tends to envision "the global" as a single, homogeneous world cultural space containing the norms and ideas that national governments try to emulate. It is a two-dimensional network of international organizations and nation states, each holding equal weight in the composition of the larger structure. Yet, through carefully tracing the structure of the world polity, Jason Beckfield finds that rather than being nonhierarchical and flat, the world polity is much more uneven, with some organizations and some nation-states carrying much more weight in the broader institutional structure than others. Beckfield's work describes a world polity that is lumpy and fragmented, with nodes of concentrated power and influence within the larger network. This point is critical for, as Nitsan Chorev observes, different international institutional arrangements have the effect of increasing the political influence of some while decreasing the influence of others.[25]

World polity theory tends to have a blind spot when it comes to these issues because it tends to presume that there is a single world culture consisting of global consensus around norms and ideas that are willingly accepted by policy makers at the national level.[26] In contrast, a recurring theme in this book is that international organizations are not just spaces where consensus is forged but are also arenas of conflict where the fundamental premises of international economic cooperation are debated. While the victors may couch their ideas and interests in the universalizing language of a "global consensus," these are still the ideas and values of particular social actors.

Coercion and Policy Diffusion

The preceding points highlight the importance of keeping power and politics central to the story of the international diffusion of neoliberalism and economic austerity, which neither competition nor emulation models of international policy diffusion leave much space for. Coercion models of policy diffusion seek to identify the specific interests that drive the spread of neoliberalism and austerity and the mechanisms by which they do so.

Showing that diffusion takes place through coercion poses difficult analytical and methodological challenges. First, a theory of coercion must be able to clearly specify coercive actors and their interests. Who is it that has power, and how do we know what their interests are? In addition, a theory of coercion must be able to identify the mechanism through which coercion takes place. While coercion is often based in some kind of resource asymmetry, such asymmetries are not, by themselves, sufficient for coercion. Rather, to be plausible, a theory of coercion must be able to show how resource asymmetries turn into power asymmetries; this, in turn, requires identifying the channels through which resources can be used to advance interests.[27]

While there are multiple cultural and material resources that can be leveraged to influence decision making around economic policy, this book focuses on how the capacity for coercion emerges from the international distribution of monetary power. "International monetary power," as David Andrews defines it, "exists when one state's behavior changes because of its monetary relationship with another state."[28] Political and economic actors acquire international monetary power when they can do at least one of two things: manipulate the use, or value, of a nation's currency or, second, control the mechanisms of international credit disbursement.

At first glance, this definition is suggestive of a competition model of policy diffusion whereby governments try to put in place policies that they think will be most likely to attract foreign investment. The critical difference is that, in competition models of diffusion, financial dependency functions more or less automatically. In the coercion model, the effect that international monetary power has on the policy-making process will depend on the varying capacities of political and economic actors to make claims to holding international monetary power; to articulate how they can exercise that power to hurt, or help, policy makers' interests; and what can be done to secure their cooperation. In other words, international monetary power must be made apparent through discursive interaction among social actors, but discourses of power must also be grounded in material relationships of dependency if they are going to have any weight.[29]

Most scholarly accounts of cases of international coercion since the end of World War II vest international monetary power with two principle actors: the United States and the International Monetary Fund. The international monetary power of the United States is a function of the "exorbitant privilege" of having the dollar at the center of the global economy.[30] In the postwar era, the dollar was institutionalized as the anchor of the entire postwar international monetary system at Bretton Woods in 1944, which gave successive U.S. governments the ability to impose the economic policies that they saw fit on other countries. Sometimes this leverage was used explicitly, as when officials in the Truman administration doled out Marshall Plan aid in exchange for cooperation in liberalizing trade flows and squashing militant leftists. More often, however, it was a more subtle mechanism, as other governments were forced to carefully monitor their macroeconomic policies to ensure that they did not disturb the exchange rate, while U.S. governments could pursue whatever policies that they wished and simply "export" any negative consequences.[31]

Even after the collapse of the Bretton Woods system in the early 1970s, some scholars have suggested that the international monetary power of the United States has not been diminished, as the dollar remains central to the global economy. This, along with U.S. military might, has driven the spread of neoliberalism under what is known as the "Washington Consensus"—an agreement among U.S. political elites and private economic actors that their interests would be better served the more the global economy is deregulated, privatized, and subjected to the logic of the market.[32]

For others, the coercive push toward neoliberalism has largely come from the International Monetary Fund, which has leveraged countries' dependency on financial assistance to force them into harsh structural adjustment programs. Created as part of the Bretton Woods settlements to provide short-term financing for countries facing balance of payments deficits, the International Monetary Fund began to attach various conditions to its loans in the early 1950s. For the most part, these conditions have stipulated specific policy measures that the borrowing government needed to undertake to, from the Fund's perspective, effect a "structural adjustment" to correct whatever economic imbalance caused the country to need to borrow in the first place.

Although the Fund was originally designed to maintain currency stability among its forty-four member countries, after the collapse of Bretton Woods the Fund's role expanded. Nearly every country in the world is now a member of the International Monetary Fund, and, with only a few exceptions, nearly every country in the world has at one point or another relied on the Fund for financing a balance of payments deficit or currency reserve crisis. In addition, the number of conditions that the Fund has attached to its loans has grown substantially. No longer limited to adjustments to broad macroeconomic policies, like total government expenditures or interest rates, the Fund's conditions now touch even the minutest details of economic and regulatory policy.[33]

These narratives of coercion, which stress the role of the United States and the International Monetary Fund, tell an important part of the story of how the global distribution of financial resources and structures of international monetary power have caused the spread of neoliberalism around the world. But they are only part of the story. One of the central arguments of this book is that, by focusing so heavily on the United States and the International Monetary Fund, scholars have in fact missed critical developments in the structures of international monetary power. As discussed in the preceding pages, one of the central goals of this book is to show how international monetary power began to shift away from the International Monetary Fund and the United States in the early 1960s and became increasingly vested primarily in central banks, but also other state monetary bodies, which have become organized along international lines. While the United States, along with other national states, and the International Monetary Fund continue to play an important role of the international economy, it is the transnational monetary authority that has most consistently pushed for an international economic order built on the tenets of economic liberalism and a global commitment to monetary stability.

Plan of the Book

Chapter 2 develops an historical account of the emergence of an international architecture of austerity in the late Bretton Woods era. The scholarship on the postwar international monetary system tends to overlook, or at least downplay, the institutional transformations that the Bretton Woods system underwent over the postwar period, yet these transformations were critical for redistributing international monetary power toward central banks and finance ministries. North American and Western European governments reduced controls over capital movements in the late 1950s that, in turn, exposed real weaknesses and limitations to the extant mechanisms for dealing with balance of payments imbalances and speculative attacks on national currencies. Into these institutional gaps stepped the state monetary authorities, which developed a dense network of cooperative arrangements to try to manage the exchange markets. As a result of these institutional transformations, national governments became financially dependent on active cooperation from central banks to protect their currencies from speculative attacks from the private financial community. These institutional innovations supported the diffusion of austerity by redistributing international monetary power into an emergent transnational monetary authority that could be used to shape the economic policies of national governments.

In addition to being a critical period of international institutional change, the era of the late 1950s and early 1960s was a critical period of debate within the international organizations of international economic governance. As Chapter 3 shows, these debates centered on the question of what the appropriate relationship between economic growth and balance of payments equilibrium should be in an increasingly liberal global economic environment. This chapter complicates the widely accepted view that the postwar international monetary system was defined by "embedded liberalism"—the belief that national economic growth needed to take priority over international monetary stability. This chapter shows how embedded liberal ideas had to fight for space against the orthodoxy of classical liberalism within key intergovernmental organizations of postwar international economic management.

Chapter 4 picks up the discussion from the previous chapter by showing how intergovernmental organizations like the OECD and the Bank for International Settlements put their ideas into practice in their discussions of Italian political and economic developments in the late postwar period. The central finding of this chapter is that, although the international community often expressed concern about the low rates of growth and high rate of unemployment in the country, these concerns were primarily motivated by fairly orthodox views about balance of payments adjustment. The international community did not encourage growth and full employment for their own sakes, as the embedded liberalism thesis would expect, but rather were encouraged or, even more tellingly, discouraged, insofar as they would help to correct for international payments imbalances.

Having traced the main dynamics unfolding in the Bretton Woods system in the late postwar period, the next three chapters look at how international monetary power was mobilized against national governments seeking an alternative, sometimes social-democratic path to growth and international stability. Chapter 5 takes the story to the United Kingdom and the global politics surrounding the Labour government's domestic economic agenda from 1964 to 1967. Returning to power after more than a decade of Conservative rule, and backed by strong popular support, Harold Wilson's Labour government promised a new social democratic model of economic growth and a defense of the pound sterling but was unable to make good on either. The pound sterling was devalued in 1967, but what was even more disappointing for Labour's supporters was that, in 1968, the party that had promised more jobs and more spending on social programs imposed what one historian has called the most austere budget in postwar history. This chapter shows how Labour's dependency on short-term financing of its payments deficits gave the international critics of Labour's economic plan leverage to compel the Wilson government to impose austerity measures.

Chapter 6 begins the case study of the global constraints on U.S. economic policy making in the 1960s by focusing on a brief, but critical, moment when, in the beginning of the decade, the Kennedy administration attempted to carve out a new growth strategy for the American economy. While the contrast between Kennedy's social democratic rhetoric and the more conservative reality of his economic policies is most often attributed to the constraints of domestic politics and the influence of a small coterie of staff policy experts, this chapter shows how the Kennedy administration was forced to compromise key aspects of its economic agenda due to the same balance of payments financing pressures that the Labour government face. This chapter pays particular attention to the debate over American monetary policy. Whereas the Kennedy administration believed that easy money was a necessary component to its tax-cut led growth program, the international community wanted to see a tighter monetary policy to stem the outflow of short-term speculative capital from the United States. A close study of these debates, in how they unfolded in both international and domestic institutions, shows the growing financial dependency of the United States on the international community to manage its payments deficit and, most critically, how the international community mobilized this newfound monetary power through the language of confidence and crisis to exert its policy preferences on reluctant American officials.

Chapter 7 explores the complexities of international monetary power in the late postwar period by looking at the rise and fall of the Great Society, which was followed shortly by the demise of the Bretton Woods system. While the international community became concerned about the high rate of American economic growth in 1966 and 1967, the Johnson administration resisted calls to slow the economy and even introduced new expansionary policies. The reason for this is that the United States had registered a couple of strong years of balance of payments surpluses in the middle of the decade and had been able to pay back many of its international debts. In addition, with the deepening crisis over the sterling, the health of the system as a whole increasingly depended on American financing of British deficits. This, however, was a short-lived respite from international pressure, and by the end of 1967 the administration was in the position of having to mobilize the specter of international financial crisis against congressional liberals and conservatives who resisted fiscal measures to slow the American economy. This finding highlights that it was not balance of payments deficits per se that put an end to national growth experiments but rather the ability of foreign monetary authorities to leverage financial dependency.

Chapter 8 returns to the larger questions that inform this book, specifically: What does this study of the politics of the 1960s tell us about the politics of austerity today? This chapter picks up the story of international institutional change that was the focus of Chapter 2 and carries it forward into the present. While much of the scholarship on international economic change from the 1970s forward focuses on the process of financial market liberalization, this chapter focuses on the evolution of global economic governance, highlighting three developments that have elevated monetary authority's role in managing the global economy: the assault on inflation in the 1970s and the spread of inflation targeting regimes, the construction of a bank-centered regulatory system for capital, and the performance of "lender of last resort" functions in times of crisis.

2 The Architects of Austerity

THE LATE 1950S AND THE 1960S WERE A CRITICAL PERIOD OF transformation in the structure of the Bretton Woods international monetary system, as North American and Western European governments reduced controls over capital movements in the late 1950s that, in turn, exposed real weaknesses and limitations to the extant mechanisms for dealing with balance of payments imbalances and speculative attacks on national currencies. Into these institutional gaps stepped the state monetary authorities, which developed a dense network of cooperative arrangements to try to manage foreign exchange markets that were increasingly vulnerable to private currency speculation.

To appreciate the significance of this development, it is necessary to situate the late Bretton Woods era within a longer historical trajectory comprised of two interrelated stories. The first is a story of emerging conflict between the economic policy ideas of the financial community, including state central banks, and national governments over whether monetary stability or economic growth and social welfare should be given priority in the policy-making process. It is conflict, in other words, between classical liberalism and embedded liberalism. The second is a story of institutional change at two levels: increasing levels of inter–central bank cooperation after World War I and the elevation of central banks to a prominent role in the management of the international monetary system after World War II. These processes redistributed international monetary power, placing it in the hands of the monetary authorities, who leveraged their position in the international monetary system to push the cause of classical liberalism.

The Embedded Liberal Vision

In the summer of 1942, John Maynard Keynes finally got his hands on the U.S. Treasury Department's plans for a postwar international monetary order. Though the fighting still raged across Europe and the Pacific, the Allied governments believed that victory would be had and so were already thinking about the process of postwar reconstruction. For the better part of a year, Keynes had been working tirelessly on his own plans for a new international monetary system, the centerpiece of which was his idea that a new institution, an International Clearing Union, would oversee and manage the settling of international payments accounts. Keynes's vision was quite radical because it essentially called on national governments to turn control over the creation and allocation of foreign reserves to an independent, international body.

Over the years Keynes had managed to overcome his most vocal critics in the British Treasury and had mollified the concerns of the War Cabinet's Reconstruction Committee, but moving forward ultimately depended on the United States. Across the Atlantic Keynes's counterpart in the U.S. Treasury department, Harry Dexter White, had also been working on the issue of postwar international monetary reconstruction. Keynes's reaction on reading the summary of White's plan in July at his home in Tilton was ambiguous to say the least. In a letter to Frederick Philips in H. M. Treasury, Keynes wrote: "I have also been making a study of the Harry White Document. Seldom have I been simultaneously so much bored and so much interested."[1] Keynes found White's presentation dull and laborious and the technical details of the plan impracticable. At the same time, however, Keynes was encouraged by the general spirit of the plan and by the underlying vision that White seemed to have for a postwar global economy. Like Keynes, White argued that the management of international money needed to be vested in a truly international body that could both settle international accounts and provide financing to countries running severe payments deficits.

Why was the international management of money so critical to both Keynes's and White's visions? On the one hand, both Keynes and White believed that the restoration of a liberal global economy, one where goods and capital flowed between nations, was necessary not only for the general level of prosperity but, perhaps even more important, to prevent the kind nationalistic and regionalistic fracturing that preceded the two world wars. On the other hand, previous periods of global economic liberalism had been built on the rigid structure of the gold standard, which compelled governments running balance of payments deficits to deflate their economies. Under the gold standard, transnational capital flows were greatly increased as stable, and fixed, exchange rates combined with the stabilization of domestic prices greatly reduced the potential risk of currency devaluations, which could destroy the value of foreign investments. Although the benefits of this system for the worldwide expansion of economic growth were lauded by many, Keynes argued that unrestricted flows of international credit placed undue burdens on national governments to adjust their economic policies in line with the need to maintain their currency's gold exchange rate.

Because the quantity of international reserves that could be used to finance payments imbalances was limited to the world supply of gold, governments facing a balance of payments deficit were compelled to raise domestic interest rates to restore payments equilibrium. Higher interest rates made it more attractive for domestic investors to keep their money at home and attracted foreign investment. In addition, higher interest rates slowed the economy, increasing unemployment, which, in turn, placed downward pressure on wages. This, in theory, would improve the trade balance by both reducing imports and making exports more competitively priced. Countries running a payments surplus, however, felt no similar compulsion to make domestic economic adjustments for international reasons. The result was that the gold standard operated with a "deflationary class bias."[2]

By freeing the international monetary system from the strictures of gold, Keynes and White hoped to decouple global economic liberalism from domestic economic austerity. This is why the international management of money was key. Rather than settling payments accounts bilaterally, an international body could manage surpluses and deficits across the system as a whole. Even more critically, in both Keynes's and White's plans this international body would also serve as a kind of bank for governments facing balance of payments deficits, providing them with ample credit to settle their international accounts so that they would not have to deplete their reserves or deflate their economies while they sought out long-term solutions to their payments deficit.

In the end, neither Keynes nor White saw their plans implemented in full, though their thinking clearly influenced the shape of the postwar international monetary order. Instead of Keynes's radical International Clearing Union, or White's more modest but still very ambitious plan for an international central bank, the delegates who met at the Bretton Woods conference in 1944 agreed to the creation of the International Monetary Fund, which had a much more limited pool of financial resources that it could lend to deficit countries and which only gave countries the explicit right to use capital controls but did not require them to do so.[3]

Despite these compromises, most scholars of the postwar international monetary system have followed John G. Ruggie's assessment that, although Keynes and White may have failed in their attempt to build a radically new international monetary system, they were nevertheless successful in imbuing postwar global capitalism with the essential core of their visions, what Ruggie terms "embedded liberalism." Concretely, this meant that the process of postwar global economic integration and liberalization was deeply embedded within a set of formal rules and informal commitments that privileged national economic policy-making autonomy over international monetary stability.[4] Postwar embedded liberalism rested on two foundations, one institutional and the other ideological.

In his influential interpretation of the Bretton Woods order, Eric Helleiner stresses the importance of the institutional transformations that were part of Bretton Woods settlements. According to Helleiner, the International Monetary Fund represented a profound success for the "embedded liberals" like White and Keynes, who wanted to protect the national welfare state from private financial capital. True, the International Monetary Fund was a more limited organization than what Keynes and White had envisioned, but the fact that the Fund's articles of agreement contained clear language on the benefits of capital controls meant that international financial interests would be subordinated to the interests of national governments.[5] With the international monetary power of private transnational capital sufficiently weakened, state officials could afford to be, as Sean O'Riain has put it, "Janus-faced" with respect to their international and domestic economic commitments: meeting international economic commitments without having to touch the levers of domestic economic management, thus allowing political officials to expand the welfare state and redistribute the fruits of economic growth to the working class and poor even when international economic conditions would suggest otherwise.[6]

Ruggie's own account of embedded liberalism stresses its ideological foundations, the commitment shared by the national governments of North America and Western Europe that protecting a government's economic growth policies should take priority over international monetary stability, particularly if those policies were framed around the goal of achieving full employment. This powerful, if informal, normative framework shored up the cause of embedded liberalism against the somewhat weak formal commitments around regulating capital flows and, even more critically, against the fracturing of the Bretton Woods institutions in the 1960s and 1970s.

Forces for Austerity

Ruggie's account of the embedded liberal compromise invokes an image of a widely shared normative framework privileging full employment and economic growth over international monetary stability, but in reality the postwar international order was defined by a deep-seated conflict between embedded liberals and those who spoke in terms of a gold standardesque classical liberalism that prioritized international monetary stability over domestic economic growth. Though these debates over core economic principles can be traced to a multitude of individual voices, the most significant sites of classical liberalism in the postwar period were central banks and the national governments of some Western European countries who were following a growth model built on the tenets of economic liberalism.

The "Barbarous Logic" of Monetary Management

One of the most striking, but rarely commented on, features of both Keynes's and White's plans for the postwar international monetary system is that both men believed that public financial institutions, specifically central banks, would actively support the embedded liberal agenda once liberated from the "rules of the game" that had been imposed on them by the gold standard. Both Keynes's proposal for an International Clearing Union and White's original plan for an international banking facility placed enormous power and responsibility for the international monetary system in the hands of the central banks. White believed that placing vast financial resources in the hands of an international central bank would give the cause of embedded liberalism a powerful weapon as member nations could be coerced into adopting full employment economic policies.[7] In Keynes's case, he believed that having balance of payments financing distributed through a central bank–managed Clearing Union would depoliticize international monetary management as technocratic civil servants carried out the monetary operations needed to achieve the full employment goals set by the national government.[8]

This shared faith in public financial authorities to carry out the embedded liberal agenda belies an important point about how both Keynes and White understood the problem of international monetary power. Both believed that managing the problem of international monetary power was really about managing *private* financial actors; state monetary authorities had been subject to the rules and pressures imposed by the international circulation of speculative capital and an overly restrictive fixed exchange rate system. Unfortunately, both Keynes and White erred in this assessment. They vastly overstated the degree to which the monetary authorities' hands had been tied by the "rules of the game" during the gold standard era and thus failed to appreciate the active role that they had played in enforcing the deflationary bias of the classical gold standard.[9]

In the nineteenth century, borrowers from international capital markets were mostly national governments with little access to domestic capital seeking to finance investments in infrastructure—particularly railroads. Between 1840 and 1910 the number of miles of laid railroad track around the world increased over 100 times, much of which was financed through government borrowing, making railroad bonds the largest outlet for long-term portfolio investment in foreign countries.[10] Because such loans went to national governments directly—or, in the cases where they went to private firms, were backed by government guarantee—foreign lenders faced little risk of outright default. They did, however, face the risk of currency devaluation. Loans made out in another country's currency could suddenly become devalued if inflation in the borrowing country triggered an alignment of exchange rates. The borrower would pay back the amount owed in their national currency, but the value of that currency to the lender would be much less in terms of their own currency, thus reducing the profitability of the loan.

The spread of the gold standard significantly reduced the currency risks associated with long-term foreign lending. For countries looking for overseas investors, adhering to the gold standard provided a kind of "Good Housekeeping Seal of Approval" on their fiscal and monetary policies, increasing international lenders' confidence that their investments would not be devalued through inflation and exchange rate fluctuations. This created a financial win-win on both sides of the ledger. For lenders, this meant that the high rates of return on foreign loans could be had with much less risk; for borrowers, this meant being able to acquire loans at lower rates of interest.[11]

Combined with the fact that foreign investment was backed by government guarantee, the gold standard dramatically decreased the riskiness of long-term foreign lending, so much so that lenders could effectively treat them as short-term investments. If the lending bank ever faced a liquidity crunch, their holdings in foreign railroad bonds and other long-term foreign investments could easily be sold for cash before their stated date of maturity. Thus, by increasing the safety of long-term foreign investments, the gold standard effectively allowed banks to increase the short-term assets in their portfolios, which gave them more flexibility in how they managed their investments, facilitating the expansion of banking and other financial activity.[12]

What is important to recognize is that the gold standard was maintained by the explicit commitment on the part of national governments and their financial agencies to prioritize exchange rate stability over full employment, not the automatic functioning of some disembodied "rules of the game."[13] National governments were not forced into austerity by the gold standard, but they willingly imposed economic austerity to tap into the growing volume of international credit. While these policies imposed real costs on the poor and the working class, the political and ideological conditions of the time made this a fairly minor constraint. As Karl Polanyi eloquently described it, this was the era when "economic liberalism burst forth as a crusading passion, and *laissez-faire* became a militant creed." The gold standard supported the laissez-faire doctrine by providing ideological cover for government policies that favored international banking profits over domestic welfare. Central banks in particular could claim to need to follow the "rules of the game" as a way of avoiding direct political agitation against their policies.[14]

This harmony of interests between national governments and their central banks fell into discord as a result of World War I. During the war, many national governments suspended gold convertibility and took control of monetary policy to finance wartime spending. When the war ended, central bankers hoped that national governments would dramatically reduce levels of spending and public debt so that they could return to the gold standard at prewar exchange rates. The Bank of England was particularly eager to see this happen. Still holding onto substantial currency reserves, the Bank wanted to quickly restore the international credit system that had been so lucrative in the prewar years. The central banks of the continental European countries, including France, Italy, and Belgium, shared the Bank of England's goal, as did the U.S. Federal Reserve Bank, which believed that restoration of a gold standard would ensure that private American bankers' wartime loans to Europe were not decimated by currency devaluation.[15]

Standing in the way of a return to monetary orthodoxy was a new "social democratic moment," a period when the radical political economy of Karl Marx was embodied in increasingly powerful left-wing political parties whose platforms were built on a fundamental skepticism of capitalism as a just, or even viable, economic system.[16] Writing about the Bank of England during this period, Gary Burn observes that the Bank's push for a return to gold was driven as much by a desire to restrain the forces of social democracy as by a belief in its economic soundness:

> Because the war, and its aftermath, had unleashed dangerous democratic forces to challenge the status quo, a return to gold would provide a value-free rationale, one based on unquestionable economic logic, with which to block such expectations, keep the City free of any future government interference and ensure a return to the pre-war social and political order.[17]

The push for a return to the gold standard became part of a broader effort of restraining the influence of increasingly popular left-wing social forces and restoring the economic policies conducive to financial profitability. In this effort, central banks were fairly successful, if only for a short period. While some countries did go back on gold in the interwar period, the global economic depression that unfolded in the late 1920s and early 1930s, followed closely by the outbreak of World War II, once again broke the link with gold.

While unable to put the world economy back on gold in the long term, the new spirit of international central bank cooperation to restore the gold standard proved to be one of the most significant developments in this period. In the era of the classical gold standard, cooperation between central banks had been sporadic, marked by periodic episodes of bilateral efforts to protect the gold standard followed by periods of acrimony as each national central bank fought to protect its piece of the global credit pie.[18] After World War I, however, cooperation became more widespread and sustained. The foundations for this cooperation had been laid during the war itself as the Bank of

England, Bank of France, Bank of Italy, and U.S. Federal Reserve Bank in-stitutionalized a set of cooperative arrangements to help each other manage their international payments.

After the war, central banks came together to deal with the interrelated issues of war reparations, currency stabilization, and the restoration of the international monetary system. Through the 1920s, central banks and private banks arranged stabilization loans, participated on the Reparations Commis-sion, and, through 1929, worked seriously at institutionalizing these coop-erative efforts by forming the Bank for International Settlements. While the issue of reparations dominated this work, these new international arrange-ments and organizations served as a foundation for a collective push for both a return to gold and the independence of central banks from the national government.[19]

Classical Liberalism after World War II

Coming out of World War II, central bankers, and the cause of monetary or-thodoxy, were squarely on the defensive. After more than ten years of eco-nomic depression and war-induced privation, the most pressing concerns of European and North American governments were reducing unemployment and raising living standards, not returning price stability or balanced bud-gets.[20] The working class had become a political force to be reckoned with in the early twentieth century and increasingly drew inspiration, and sup-port, from the socialist and communist left, adding a radical tenor to their demands. In addition, the diffusion of Keynesian economic theory gave intel-lectual support to the idea that unemployment was best dealt with through active government intervention.[21] Faced with the economic and political dan-gers of depression, many national governments after World War II broke with the orthodoxy of economic liberalism and attempted to bring the left into a new "embedded liberal" economic policy paradigm.

As already discussed, in forging the embedded liberal compromise, the power and influence of state monetary authorities was sharply curtailed. In some cases, as in Italy and Germany, the power of the central bank was strengthened at the war's end, supported by conservative political coalitions that pursued aggressive deflationary policies. In other countries, however, center-left and socialist political parties rightly saw independent central banks as a threat to their policy agendas and thus took over many of their central banks' powers with respect to managing money and credit and placed institutional constraints on their autonomy. In the United States, the Treasury Department took control over monetary policy from the Federal Reserve and pushed interest rates artificially low to help reduce the cost of the government's wartime borrowing. In the United Kingdom, the Labour government that came to power at the war's end set as one of its highest priorities the nationalization of the Bank of England, as did de Gaulle's government in France, which feared that an independent Banque de France, focused on combating domestic inflation, would undermine his plans for renewed economic growth.[22]

The central banks of the postwar years were not the same as the central banks of decades past. As John Singleton observes, whereas the central bankers of the nineteenth century came out of the banking profession and shared the same concerns as the private bankers, by the early 1950s central banks occupied a space somewhere between private bankers and civil servants.[23] Central banks were now responsible for much more than looking out for their private shareholders; they were part of a larger state apparatus of macroeconomic management. Nevertheless, central bankers did not embrace their new subservient status and continued to push for moderate, fiscally conservative economic policies that would not threaten price stability and the value of bankers' investments.[24]

The Swiss National Bank, for example, was founded in 1905 without any profit-maximizing statutes but with the expressed purpose of managing the domestic money supply and facilitating international payments. Similarly, the 1957 Bundesbank Act made protecting the currency and facilitating international payments the primary function of Germany's central bank. In addition, countries like the Netherlands, Switzerland, and the United Kingdom had functioned as major international financial centers before the war, and central banks worked hard to ensure the stable monetary conditions that would allow financial interests to reclaim this position. Finally, while the fear of a return to depression motivated the push for fiscal activism, at the same time many countries came out of World War II struggling with hyperinflation, which, for the central banks, demand a harsh round of deflation. Both the Bank of Italy and the Bank of Belgium overcame proponents for liberal Keynesian growth measures and, in the immediate postwar years, put their countries through a harsh round of monetary tightening to bring price levels under control.[25]

Central banks thus remained the champions of classical liberalism and worked to reclaim their ability to keep macroeconomic management on the path of monetary and fiscal orthodoxy. For central banks like the Federal Reserve and the Bank of England that had either seen their policy-making autonomy sharply curtailed or been nationalized outright, the first goal was to reclaim some independent say over monetary policy. In the United States, the Federal Reserve Bank persistently resisted the Truman administration's efforts to use monetary policy as a tool of domestic economic expansion, a conflict that finally culminated in the Federal Reserve–Treasury accord of 1951 that formalized the central bank's independence from the executive branch. After the accord, the Federal Reserve performed its open market operations independent of Treasury consultation and with regard to economic stabilization rather than economic growth. The Bank of England was likewise eager to regain control over monetary policy, more interested in protecting the international value of sterling than "Facing the Future" with the Labour Party. What resulted was persistent conflict between the Bank of England and the Treasury, a conflict manifested in the schizophrenia of British monetary policy over the course of the 1950s.[26]

In addition to waging these wars of position with their respective governments, central banks increasingly turned to the international arena to discuss issues of common concern, with the Bank for International Settlements serving as a focal point for this activity. Like the national central banks, the Bank for International Settlements, through its Research Department and its published annual reports, forcefully argued for a return to "sound money" and against domestic policies that would lead to price inflation. In the Bank's view, monetary stability was paramount and required a balanced approach to growth where wages did not exceed productivity and public expenditures did not exceed revenues. In particular, the Bank raised concerns about inflation during the Korean War boom of the early 1950s and during the broad economic expansion that took place in the middle of the decade. With respect to the latter, the Bank urged national governments to adopt tight monetary policies and fiscal austerity to drive down not just actual inflation, but even inflationary expectations.[27]

After World War II, monetary policy had thus become deeply politicized. Domestic social forces across North American and Western European countries were threatening domestic and international price stability, the primary charge of the public monetary authorities. It was a conflict that embodied the central tension of the embedded liberal compromise.

The Limits of Bretton Woods

The postwar international monetary system was not set in stone in Bretton Woods. Rather, it was a system that continued to evolve, particularly on the issue of capital controls. Embedded liberals like Keynes and White had managed to eke out a modest commitment to controlling short-term, speculative capital movements during the Bretton Woods negotiations. But, in interpreting this period, scholars like Eric Helleiner have overstated the degree to which the restrictions on capital controls in the International Monetary Fund's articles of agreement represented the victory of the embedded liberals and the defeat of the international financial community. In reality, those who advocated for strong capital controls had not been able to get a firm commitment on the issue from the main negotiating governments of the United States and Great Britain. Rather, the financial community had been able to soften White's and Keynes's proposals for the postwar international monetary order, preventing the creation of bilateral and, most important, obligatory capital controls that both men felt were essential if the domestic welfare goals of individual states were going to be protected from the pressures of global capital movements.[28]

True, Keynes and White had a great deal of influence over both the U.S. and the U.K. initial plans for the postwar monetary system, but, by many accounts, their influence was also relatively short lived. Keynes died just two years after the Bretton Woods agreements were signed. In the United States, Harry Dexter White's influence over the Bretton Woods negotiations derived from the fact that Franklin Roosevelt favored the foreign economic policy views of White's boss, Treasury Secretary Henry Morgenthau, over the competing views of the State Department. However, following Roosevelt's death in 1945 and the escalation of Cold War tensions with the Soviet Union, the balance of power over foreign policy making shifted to the State Department, which was more concerned with opening up the world economy than it was with complex monetary arrangements to promote embedded liberalism.[29]

But it was not just the U.S. government that worked to undermine the embedded liberal compromises of Bretton Woods. Among many of the key parties to the Bretton Woods agreements the commitment to capital controls was not as complete or as principled as is frequently asserted in accounts of postwar embedded liberalism. Transnational flows of capital were intentionally limited in the immediate years following the end of the war, but this was more a pragmatic position reflecting the fact that many Western European economies were still recovering from the war, and their currencies were too weak to be used in global transactions. In principle, however, the governments of the postwar Atlantic community—the United States, Canada, the United Kingdom, and the countries of Western Europe—were committed to the liberalization of global capital flows once economic reconstruction had taken place and, most critically, European currencies were strong enough to be fully convertible under the Bretton Woods rules.

The British worked very quickly to remove restrictions on transnational capital movements. The Bank of England, which had never supported the work of Keynes, hoped to restore the pound sterling's role as a key international currency and, in doing so, protect the imperial vestiges of the sterling bloc.[30] After Keynes's death in 1946, the Bank of England had a much easier time pursuing this agenda. Efforts to soften restrictions on capital movements were also under way in Western Europe, though there progress was slower. In 1954, Western European governments, working through the European Payments Union and the Invisibles Committee of the Organization for European Economic Cooperation, also began to explore liberalizing transnational flows of investment capital. Building on this initial work, just one year after full currency convertibility was restored in 1958 the OEEC agreed to adopt a Code of Liberalization of Capital Movements. While the Code maintained restrictions on short-term speculative investments abroad, it did provide important provisions for removing restrictions on foreign direct investment and foreign portfolio investment and, perhaps most critically, set the stage for further liberalization efforts.[31]

Even the International Monetary Fund, within which the power to enforce capital controls was vested, quickly relaxed its strictures against governments using the Fund's resources to finance transnational capital movements. The Fund's 1946 charter clearly stated that the Fund's resources were not to be used to help finance balance of payments deficits stemming from short-term speculative capital flows. Yet, in just a few short years the International Monetary Fund began to change its views on the dangers of speculative capital flows and softened its commitment to capital controls. This shift came about for two reasons. First, the Fund's analytical staff adopted a new "monetary approach" to analyzing balance of payments deficits that suggested that balance of payments deficits were rooted in the failure of national governments to manage productivity and total economic demand, not unregulated global capital markets. Developed by Jacques Polak of the Fund's research staff over the course of the 1950s, this new approach effectively blamed the domestic economic policies of deficit countries for their own balance of payments problems. Domestic adjustment, not capital controls, was needed to correct payments imbalances. Second, Per Jacobson, the Fund's managing director, was deeply skeptical of the classic Keynesian claim that speculative capital flows were inherently problematic. Although agreeing that such flows needed to be managed, Jacobson would not go as far as the original drafters of the Fund's charter and say that short-term speculative flows needed to be eliminated. Under the weight of these internal developments, by the early 1960s the Fund was seriously debating the question whether, and how, to relax controls on capital.[32]

The consensus that emerged in the official circles of international monetary management over the course of the 1950s was that economic development would be better served if capital could flow more freely across borders. It is difficult to know the degree to which this shift in the underlying ideas about international monetary management manifested in actual developments in transnational capital markets. Capital movements are notoriously difficult to trace and were especially so in the late 1950s and early 1960s. Many transactions went unrecorded, falling under the category of "errors and omissions" in official balance of payments ledgers. Yet, even with the highly imperfect ability to classify and record short-term capital transactions, it quickly became clear not only to government officials, but to officials and expert analysts at the International Monetary Fund and the OECD, that the relaxation of capital controls had profoundly altered global economic landscape by unleashing a wave of private, transnational, short-term investment.

The Consequences of Capital Liberalization

By the late 1950s the increasing volume and speed of global capital flows had created a real dilemma for the national governments and international organizations charged with managing the postwar international monetary order. On the one hand, no one was willing to go back to a time when transnational capital flows were more closely restricted On the other hand, for many North American and Western European governments the acceleration of short-term capital movements wreaked havoc on their balance of payments accounts. In the United States, for example, before 1959 short-term capital flows had been a check in the positive column of the country's balance of payments ledger as funds from abroad sought the stability of investment opportunities in the United States. After 1959, short-term capital began to pour out of the country as American financial institutions were attracted to higher European interest rates and newly stable currencies. By 1964, over $2.5 billion worth of short-term liabilities were held abroad. The French and Italians also began to show substantial short-term capital outflows after 1959. For other countries—the United Kingdom, Canada, the Netherlands, and Germany—the relaxation of capital controls brought a massive inflow of short-term capital.[33]

The current system of international monetary management was not designed to handle the scale and scope of these kinds of global capital flows. In 1958, the United States experienced its largest ever drain on its gold supply of over $2.2 billion with, even more significantly, a $2.3 billion outflow of gold to Western European nations. In 1959, gold continued to flow out of the country at an alarming rate, exposing the limitations and vulnerabilities of the international monetary system that had been put in place at Bretton Woods. In an effort to halt the gold outflow, the outgoing Eisenhower administration engaged in lengthy discussions with European countries to convince them to refrain from converting their growing surpluses of dollars into gold. Although European central banks were willing to help Eisenhower out, private investors were not so easily placated, and gold was driven up to $40 per ounce by the fall of 1960. On taking office, President Kennedy took a series of immediate measures to try to restore confidence among private investors. He appointed two of their own, investment banker Douglas Dillon and member of the Federal Reserve Bank of New York Robert Roosa, to the Treasury Department and publicly avowed to defend the dollar value of gold set at Bretton Woods.[34] While these symbolic steps were sufficient to restore order to the private gold market in the immediate term, they did not address the more fundamental problem of how to maintain exchange rate stability in what was now a much more open, and volatile, global economic environment.

Efforts to deal with this problem resulted in a near decade-long process of institutional innovation, the central goal of which was to buttress the original Bretton Woods institutions with new international credit facilities that could be drawn on to finance balance of payments deficits. The scholarship on the postwar international monetary order tends to gloss over this period of institutional innovation, seeing it as mere scribbling in the margins while the story of Bretton Woods was rapidly coming to a close. However, although the managers of the postwar international monetary system may have been unable to save Bretton Woods, in their efforts to do so, state officials and the heads of intergovernmental organizations vastly expanded the public financial authorities' role in managing the international monetary system, which had important, and long-lasting, consequences for the relationship between national governments and global finance.

The Evolving Bretton Woods Order and the Institutionalization of Central Bank Cooperation

As a first step toward strengthening the Bretton Woods system against capital liberalization, the Atlantic community increased their payments into the International Monetary Fund so that it would be able to finance what were likely to be increasingly frequent, and more severe, international payments imbalances. By 1961 the Fund's managing directors were weighing proposals that would allow the Fund to vastly increase its capacity to borrow directly from member governments. From these discussions came the General Arrangements to Borrow, which were formalized in January of 1962.[35] As Jeffrey Chwieroth observes, the General Arrangements to Borrow were explicitly designed to realign the mechanisms of balance of payments financing with the new push for capital account liberalization.[36] This was a significant step not only because it increased the financial resources that the Fund could use to fend off speculative attacks against national currencies but, more importantly, because negotiations over the Arrangements set off a serious discussion about the basic principles of balance of payments financing.

Staff at the International Monetary Fund preferred that any changes to its borrowing arrangements maintain the principle of multilateralism that had informed the Fund's creation: Resources would be contributed by all member governments and would be available to all member governments on equal terms. Many lenders, particularly the continental Europeans, were hesitant to lose control over any further resources that were committed for the purposes of balance of payments financing and proposed various alternative arrangements that would give lending governments the capacity to decide whether, and how, their money would be used. In the end a compromise was reached whereby the use of additional standby borrowing would be coordinated through the ten countries—specifically their central banks—that contributed additional money to the International Monetary Fund's reserves under the new agreement. It was here that the Group of Ten was born.[37]

Although a major achievement, the General Arrangements to Borrow ultimately proved insufficient for solving the problems of payments imbalances, though not for a lack of financial resources. The issue was that, although the International Monetary Fund had been created at Bretton Woods to serve as the main source of balance of payments financing, capital account liberalization was making national governments very hesitant to make drawings on the Fund when facing a severe payments deficit. The reason was that when governments made a drawing on the Fund it was a dramatic and highly visible affair potentially signaling to private investors that the payments deficit of the borrowing country had reached crisis proportions.

Given the strong connection between the official central bank–run market for gold that was formalized at Bretton Woods and the private market for gold located in London, governments running payments deficits had reason to be concerned about their image in the eyes of private investors. According to the Bretton Woods rules, governments, through their central banks, could purchase gold from the United States at the fixed rate of $35 per ounce. In addition, private investors could also purchase gold through the London gold exchange at whatever price was set therein.[38]

The existence of a private market for gold operating in parallel to the official market for gold created opportunities for financial gain through arbitraging the price differential between these two markets. Because the United States was committed to selling its gold at a fixed price there was a floor beneath which the price of gold could not fall. This created a tendency for the price of gold on the London exchange to be either at, or above, the official rate of $35 per ounce. When the London market gold price rose substantially above $35 per ounce, foreign central banks had an incentive to engage in price arbitrage: buying gold from the Federal Reserve and then reselling it on the London market. In addition, heavy gold purchases by the central banks raised concerns that the United States would be forced to raise the dollar price of gold, thus deflating the value of the dollar. Fearing a deflated dollar, private speculators would exchange their dollar-denominated assets for those denominated in other currencies, causing further disruption in the exchange markets.

Thus, in an ironic twist, although the need for a financing mechanism like the Fund had become even greater once currency convertibility had been achieved and capital controls were relaxed, and although national governments were putting all of this time and energy into negotiating over how to increase the financial resources available to the Fund, the liberalization of short-term capital movements also increased states' sensitivity to the concerns of international investors, making them more hesitant to use the Fund's resources.

What was really needed was a different kind of balance of payments financing mechanism, one that was sensitive to the fact that swings in countries' balance of payments positions were increasingly dependent on investor confidence. It was for this reason that central banks or, more specifically, international coordination across central banks became the central mechanism of balance of payments financing after the 1950s. By manipulating a currency's relative value, a government could increase the financial incentives for holding onto their currency and thus could make gold a less attractive financial asset. The early 1960s thus saw a rapid growth in direct, and initially secret, coordination and cooperation between the central banks of Western Europe and those of North America. This new cooperative spirit manifested, initially, as closer coordination between the United States and the central banks of Western Europe to craft a network of financial arrangements that were designed to supplement—or in some cases circumvent—the existing machinery of balance of payments financing.

These manipulations, however, required a great deal of cooperation and coordination among central banks, finance ministries, and treasuries. For this reason, it did not matter whether weak currencies were held by private investors or by public financial authorities; preventing speculative attacks on their currencies required countries running severe payments imbalances to garner the willingness of foreign central banks to engage in complex transactions in foreign exchange markets so as to alter the material incentives of holding different kinds of reserve assets.

The first concrete result of this new spirit of cooperation was the establishment of the London gold pool, the brainchild of Treasury Secretary Douglas Dillon and his counterpart in the United Kingdom. The idea behind the gold pool was that countries would commit a portion of their own gold reserves to the Bank of England, which the Bank could then use to buffer major movements in the London gold market. As with the negotiations around the General Arrangements to Borrow, it was not easy to convince the heads of the other central banks to sign on to this arrangement. In essence, the U.S. Treasury and the Bank of England were asking other countries to give up control over some of their own gold reserves and place them in the hands of the

British for the purposes of defending the dollar. Even the British needed to be assured that the gold pool would not undermine London's free market in gold, which was central to the country's position as a major international financial center.[39] In the end, the doubts of the British and the Europeans were assuaged, and the gold pool was formed, with the United States committing $270 million worth of gold and the other seven participating countries each contributing between $5 million and $35 million. Paralleling the role that central bankers played in monitoring the General Arrangements to Borrow, the Bank of England was given responsibility for conducting gold pool operations, but oversight of the arrangement was given to the Bank for International Settlements, where central bankers could review, and discuss, those operations on a monthly basis.[40]

The gold pool was one of those big public displays of coordinated central bank financial power. In the background, a quieter system of central bank cooperation to regulate currency markets was established via a multilateral network of currency swap arrangements. In simplest terms, a currency swap is an agreement between central banks such that each opens an account in its own currency in the name of the other bank. Hypothetically, under a currency swap between the United States and Germany, the United States would make available to the Germans $100 million in an account at the Federal Reserve Bank and the Germans would make available to the United States $100 million worth of Deutschmarks in an account at the Bundesbank. In this way, the United States could meet a temporary demand for Deutschmarks without having to have built up its own supply of currency reserves.

As American officials wrestled with their balance of payments deficit in the early 1960s, they established several bilateral currency swaps with other central banks to finance short-term balance of payments deficits. Unofficially, the first of these arrangements was put into place by the Treasury Department in the spring of 1961 by borrowing approximately $1 billion worth of German marks, Swiss francs, and Italian lira. This was a very significant development, being the first time since 1919 that the U.S. Treasury had borrowed in foreign currency.[41]

A more formal process for negotiating and establishing foreign currency operations between the Federal Reserve and European central banks was put into place in February of 1962 and was conducted, on the American side, within the Federal Open Market Committee of the Federal Reserve Board. In March, the Federal Reserve purchased $50 million worth of French francs and $25 million worth of German marks from the Bank of France and the Bundesbank, respectively.[42] In May, the Federal Open Market Committee entered into formal currency swap arrangements with the English, Dutch, Belgians, and Swiss worth $300 million.[43]

The British government likewise turned to borrowing arrangements outside of the International Monetary Fund's loan facilities to try to carry them through recurring balance of payments crises in the 1960s without having to resort to currency devaluation. Concern for the pound sterling arose in early 1961 as speculative attacks raised the possibility that the British would have to revalue the currency. In an effort to support the British government's commitment to its exchange rate, central banks committed some $900 million, including a $150 million gold swap arranged by the Bank for International Settlements. While these efforts defused the threat against the pound sterling for some time, speculative pressure returned again in 1963 and 1964. This time the Bank of England arranged a three-month swap arrangement with the Federal Reserve Bank of New York worth $500 million and a set of swap arrangements with the central banks of Canada, Germany, France, Switzerland, Holland, and Belgium totaling $500 million. Reginald Maudling, Chancellor of the Exchequer, hoped that these short-term credit arrangements would ward off speculative runs against the pound sterling long enough for the trade balance to improve and the balance of payments situation to become less dire.[44]

The year 1964 was also when swap arrangements were put into place to defend the Italian lira. While Italy had consistently run balance of payments surpluses throughout the 1950s, in 1963 a substantial payments deficit emerged that threatened the value of the currency. Unlike the United States and the British, which had organized their swap arrangements on a multilateral basis, the governor of the Banca d'Italia, Guido Carli, downplayed his country's need for assistance in front of the Bank for International Settlements while simultaneously working with the Federal Reserve Bank of New York to arrange a $1 billion package of currency swaps, which included swaps with the Bank of England and the German Bundesbank. While Carli's decision to forego multilateral discussion and consultation drew the ire of many financial officials in Europe, soon thereafter pressure against the lira abated.[45]

Two critical consequences followed from this steady and somewhat haphazard process of institutional transformation in mechanisms of balance of payments financing. First, the management of the postwar international monetary system began to look a little bit like what Keynes and White had envisioned back in 1944: international monetary management through central bank cooperation. Through the General Arrangements to Borrow, the establishment of the London gold pool, and the ever-growing network of currency swaps, the central banks of the United States, Canada, the United Kingdom, Japan, and several countries in Western Europe became the de facto managers of this new architecture of balance of payments financing. True, it was not a single world central bank, but these separate national monetary bodies were also becoming increasingly connected through close collaboration under the framework of official, international organizations like the Bank for International Settlements, the Group of Ten, and the Organization for Economic Cooperation and Development.

Second, in an important consequence of the development of these new networks of financial arrangements and the evermore frequent meetings between central bankers that were required to manage them, the institutional and nationalistic differences that used to divide central banks began to shrink. The members of the Group of Ten were now meeting monthly at the Bank for International Settlements, which was also working much more closely with the International Monetary Fund. Writing on this period, Richard N. Cooper has recently observed that it was the 1960s "which saw the real birth of multilateral central bank cooperation envisioned but stillborn in the 1930s," a view supported by John Singleton, who describes the emergence of "a central bank circuit" in the 1960s, "with stops in Washington, New York, Basel, London, Paris, and Frankfurt." Through these routines of international monetary management, policy views among the central bankers of North America and Western Europe converged and often trumped a central bankers' nationalistic sentiments.[46] As Chapters 5 and 6 will show, although these financing mechanisms were critical for defending both the pound sterling and the dollar by maintaining their currency reserves during times of severe deficit, they also had the effect of bringing foreign central banks, and their ideas and interests, into the conversation about domestic economic policy making.

Central Banks, International Monetary Power, and Austerity

This chapter has brought together two interrelated stories about the evolution of the public monetary authority from the gold standard era through the postwar period. One part of this story, told in the first section of this chapter, is that of a growing politicization of the domestic economic and social costs of international monetary stability. Throughout the postwar period, central banks remained committed to the kind of austere economic policies that they had supported under the classical gold standard. What changed was that at the end of the Second World War the interests of the central bankers in promoting international economic stability through domestic austerity had become politically fraught. Although the trade-off between monetary stability and social welfare had always been understood, during the classical gold standard and even through World War I the forces lined up to oppose the financial community were fairly weak. By the 1950s, however, banking interests had to confront the increased organization of the working class and the institutionalization of their interests within state agencies willing, and empowered, to push for full employment economic policies and the expansion of the welfare state. One way that central banks tried to reassert themselves was in their efforts to recapture control over monetary policy. Central banks that lost their independence during the Second World War tried to take it back over the course of the 1950s, some more successfully than others.

The second part of this story takes place at the international level and can be described as two parallel trajectories: increasing levels of inter–central bank cooperation after World War I and the elevation of central banks to a prominent role in the management of the international monetary system after World War II. At the international level, central bankers' views about the best practices for aligning the management of domestic money with the management of international money coalesced around classical orthodoxy; domestically, however, classical orthodoxy had to contend with a wide host of "heretics": trade unions and socialists who wanted higher wages and more social benefits, elected leaders who were willing to go into debt to meet these demands, and a new generation of economists who wanted to do away with the stodgy focus on economic stability.

In laying out these two narratives, it is clear that it is inaccurate to see the postwar period as the era of embedded liberalism triumphant. Yes, embedded liberal sentiments were strong, but they had to fight for position against those who pined for a world of stable prices and stable currencies. In the standard accounts of the political economy of the postwar period, the Bretton Woods international monetary arrangements favored the side of social welfare by keeping the private international finance community out of the policy-making equation. Yet, as already discussed, the mechanisms enshrined in Bretton Woods that were supposed to support embedded liberalism quickly became inadequate for dealing with the erosion of controls on transnational capital flows and currency speculation. To support the Bretton Woods international monetary system, a series of new balance of payments financing arrangements were established, each of which placed central banks at the center of the management of the international monetary system.

The key consequence of these developments was the redistribution of international monetary power to an increasingly cohesive group of public monetary authorities. In this new institutional context, resolving the recurring crises of the Bretton Woods system—which hit the United States the hardest but that were also felt in other countries like the United Kingdom and Italy—now depended on the active cooperation of a tightly networked group of central bankers who controlled the financial resources that countries running balance of payments deficits needed to stave off speculative runs against their currencies. This is the critical development missed by the scholarship on postwar embedded liberalism, which emphasizes the way in which Bretton Woods system limited the international monetary power of *private* financial institutions but misses the growing influence of *public* financial institutions over international credit and currency markets.

3   The Question of Growth in
a Global Economy

F OR A PROCESS THAT IS SO DEEPLY CONTENTIOUS, SO THOR-
oughly counter to powerful notions of national sovereignty, the restructuring of national economic policies to make them fit with the demands
of international economic pressures goes by a fairly benign name: adjustment.
While countries who undertake adjustment frequently do so under some kind
of duress, having, for example, accumulated massive piles of debt and needing
assistance from public or private financial institutions, the actual process of
adjustment is structured by a set of ideas: ideas about when economic conditions warrant, or even demand, adjustment; ideas about what policies and
practices will result in a successful adjustment; and, looking forward, ideas
about what policies and institutions need to be put in place to prevent the
need for future financial assistance.

Economic historians and scholars of international political economy frequently point out that one of the key differences between the system of international monetary cooperation of the classical gold standard era and the
Bretton Woods system of international monetary cooperation was a fundamental shift in the ideas about adjustment. In the era of the classical gold
standard, economic liberalism dictated that governments should barely intervene in their economies lest they spend too much money and create price
inflation; instead they should let market forces dictate the ebb and flow of
economic growth and decline. This idea fit neatly within an adjustment model
based on the gold standard "rules of the game" whereby the national mon-

etary authorities—central bankers and government finance officials—were expected to conduct monetary policy with the goal of maintaining equilibrium in the international accounts, allowing the supply and cost of credit to fluctuate "naturally" with the balance of payments.

After World War II and the diffusion of Keynesian economic thinking, this "barbarous logic," as Keynes called it, was replaced by a new ideational couplet, one that called on national governments to actively intervene in the economy to promote economic growth and high levels of employment and that sought to protect these policy goals from international economic pressures by doing away with the "rules of the game" by building flexibility into the system of international payments.

Painted in such broad strokes, this narrative captures some of the key distinctions that defined these two eras, but closer investigation into the historical record of postwar international monetary cooperation shows that such a clear-cut distinction is vastly overdrawn and obscures important tensions between classical liberal and embedded liberal views on international monetary cooperation and domestic economic policy. The major sources of these conflicts were twofold. The first, as discussed in the previous chapter, was the conflict between national governments and their monetary authorities, the former facing increasing domestic political pressures for high levels of employment and improved living standards while the latter pushed for a return to domestic and international monetary stability. The second source of conflict was the different growth strategies that countries had adopted at the end of World War II. Scholars have already recognized that there were real cross-national differences in ways that the new Keynesian spirit of growth was put into practice by national governments in Western Europe and North America in the early postwar years.[1] What has been less appreciated, however, is that these different growth strategies were built on different relationships to the international economy and thus yielded very different interests when it came to the issue of international economic cooperation.

In the early postwar years, the conflict between these competing liberalisms was largely kept at bay as capital and exchange restrictions limited the degree of international economic interaction and interdependence. However, once full currency convertibility was achieved across the OECD area it forced a dialogue on the issue of international economic cooperation. As the Bank for International Settlements noted in its 1960 *Annual Report*: "Once convertibility had been introduced, it clearly became of much greater importance that the national economies should move in step in order to minimize the changes of such conflicts arising; the need for international cooperation in this field has thus become more urgent than it was before."[2] On this basic point, there was no disagreement, but there were clear lines of division within the OECD member countries when it came to precisely what form this cooperation should take.

This chapter traces the manifestation of these two sets of ideas within one of the main intergovernmental organizations of postwar economic governance: the Organization for Economic Cooperation and Development. From a research and analysis standpoint, the OECD's position in the formal structure of postwar international monetary management offers a window into the competing ideas and interests that framed official discussions of how best to reconcile the desire for a liberal global economy and the desire for steady, strong economic growth. As an intergovernmental organization, the OECD served as a kind of arena where competing interests with respect to economic growth, balance of payments equilibrium and monetary stability could be debated.

The International Politics of Growth in the Late Postwar Era

Although all of the OECD member countries had emerged from the Second World War with a new commitment to economic growth, they varied considerably in their domestic political institutions, position in the global economy, and experience with the war itself, all of which, in turn, resulted in substantial differences in how each country set about trying to rebuild and grow their economies after the war's end. These differences did not matter so much in the early postwar years of reconstruction, when economic interdependence across the OECD was quite low, but did not so easily fit together in the more liberal global economic environment that emerged in the late 1950s. Though each of the OECD countries had its own distinct set of interests with respect to the process of international economic cooperation, the conflict that was at the core of the debate in this period was that between the imperial Keynesianism of primarily the United States, but also the United Kingdom, and the social market conservatism of primarily Germany but also the Netherlands and Switzerland.

Although the United States came out of World War II with perhaps the strongest economy in the world, government officials worried that the war's end would send the country back into depression. For this reason, the Truman and then Eisenhower administrations managed the domestic economy through Keynesian demand management but also pushed for the rapid economic reconstruction of Western Europe. Domestic Keynesianism was thus coupled to an imperial sort of Keynesianism in that the objective was an open world economy that would provide new sources of demand for U.S. goods and U.S. investment capital. Also Keynesian was the way that the whole project was premised on an initial period of balance of payments deficits to finance not only reconstruction in Western Europe but also development in the former European colonies, which would be balanced as soon as Europe could use its supply of dollars to purchase goods from the United States.[3]

Although the scholarship on the postwar settlements stresses U.S. interests in global economic liberalism and export promotion, it was really the social market economies of Germany, the Netherlands, and Switzerland whose postwar economic growth was highly dependent on their vibrant export sectors. Compared to the OECD area as a whole, the real value of U.S. and U.K. exports increased fairly modestly in the postwar period. On the other hand, the value of exports coming out of Germany increased at nearly five times the OECD average, and both the Netherlands and Switzerland saw export growth well above the OECD average.[4]

Three factors stand out as far as explaining these countries' success in global markets. First, all three were already well positioned to compete in world markets. Germany and the Netherlands had competitive firms in machine tools and chemicals, and Switzerland's business community was very internationally oriented. Second, all three countries came out of the war led by political parties that put a high priority on market competition and private investment and had strong independent central banks that put the highest priority on domestic price stability and exchange rate stability. Germany is the model case where, under the guidance of Ludwig Erhard in the Ministry of Economics, the Christian Democratic Union modeled its economic agenda on the idea of a "social market economy," one that balanced a primary commitment to economic liberalism with a recognition that the state needed to support basic social needs. The core values and ideas at the heart of Germany's "social market economy" also defined economic policy in the Netherlands, which was heavily influenced by Catholic and Protestant notions of "private responsibility" and in Switzerland, which followed a "market-driven process of adjustment." Third, in all three countries, labor unions were fairly weak and entered into corporatist bargaining arrangements with the government and business that kept wage increases in check.[5]

Together, these factors produced an institutional environment and set of macroeconomic policies that were very conducive to internationally oriented businesses. Strong deflationary action in the late 1940s brought prices and wages down dramatically. As a result, compared to not just the United States and United Kingdom, but other European countries as well, Germany, the Netherlands, and Switzerland all emerged as low-cost producers, with unit labor costs in Germany and the Netherlands nearly half of those of France.[6]

The linchpin of this growth model was domestic price stability. Stable prices not only helped to keep export prices low but, equally important, helped to keep the corporatist political bargain together by letting workers see their real incomes grow even as nominal wage increases were kept closely in check. Through the 1950s this model worked quite well, producing rapid growth and a real improvement in the standard of living. The high volume of exports produced consistent balance of payments surpluses, which threatened to tip the scales of these delicately balanced economies, but their central banks were able to keep economic expansion under control through a policy of tight money and high interest rates. By the end of the decade, however, this system came under pressure from the liberalization of capital flows. The central banks' strategy of monetary tightness to keep domestic expansion in check had the perverse effect of expanding the money supply as international investors sought to take advantage of high German, Dutch, and Swiss interest rates. This rapid influx of liquidity threatened to overheat, and inflate, economies that were already growing rapidly.[7]

Thus, by the late 1950s the U.S. imperial Keynesianism was beginning to clash with the economic liberalism of the social market economies. Whereas the United States wanted assistance in financing its balance of payments deficit, which it saw as vital for both holding the Bretton Woods system together and protecting world capitalism from the threat of communism, for the social market economies economic integration meant accepting the discipline of monetary orthodoxy.

Growth, Stability, and the OECD

The intergovernmental organizations that were crafted out of the Bretton Woods negotiations were created to be more than just institutional agents overseeing, and lubricating, the machinery of the postwar monetary order. They were also designed to be spaces where state officials from North America and Western Europe could meet and discuss issues of common concern. In the early postwar years, the International Monetary Fund served this role, but by the end of the 1950s the Organization for Economic Cooperation and Development had become the primary intergovernmental organization hosting debate and discussion over issues of international monetary management.

The OECD began life as the Organization for European Economic Cooperation, which was formed to aid in the disbursement of Marshall Plan aid to Western Europe from the United States and, more broadly, with guiding the process of postwar economic recovery in Western Europe. The organization's name changed to the Organization for Economic Cooperation and Development in December of 1960 when the United States and Canada joined as full members. As European economies recovered in the 1950s, American and Canadian officials grew concerned by what they saw as a burgeoning European regionalism whereby free trade was promoted within the European community but not between Europe and North America. Anxious to derail these troublesome developments, American policy makers were keenly interested in gaining access to the institutions of European economic cooperation.[8]

What make the OECD such a compelling window through which to view the history of postwar international economic cooperation are the institutional and organizational features that distinguish it from the other international intergovernmental organizations that were formed in the early postwar years. Like its cousins, the International Monetary Fund and the World Bank, much of the OECD's work involves analyzing and forecasting economic trends and passing along advice and policy recommendations to member governments. However, unlike the other two bodies, the OECD does not command financial resources that can be used to compel governments to actually adopt its recommendations. In addition, like many other intergovernmental organizations, the OECD maintains a large, permanent, bureaucratic staff to oversee day-to-day operations, gather and analyze data, and assist with reports and recommendations. However, whereas in other bodies, like the International

Monetary Fund, the permanent staff has a great deal of influence over the work and recommendations of the organization, in the OECD much of the policy discussion takes place within committees and working groups that are comprised of state officials from member governments.[9]

These two features—lack of a direct mechanism of financial coercion and frequent interaction between high-level state officials—make the OECD a good example of what political scientists David Soskice and Peter Hall call a "deliberative institution." Deliberative institutions can influence the decision making of national political leaders by shaping the perceived costs and benefits of members' policy actions through routine and frequent social interaction among policy elites. Through debate and discussion, participant members learn other members' interests, and, perhaps most important, what steps they are willing to take to achieve those interests. In this way, while the OECD did not have its own autonomous means of exercising coercive power, it was a critical space where power and interests were articulated among the OECD members.[10]

Much of the scholarship on the postwar international monetary system glosses over the OECD, focusing instead on the development of ideas about adjustment within the International Monetary Fund and the mechanisms through which the Fund's ideas diffused across the globe. However, although the International Monetary Fund has played a critical role in pushing poor countries down the path of economic orthodoxy, Western governments preferred the OECD for discussing issues of international economic cooperation. This was for two reasons, the first of which was political. The International Monetary Fund was dominated by the United States, and so many European governments resisted using it as a site for negotiating solutions to periodic and, by the later half of the 1950s, recurring problems in the international monetary system. Second, whereas the dealings of the Fund often attracted public attention, negotiations and deals struck within the OECD were often conducted in secret, something that was increasingly valued in the later Bretton Woods years as major reforms to the system were being debated.[11]

The hub of the OECD's activity on the analysis, discussion, and debate of matters of economic policy was the Economic Policy Committee and its various subcommittees and working groups. Created in April of 1959, the Economic Policy Committee was defined by two often competing tasks: devising policy recommendations for achieving domestic price stability in order to foster a climate conducive to international payments equilibrium, and devising policy recommendations to achieve high levels of economic growth. Given that these two policy goals can often come into conflict, the Committee gave priority to ensuring a balanced and stable international monetary system, a choice that was reflective of the Committee's origins as a meeting ground for finance ministers.

In July of 1956, the OEEC Ministerial Council was looking ahead to a future when European currencies would be fully convertible under the Bretton Woods rules and created a subcommittee called Working Party 19 to begin planning for this critical stage in the larger effort toward rebuilding a liberal global economic order.[12] The membership of Working Party 19 was comprised of the finance ministers from several Western European and North American governments whose primary concern was ensuring that domestic price inflation did not destabilize the fixed exchange rate system. In April of 1959, the OEEC Ministerial Council changed the name of the working party to the Economic Policy Committee, which, in its early years, continued to focus on what its members saw as the critically related issues of domestic price stability and international monetary stability.

It was in 1962 that the Ministerial Council asked the Committee to expand its focus to include a study of policies to promote economic growth and high levels of employment in a way that was consistent with financial stability. This was all part of the Ministerial Council's larger goal of achieving a 50 percent increase in the combined gross national product of the twenty member countries by the year 1970, or an average growth rate of 5 percent a year for the decade as a whole.[13] In this context the Economic Policy Committee was given responsibility for analyzing member countries' growth records and growth prospects and for issuing policy recommendations to promote growth.

Through these developments, the Economic Policy Committee came to embody the tension between growth and stability that was at the heart of the conflict between postwar embedded liberals and classical liberals. In addition, the Economic Policy Committee was forced to wrestle with this tension at that precise historical moment when the return of full currency convertibility and the steady relaxation of capital controls made OECD member countries increasingly interdependent, raising anew fundamental questions about adjustment.

The remainder of this chapter examines two ways in which the Economic Policy Committee was central to the resolution of questions raised by international economic cooperation in a liberal global economy. In one respect, the Committee operated as an organizational agent producing and disseminating its own ideas about the sources of price instability and its relationship to economic growth. In addition, the Committee served as a space where a series of debates over whether a new set of "adjustment rules" needed to be put into place to ensure that governments' domestic policies would not lead to destabilizing payments imbalances. In both of these ways the Economic Policy Committee supported the classical liberal agenda, first by articulating a very orthodox set of ideas about the causes and effects of price inflation and second by taking up, and therefore legitimating, the question of a return to firm and formal adjustment rules akin to those that held during the era of the classical gold standard.

Growth, Monetary Stability, and Global Capitalism

A lot can be learned about organizational norms and values by looking not just at how issues are discussed but also at which issues even come up for discussion. Given the vast range of questions raised when trying to balance economic growth and price stability while moving toward greater economic liberalism, it is telling that one of the Economic Policy Committee's very first items of business was to commission a study on the "problem of rising prices" from a panel of economic experts in May of 1959.[14] Looking ahead to the new decade, the Committee members were growing concerned that economic expansion in Western Europe, which had succeeded in the 1950s largely by absorbing unused productive capacity, was now bumping up against those limits. This created the potential that demand would exceed the economy's capacity to supply, resulting in rising prices.[15]

After two years of work, the expert panel presented its findings to the Economic Policy Committee in October of 1961. While drawing attention to several one-off factors that had contributed to periodic bursts of inflation, such as poor harvests and monopolistic pricing in some economic sectors, the experts' report focused on what they identified as the two primary causes of rising prices in Western Europe, excess demand and excessive wage increases. To address the problem of excess demand, the experts' report urged national governments to be more flexible in their use of fiscal and monetary policies to more precisely manage the pace of economic growth. Excessive wage increases were a more difficult matter. The report rejected deflationary action to drive up unemployment and also cautioned against attacking unions' legal rights as policy options. Instead, the experts' report called on national governments to develop clear, robust income policies that would keep labors' demands in line with productivity increases.[16]

The report's call for the flexible use of fiscal and monetary policies was very much in line with a basic Keynesian understanding of the relationship between growth and inflation. This is not surprising given that, although Keynes's specific economic ideas were adopted in a variety of ways, at variable speeds, across North America and Western Europe, nearly all of these governments accepted Keynes's core idea that growth was a function of aggregate demand and that demand could, and should, be manipulated by economic policy.[17] At the same time, the underlying premise of the report, the so-called problem of inflation, was a departure from Keynesianism. True, Keynes had issued strong warnings about the dangers of hyperinflation, such as that which preceded the rise of fascism in Germany, but the degree of inflation that the Economic Policy Committee was concerned about was quite moderate in comparison. So, when the report drew attention to the "excess demand" building up in Western Europe, this reflected not the ascendancy of the new Keynesian orthodoxy but rather the still-powerful legacy of the old classical orthodoxy.

These subtle points of emphasis reveal something important about how the Economic Policy Committee saw its own work. From its inception, the Committee resolved the tension between growth and stability in favor of the latter. The Committee's goal was not to promote policies to achieve maximum levels of demand, or even high levels of demand, but rather, as they so often stated in their policy documents, to maintain an "adequate level of demand," a level of demand that was high enough to sustain robust economic growth but not so high as to trigger even moderate levels inflation or produce international payments imbalances.

The concept of "adequate demand" resolved the tension between growth and inflation in theory, but by itself it gave little guidance as to how an adequate level could, or should, be maintained. Total economic demand comes from the combined demand-generating effects of activity in all economic sectors. Governments generate economic demand when they spend, whether on social services or infrastructure or the military, as do private businesses when they invest, as do workers when they spend their wages. Like any other macroeconomic indicator, total demand is an aggregation of numerous, diverse, and interconnected forces in an economy. Government transfer payments can support consumer spending, and increased consumer spending can spur a business to invest in new productive capacity.

This complexity makes it very difficult to isolate single, causal factors driving the level of total economic demand. While this point may seem obvious, the experts reviewing the problem of rising prices were careful to make it explicit, noting in their report to the Economic Policy Committee: "To attribute to some particular economic policy measure a particular growth effect is largely arbitrary. Such reasoning could only be valid if it were possible to distinguish the effect of each factor 'all other things being equal.' This condition is never fulfilled in practice."[18] Despite the expert report's warning about the inherent difficulty of trying to generate clear policy prescriptions regarding economic demand, difficulties compounded by the wide variety of national political and institutional settings that they were dealing with, the Economic Policy Committee very quickly settled on one primary culprit for domestic price inflation: the "excessive" wage demands of organized labor.

For example, in commenting on data showing large percentage wage increases in Germany, the United Kingdom, the Netherlands, and Sweden, the Economic Policy Committee observed with dismay that "there is a clear danger that wage increases will outrun productivity gains."[19] As growth rates across Western Europe began to decline, the Committee grew even more concerned that wage increases would have a powerfully inflationary impact, noting in its review of economic prospects in February of 1962 that "the rate of growth of productivity has moderated substantially and the problem of policy is to secure a corresponding moderation in the rate of growth of wages."[20] The Economic Policy Committee's concern was shared by the central banks, as shown by the Bank for International Settlements's own assessment of economic developments in Europe. In its 1962 *Annual Report*, the Bank suggested that rising wages were cutting into corporate profits and therefore weakening the foundations for future growth. Commenting on trends over the previous years, the *Annual Report* notes:

> While industry on the Continent has been in a position which enabled it to absorb some weakening of its competitive standing, there is no doubt that the wave of wage increases is reaching dangerous proportions; if it continues it will threaten the high level of demand needed for economic growth as well as the balance on external account.[21]

Two years later, as unemployment rates across Europe fell to historic lows, the Bank suggested in its 1964 *Annual Report* that overly aggressive trade unions were exploiting this favorable position and winning excessive wage increases that threatened the continent with an "inflationary eruption."[22]

The tight parallel between the Bank for International Settlements's analysis of European economic developments and the Economic Policy Committee's analysis indicates how closely the latter body remained tied to its origins in finance. Price stability, more than anything else, needed to be maintained such that even moderate bouts of inflation were cause for alarm. In addition, although few would dispute that the level of economic demand and domestic price movements were closely related, the Economic Policy Committee interpreted inflationary developments through what economists would now call a wage-push theory of inflation. This theory put aggressive trade unions at the center of Western European inflation and made readily apparent the distributional, and therefore political, implications of the Committee's analyses and recommendations.

Challenges to the Idea of Wage-Push Inflation

One could object to the above interpretation that the Economic Policy Committee's perspective was shaped by its origins in pubic finance on the grounds that their wage-push story of inflation was, in fact, the technically superior one. Although a plausible argument, it does not hold up to the historical record, which shows that the Economic Policy Committee's own working groups and subcommittees were generating data and reports that contradicted the view that price inflation was primarily driven by wage pressures. In early 1962 the Economic Policy Committee created a subcommittee called "Working Party 4," which it charged with producing a detailed study of the relationship between costs of production and prices. Like the committee of independent experts, Working Party 4 began its work with an investigation into the relationship between excess demand and prices. However, whereas the expert committee's report had focused rather narrowly on the need to regulate wage income, Working Party 4 took a broader approach by investigating the effects of total income—which included income from wages but also included income from rents and corporate profits—on total economic demand and rising prices. When the Working Party issued its first major report to the Economic Policy Committee in February of 1964, it followed the committee of independent experts in recommending that member countries adopt income policies to help keep the growth of income in line with productivity increases. However, whereas the committee of economic experts limited its recommendation to wage income, Working Party 4's report suggested that other forms of income, specifically corporate profits, needed to be regulated by an income policy as well.

Working Party 4's recommendation was based on a more careful reading of macroeconomic data than that which informed the wage-push story of inflation. To support its assessment that excessive wage increases were driving inflation, the Economic Policy Committee drew attention to a simple correlation between two trends: Data showed that prices were rising in countries where wages were also rising. Working Party 4's report added a new variable to this mix, observing that "profits and other non-wage incomes is an important cause of rising prices, either in isolation or in supporting and reinforcing a rise in wages."[23]

To support this assertion, Working Party 4 pointed to data showing that in 1962 nonwage income in OECD member countries ranged from a low of 25 percent of net national income in the United Kingdom to a high of 44 percent in Ireland. True, wage income was still the largest contributor to total demand, but it was by no means the only relevant factor. More critically, the Working Party's report suggested that wage growth may be epiphenomenal, simply the result of rapid economic growth driven by high rates of private investment and not the result of overly aggressive unions. If this were true, then profit income, not wage income, was the primary factor driving price inflation.

Additional data gathered from other Economic Policy Committee working groups supported this interpretation. Related research was being conducted by Working Party 2, which was tasked with studying the growth experiences of OECD countries over the previous decade and, in an effort to meet the OECD Ministerial Council's growth target for the end of the decade, was given the responsibility for offering guidance on policies to promote economic growth. In 1965 the Working Party issued a midterm report on progress toward the 50 percent growth target based on a detailed study of individual country experiences. This report included the most thorough study of patterns of total demand across the OECD member countries and tried to capture the full array of member countries' diverse growth experiences and the relationship between growth and a wide range of related indicators—social welfare, population dynamics, industrial restructuring, the movement of prices, and evolving patterns of trade.

A key section of the report presented the Working Party's analysis of the demand components of gross national product from 1950 through 1963.

Whereas the Economic Policy Committee and the Bank for International Settlements had consistently argued that excessive consumer demand was causing the European economies to overheat, leading to price inflation, data presented in the Mid-Term Review showed that, although personal consumption remained the largest component of demand, personal consumption as a share of total demand had actually been declining over the last five years. In other words, if demand pressures were increasing, it was not because of increased personal consumption. Rather, the report found that "a major offset to the decline in private consumption has been a fairly general rise in fixed asset formation." Looking forward, the report projected that these trends would continue with fixed investment growing faster than gross national product in most OECD countries over the rest of the decade.[24] This finding lent considerable weight to Working Party 4's claim about the need for broad income policies.

In framing its recommendation for a broad approach to income policies, Working Party 4 showed a real appreciation for the political implications of their work. As the group's report to the Economic Policy Committee pointed out, there was a "need to complement a wages policy with a parallel policy towards other incomes, aimed at correcting what are regarded as undesirable or unacceptable trends in the evolution of the different classes of income."[25] These political concerns were not abstract speculations but grounded in economic reality. In a report published in June of 1964, the Economic Policy Committee secretariat noted that, with corporate profits projected to increase by 10 percent after taxes, trade unions might be less willing to go along with any income policies.[26] There was really no need to speculate on the views of the trade unions. The Economic Policy Committee's own Trade Union Advisory Council had submitted a formal response to the experts' report on rising prices that, while not disputing that wage increases could cut into profits, put the onus back onto business owners to "improve his organization and production capacity in order to re-establish his previous rate of profit."[27] In other words, if prices went up it was because business owners failed to do the thing that was supposed to make the private ownership of productive wealth beneficial to society: reinvest and innovate.

Working Party 4's recommendations for how to manage inflation were based on a more nuanced analysis of the macroeconomic data than the wage-push story and also suggested a means of avoiding the political fallout of an incomes policy that targeted workers and consumers. Despite this, Working

Party 4's call for a broad income policy that would cover both wages and profits never really made it into the discussions of the top levels of the Economic Policy Committee or the OECD Ministerial Council. Rather, the dominant narrative clung to a simple wage-push story even when the economic reality was much more complex.

Why was the Economic Policy Committee so fixated on the barriers, real or imagined, that wage increases posed for economic growth? One reason seems to be that the Committee's assessment of the prospects for continued growth across in the OECD was based on what might be called a prototypical supply-side model of economic growth. Liberal Keynesian, demand-side growth models suggest that investment, business expansion, and rising levels of employment follow from consumer demand. In the liberal Keynesian framework, wage growth is necessary for broader economic growth. In the supply-side model, growth begins with capital investment, and investment depends on whether the economic climate gives firms confidence to believe that their investments will turn a profit. Wage growth, by cutting into profits, is inimical to business confidence.

This distinction helps to make sense of why, despite data showing that private investment had been the major contributor to total demand and thus inflationary pressure in the first half of the decade, the Economic Policy Committee was uninterested in restrictions on business incomes. From the supply-side perspective, future growth depended on an even greater volume of investment, and, in a zero-sum economic system where total national income for investment is divided among consumers, firms, and the state, the share going to consumers would necessarily need to shrink.

Supply-side growth models thus held considerable influence long before the much-commented-on supply-side ascendancy of the 1980s. Moreover, while Cathie Jo Martin has made similar claims about the transformation of economic thinking in the United States in this period—a point that will come up again in later chapters—the emergence, or perhaps reemergence, of supply-side thinking was not strictly a U.S. phenomenon.[28] The organizations of postwar international monetary management were not, as the embedded liberalism thesis sometimes suggests, the bastions of liberal Keynesianism, working to protect national governments' social democratic agendas from global capitalism. Rather, the OECD, like the International Monetary Fund and the Bank for International Settlements, was more likely to see high levels of growth and low levels of employment as threats to, rather than signs of, a healthy economy.

Adjustment Rules Redux: The "Code of Good Behaviour" and the Adjustment Process Report

If, by the early 1960s, the first pillar of embedded-liberal ideology, the rapprochement with labor and the belief that full employment was good for the economy, showed signs of weakness, the second pillar, the belief that national economic governments should be protected from international economic pressures, was on the verge of collapse. The return of currency convertibility combined with the steady relaxation of capital controls brought renewed interest in the formulation of adjustment rules for countries running persistent payments deficits and surpluses.

The International Monetary Fund had already begun following what were essentially classical adjustment rules in 1952 when it began to make drawings on the Fund conditional on governments taking concrete policy measures to address their payments deficits. Over subsequent decades the scope of the conditionality agreements broadened to cover not just broad macroeconomic policy measures but also social welfare policies and regulation. At its core, the Fund's approach to conditionality was informed by a monetary view of price inflation and payments deficits. Developed by Jacques Polak in the Fund's research department, the monetary view argued that payments deficits and price inflation could largely be explained by excessive credit creation in the economy. Countries in deficit were "absorbing" more money and more goods than they created, the difference made up for through borrowing. The solution, then, was for governments to reduce total demand in the economy by using monetary policy and credit controls to both dampen the business cycle and manage payments imbalances.[29]

The International Monetary Fund, and the ever-expanding terms of its conditionality agreements, has been rightly implicated as a major driving force behind the spread of neoliberal economic policy across the developing world, particularly in the 1970s, 1980s, and 1990s, when many countries in Latin America, Africa, South Asia, and Eastern Europe experienced devastating debt crises that forced them to turn to the Fund for assistance. That being said, placing too much emphasis on the International Monetary Fund in the international debate over balance of payments and adjustment misses the critical role that other organizations played in this process. For one, forays by researchers into the inner world of the International Monetary Fund of the early postwar years paint a more complex picture than that of a simple "proto-neoliberalism." Through the 1960s, top Fund officials like Jacques Polak were still working within a broadly Keynesian framework and held onto some notion that the process of balance of payments adjustment should leave adequate space for national economic policy goals—at least for developed Western countries.[30]

In addition, although by the late 1950s the Fund had developed a fairly clear set of adjustment rules, those rules could be applied only when countries needed to make drawings on the Fund. This meant that the Fund's adjustment rules were far more likely to be applied to poor countries, who had little recourse to other sources of balance of payments financing, than they were to the wealthy countries of the OECD area, who were not only very hesitant to make drawings on the Fund but, as discussed in the previous chapter, could draw on non-Fund sources of payments financing.

Indeed, it was precisely because these non-Fund credit mechanisms had grown so much that monetary authorities and other government officials from OECD member countries, particularly those countries that were pursuing some version of a social market growth strategy, felt that the system needed a clear set of adjustment rules to ensure that new financing mechanisms would not replace sound domestic economic management. While neither the OECD Ministerial Council nor the Economic Policy Committee actively took up this issue, the Economic Policy Committee did become a central forum for discussion and debate over renewed calls for formal adjustment rules.

Dedicated discussion on this issue began in 1961 when Professor Alfred Mueller-Armack, who was currently serving as Germany's undersecretary of state for European affairs, submitted a formal proposal for an international "Code of Good Behaviour." From his position in the German government, Mueller-Armack had assisted in the process of European economic reconstruction and integration and had witnessed firsthand the complex ways in which national economies had become economically interdependent. It was also Mueller-Armack who had coined the phrase "social market economy" and who served as a key economic advisor to Ludwig Erhard in the late 1940s as he sought to rebuild the German economy on the principles of economic liberalism.[31]

Mueller-Armack premised his presentation of the Code on what was an all-too-obvious fact about the global economy: International economic interdependency had grown considerably with the achievement of European currency convertibility, binding the economic fortunes of one country to the economic policies of others. Without cooperation, Professor Mueller-Armack feared, governments who set policy only with regard to their national economy could quickly undermine the economic goals of others—especially countries like Germany, whose growth was very dependent on stability in foreign markets. To try to avoid this situation, Mueller-Armack proposed a Code of Good Behaviour that would serve as a framework for greater economic cooperation between the OECD members. He took pains to make clear that the goal of the code was not to establish a binding set of policy rules but simply to lay out some broad principles of economic coordination that would "ensure that countries in economic difficulties should avoid taking action which would harm their neighbors."[32]

At first glance, the proposed code seems completely innocuous. It called on member nations to use countercyclical economic policy to maintain a rate of growth that produced high levels of employment while, at the same time, using the same policies to avoid inflation and to maintain reasonable equilibrium in the balances of payments accounts. Where the Code drew controversy was its suggestion of some fairly broad, but nevertheless clear, ideas about the proper role and use of domestic economic policy in an integrated global economy. Rather than being strictly an instrument of national economic management, Mueller-Armack's Code stated that how governments used their fiscal and monetary policy tools was now "matters of common interest." In addition to using countercyclical policy to maintain a stable, noninflationary growth path, countries running severe payments imbalances were asked to make adjustments to their economic policies to restore equilibrium. Indeed, whereas the opening language of the Code recognized the full variety of policy objectives that governments strive to meet, in determining which policy goals should receive priority when they come into conflict, the code struck out a clear position, stating that surplus and deficit countries needed to "give priority to policies which will effectively contribute to a real equilibrium in their external payments."[33]

Revised versions of the Code spelled out more clearly the precise way in which countries were to go through the process of internal adjustment to restore international equilibrium. Countries running a payment surplus were asked to take steps to grow their economies, not to discriminate against imports, and to encourage the export of capital. Countries running a payment deficit needed to "secure internal financial stability and demand conditions which would prevent excessive imports"—in other words, slow the rate of economic growth and take steps to combat inflation.[34]

It is this language that makes the Code of Good Behaviour so significant. Whereas other Economic Policy Committee documents gave equal weight to the three goals of high employment, price stability, and international payments balance, the Code of Good Behaviour took a clear position on how the achievement of policy goals should be prioritized when they came into conflict with each other. Faced with international economic pressures stemming from payment imbalance, countries needed to sacrifice their domestic policy agendas and go through a process domestic adjustment to restore payment equilibrium. To be clear, this was fairly mild language; it was not a new "rules of the game" in that the Code did not specify the precise circumstances under which adjustment should take place, which policy instruments should be used, and in what way, in the adjustment process. Nevertheless, the Code did share something critical in common with the old gold standard conception of "rules of the game," and that was the belief that countries running balance of payments deficits should restore equilibrium even if it meant deflating their national economy. From this standpoint, the proposed Code of Good Behaviour ran completely contrary to the spirit of embedded liberalism.

Seen in this light, what is particularly surprising is that the Code of Good Behaviour was not more controversial than it was. In fact, it seems to have been accepted by most of the members of the Economic Policy Committee, with only the United States registering any official criticism of the document. In an effort to present the OEEC Ministerial Council with an alternative to Professor Mueller-Armack's Code, the United States offered its own draft set of principles that, while subscribing to the basic goals of the Code—high employment, price stability, and payments balance—did not set priorities among these goals, lacked any policy prescriptions for surplus and deficit countries, and had very soft language on the questions of when countries were expected to orient their own policies with an eye toward their effects on other countries.[35]

In the end, it was the revised version of Professor Mueller-Armack's Code, not the U.S. document, that was supported by the broader Economic Policy Committee membership and sent off to the OECD ministerial council. The

U.S. objections had little effect on the final document; its various criticisms of the code only received brief mention in a few, scattered footnotes. Nevertheless, it does not appear that the Code had any direct lasting effect on future discussions that took place within the Economic Policy Committee. It was never raised again by the Committee, nor was the language of the Code mobilized by member governments.

Although the Code was short-lived and largely forgotten, this episode surrounding the Code of Good Behaviour is significant for two reasons. First, it shows that by the late 1950s officials dealing with international economic management and coordination were open to the idea that some new adjustment rules needed to be put in place and, even more significantly, that rather than protecting the autonomy of national governments, these adjustment rules should give greater importance to maintaining international monetary stability. Second, this episode surrounding the Code shows how different governments, pursuing different models of capitalism, used the Economic Policy Committee as a space to assert their interests with respect to questions of international economic cooperation.

While the Code of Good Behaviour did not get very far, it did not mark the end of efforts to formulate clear, binding adjustment rules. Only a few short years later the question of adjustment rules reemerged, though this time with renewed vigor and with the support of the finance ministers and central bankers of the OECD countries.

The Adjustment Process Report

When Professor Mueller-Armack distributed his proposed Code of Good Behaviour, the weaknesses in the Bretton Woods system were only just percolating to the surface. Three years later the system seemed to be lurching from one crisis to another. The Gold Pool, General Arrangements to Borrow, and the swap network had so far kept a major speculative crisis at bay, but by 1964 it was becoming clear that something more had to be done if the Bretton Woods system was going to have a future. To this end, government officials from finance ministries and central banks began to systematically review the state of the international monetary system and searched for a new set of principles of international monetary cooperation.

On June 15, 1964, the finance ministers and central bank governors of the Group of Ten met at the offices of the French Finance Ministry in Paris to discuss a report on the future functioning of the international monetary system. The report made three major recommendations: first, that the system of balance of payments financing needed be brought under multilateral surveillance; second, that serious study needed to be given to the question of the future of reserve asset creation; and, third, that study needed to be given to the process of balance of payments adjustment. The task of multilateral surveillance was handed over to the Bank for International Settlements, and the study of reserve asset creation was given over to Rinaldo Ossola, Vice Chairman of the Bank of Italy. The study of the adjustment process was handed over to Working Party 3 of the OECD.[36]

Working Party 3 had been formed as part of restructuring of the Economic Policy Committee in 1961 and was tasked with reviewing countries' balance of payments positions and, most important, with making recommendations of steps to be taken in times of serious payments imbalance. Given the Working Party's focus, its discussions frequently touched on the issue of balance of payments adjustment. This was the first time, however, that the Working Party took on the question of adjustment formally and systematically. Official study of the adjustment process within the Working Party began with a paper submitted by the Dutch delegation on the relationship among internal liquidity, capital flows, and the balance of payments. Like Germany, the Netherlands had built its postwar economic recovery on social market economic principles and was also very export dependent.

Whereas the Group of Ten had charged Working Party 3 with analyzing the full spectrum of economic policies that could have an impact on the adjustment process, the Dutch paper restricted its focus to monetary policy. In addition, the Dutch paper took the idea of adjustment rules much further than Alfred Mueller-Armack's Code of Good Behaviour had. Mueller-Armack had danced delicately around specifying concrete monetary policy rules. In contrast, the Dutch paper was much more direct and explicitly suggested that the gold-standard "rules of the game"— whereby monetary policy was dictated by the changing tides of transnational capital flows—needed to be revived to deal with the persistent problem of international payments imbalances.[37]

As a first stroke, this was a bold one, as it made explicit the tensions and conflicts over the idea of adjustment that had previously only occasionally risen to the surface. When this paper was taken up for discussion at the June meeting of the Working Party it, perhaps not surprisingly, received strong support from the German delegation. Dr. Gocht from the German Ministry of Economics used the Dutch paper to make his own case for strengthening the rules of international monetary cooperation. As the minutes of that meeting note, he clearly meant a return to classical formulas: "In [Dr. Gocht's] view the problem was how to make internal liquidity creation a dependent variable as it was under the gold standard."[38]

This was an extremely controversial position, one that called into question the very essence of the Bretton Woods compromise. As such it drew a significant amount of criticism. Whereas only the U.S. delegation had registered strong criticism of the Code of Good Behaviour some years earlier, this time it was clear that the Dutch and German positions were in the minority. Even those who came to the meetings representing state monetary authorities were not willing to turn the clock back to 1870. Robert Roosa from the U.S. Treasury department argued that the current international monetary system was too unstable, with too many structural imbalances, to make such rules practicable. R. W. Lawson from the Bank of Canada argued that "a mechanistic quantitative approach was not satisfactory," a view shared by M. M. Perouse of the French Treasury, "who did not agree with the idea of establishing automatic rules," and Salvatore Guidotti of the Bank of Italy, who "considered the idea of automatic quantitative rules quite unacceptable."[39]

Faced with such strong divisions within the Working Party, the possibility of preparing a consensual report for the Group of Ten seemed dim. Through 1964 and 1965, work proceeded on an official Adjustment Process Report within a subcommittee chaired by Lawson of the Bank of Canada. Marred by internal conflict, the subcommittee had a very difficult time drafting anything that might represent a consensus, or even a compromise, position. When the work of the subcommittee was brought up for discussion within the larger Working Party, Dr. Gocht complained that "discussions had revealed some lack of will of tackling the problem seriously" and that the group had not given due consideration to his ideas. Fred Deming, representing the United States, continued to stake out the opposite terrain by arguing that individual country circumstances were too diverse to make fixed monetary policy rules practicable.[40]

The subcommittee returned to the broader Working Party in March of 1966 with a draft conclusion of the report that was circulated for wider discussion. The resulting document was essentially a compromise between the U.S. "flexibility" position and the Dutch and German "rules" positions. Although making the case that no clear, quantitative rules could be established, the Adjustment Process Report did articulate guidelines of appropriate policy measures that governments should follow in cases where payments imbalances could clearly be attributed to "pure" circumstances of internal demand pressures, problems of international trade competitiveness, and capital flows.[41] After a brief discussion at the May meeting of Working Party 3, the report was finalized and sent to the ministerial council of the OECD without any further changes.

On July 7, 1966, Otmar Emminger, member of the Board of Managers of the Bundesbank and chairman of the deputies of the finance ministers of the Group of Ten, transmitted a report to the Group of Ten on the outcomes of the discussions that had taken place on the future of the international monetary system. The report contains a fairly lengthy discussion of the process of multilateral surveillance and on the possibility of new reserve asset creation, but on the adjustment process it says very little. At most, Emminger could write that the members of the Working Party 3 "agree that improvements in the adjustment process are needed and possible" but could report nothing of substance. In fact, in the entire twenty-five-page report to the Group of Ten discussion of the adjustment process was given just two paragraphs.[42]

This rather anticlimactic outcome bespeaks a parallel story to that of the Code of Good Behaviour: those in favor of precise adjustment rules clashing with those arguing for flexibility, resulting in a hopelessly compromised document that comes out in favor of neither side. Unlike the Code of Good Behaviour, which seems to have completely vanished from the ideational and discursive landscape of the Working Party, the Adjustment Process Report did frame future discussions of payments disequilibria and policy responses. After 1966, Working Party 3 delegates would often reference the success, or failure, of other countries' adjustment processes in their assessment of payment imbalances. Occasionally, a delegate or a secretariat paper would use the language of the Adjustment Process Report's "pure causes" to evaluate a payment imbalance. However, while the language of the report could occasionally be used as an assessment device, using those assessments as a means of prescribing clear policy responses was much more difficult.

No doubt one reason for this was the controversial nature of the Adjustment Report itself, but another factor was that after 1964 the question of adjustment was superseded by renewed concern over the question of liquidity in the global economy. As already noted, the impetus for the Adjustment Process Report was a deeper concern within the Group of Ten that new forms of international liquidity were emerging, like central bank swaps and other forms of official credits to deficit countries, which could "obscure the need for active adjustment policy measures."[43] In other words, although the finance ministers and central bankers of North America and Western Europe were willing to take on a large role in patching up the Bretton Woods system, they were not willing to allow these new arrangements to let countries off the hook by plying them with short-term balance of payments financing. Indeed, if the monetary authorities ever became unwilling to provide short-term financing to a deficit country, then the question of adjustment was somewhat moot.

A crucial difference between the Adjustment Process Report and the Code of Good Behaviour is that, when Dr. Mueller-Armack proposed his Code, state officials and policy experts certainly understood that, at times, international considerations may warrant a change in course of domestic policy, but the idea that domestic policies would be constantly evaluated in terms of their international impacts was certainly not an accepted one. The Adjustment Process Report marks a shift in this basic paradigm. Once state finance officials made it clear that there would be no new major infusion of liquidity into the international monetary system, adjustment went from being an occasional thing that governments had to do to correct for short-term payments problems to a permanent part of the institutional architecture of international monetary cooperation. True, advocates for a return to something akin to the classical gold standard may not have won agreement to a new set of monetary rules, but what they did have agreement to was more subtle, but perhaps more important: that domestic policy concerns give way to protecting the health and integrity of the international monetary system.

The Tenuous Hold of Embedded Liberalism

Even as late as 1961, more than fifteen years after the signing of the Bretton Woods agreements, the central tenet of embedded liberalism—that domestic economic policy should be geared toward full employment, not toward maintaining international payments equilibrium—still had to fight for space in the organizations of postwar international monetary cooperation. The gold standard had long since passed, but the belief that international monetary cooperation should be rule bound with national economic policy given over to the ebbs and flows of international transactions still had many adherents.

How was classical economic liberalism able not only to resist the post-Depression, postwar progression of embedded liberalism, but also to maintain a sufficiently resonant legitimacy such that one could, without fear of scorn, suggest in the most official organizational forums of intergovernmental cooperation that the best way to structure the international monetary system was according to the same "rules of the game" of the gold standard era? Other scholars who have noticed this weakening of the embedded liberal compromise during the late 1950s and 1960s have suggested that state officials begrudgingly accepted the tenets of economic liberalism either because they were foisted on them by powerful American officials or because it was the only sensible thing to do given the pressures of an increasingly liberal global economy. The historical record shows both of these interpretations to be incorrect.

American officials by the late 1950s were persistently saddled with balance of payments deficits and therefore had no interest in supporting adjustment rules that would require them to abandon their domestic economic programs to correct that deficit. Of the national governments, it was the Germans and the Dutch who had already embraced economic liberalism in building their social market economies and who had the most to gain from a stricter set of international monetary rules. Classically liberal ideas about the relative importance of growth versus inflation, the causes of inflation, and the need for firm adjustment rules were being advanced before national governments began to face the pressures of economic globalization. These ideas, in other words, were about *shaping* the emerging liberal, global economy, not reacting to it.

The OECD, which by the early 1960s had become perhaps the central forum for intergovernmental dialogue over domestic and international economic issues, influenced the shape of these debates in two important ways. First, the OECD and its Economic Policy Committee had its own set of clear ideas on questions of economic management—ideas that hewed to the Committee's origins as a talking shop for government finance officials and that seemed fairly impervious to alternative perspectives. So, in addition to providing a deliberative space for member governments, the Economic Policy Committee actively constructed that space both by asserting its own views and, perhaps most critically, by actively encouraging and legitimating particular lines of discussion.

If national governments were going to pursue a social democratic path to growth they would have to do so in spite of the prevailing ideas held by the international community. Growth, employment, social welfare—these were all goals frequently lauded in the reports of the Bank for International Settlements, the communiqués of the Group of Ten, and the policy statements of the OECD. But they were secondary goals, goals to be pursued only on the condition that they did not interfere with the primary concern with price stability and international payments balance.

4 Adjustment in Practice

Opening and Closing the Door on the Italian Left

THE PREVIOUS CHAPTER SHOWED THAT THE DISCUSSIONS around the basic principles of postwar economic management and balance of payments adjustment that took place within the OECD, particularly its Economic Policy Committee, were characterized by an underlying tension between a commitment to economic growth and fairly orthodox views about the relationship between domestic and international economic stability. This tension was never resolved in the abstract, and no formal agreement was ever reached on the underlying question of adjustment—at least while the Bretton Woods system was still up and running. But what about in practice, when push came to shove and the members of the various committees and working groups had to give clear, concrete interpretations of, and solutions to, pressing economic problems? Which paradigm, embedded or classical liberalism, prevailed in those instances?

This chapter begins to answer this question with a study of Italian political and economic developments during the 1950s and 1960s. Italy does not feature prominently in most studies of postwar political and economic developments. This is most likely because, from an international relations perspective, Italy was not a dominant player on the world scene. True, the country did have the distinction of being grouped as one of the "major countries" of the Western World, but it was certainly the least major of the majors. The United States and the United Kingdom were the reserve currency countries, where developments in the markets for dollars and sterling reverberated across the

Bretton Woods system. The Federal Republic of Germany was the economic powerhouse of Western Europe and the anchor of the European Economic Community. France, though not as economically dominant as Germany, consistently threw itself on the international stage by openly challenging American hegemony and the centrality of the dollar in the postwar international monetary system.

From the standpoint of the study of "great power politics," developments in Italy therefore do not attract a lot of attention. But as a case study in how prevailing ideas about growth and balance of payments adjustment manifested in practice, Italy is a compelling site of inquiry. First, like Germany, the Netherlands, and Switzerland, Italy achieved a high rate of economic growth after World War II through a fairly conservative policy framework that was powerfully influenced by the tenets of classical liberalism. However, whereas the success of the social market model was predicated, in part, on very low rates of unemployment and a corporatist model that integrated a fairly weak labor movement into the political and economic system, Italy struggled with very high rates of unemployment, a sharp regional divide between the prosperous North and the underdeveloped South and, perhaps most critically, a mobilized, radical, and popular left-wing movement of communists and socialists that constantly threatened the center right's economic agenda.

In terms of its international position, Italy consistently ran a balance of payments surplus and steadily accumulated a massive pile of foreign reserves. The one year that the Italian surplus went into deficit, 1963, was during the short-lived "opening to the left," a brief moment when the ruling Christian Democratic Party formed a center-left coalition government with the socialists and injected a strong dose of social democracy into its economic agenda. Although Italian foreign reserves were high, and although a significant portion of the deficit could be blamed on a poor harvest that drove up food imports, in the face of speculation against the lira the Christian Democrats and the Bank of Italy quickly abandoned their expansionary fiscal and monetary policies and aggressively deflated the economy. Though the payments surplus quickly recovered, government policy remained cautiously expansionary for the rest of the decade.

Although a rather brief episode in the longer trajectory of Italy's postwar economic and political development, the "opening to the left" and its aftermath reflected the deep and growing tensions between the country's domestic and international pressures and, as such, provides a sort of testing ground to see through which of the competing paradigms, classical or embedded liberalism, the international community would approach the problem of how to balance international payments adjustment against economic growth and high employment. Had Keynes's vision of the international monetary order prevailed within the postwar international monetary system, the Italian government would have been lauded for directly taking on the country's high rate of employment, and the speed with which short-term credit facilities ended the speculative run against the lira would have been interpreted as a successful effort of international monetary cooperation to protect this important, and necessarily tumultuous, economic experiment.

Such was not the case. This scenario of embedded liberalism in action exists only in the parallel universe of counterfactuals and historical speculation. As the rest of this chapter will show, in discussions of Italian growth and balance of payments, the Economic Policy Committee and the Bank for International Settlements framed their analysis of Italy's domestic economic development within a prevailing concern about the state of the country's international payments accounts and, more broadly, its effect on international monetary stability. Growth, employment, and the distribution of national income were discussed and even supported at times, but not because they were seen as values in their own right. Rather, they were factors that facilitated or hindered the equilibration of payments flows.

Indeed, throughout the late 1950s and early 1960s the international community was conspicuously silent on the high rate of Italian unemployment. The fact that Italy had managed to achieve rapid economic growth, relative price stability, and a balance of payments surplus was seen as the product of sound economic management. By the latter half of the 1960s, after the Christian Democrats had abandoned the policies associated with the opening to the left, the international community did begin to express concern about low rates of Italian growth, but not because they were concerned about stubbornly high rates of unemployment. Rather, with the international monetary system looking ever more fragile, members of the Economic Policy Committee worried that Italy's large balance of payments surplus and accumulation of foreign reserves was placing further strains on the Bretton Woods system. If they felt that Italy needed to grow, it was not for the sake of the unemployed, but rather for the sake of international monetary stability.

Closing the Door on the Left

The immediate problem that many countries faced after World War II was re-building the physical infrastructure lost to years of heavy combat. Italy, how-ever, had managed to exit the war without total devastation of its economic infrastructure. This was largely due to the resistance movement led by trade unionists, communists, and socialists who, in putting up an effective resis-tance to the authority of the axis powers in the Northern industrial areas of the country had managed to protect many factories from being destroyed or stripped.[1] Yet, while the productive base of the country was largely intact, the task of forging a united nation out of the fascist experience was plagued by deep cleavages along political, economic, and regional lines.

Politically, the country was sharply divided between a conservative lean-ing center and the far left. The center was organized in the country's largest political party, the Christian Democrats, which was a broad-based party that had strong support among both the urban middle class and small farmers. In addition, the Christian Democrats enjoyed the support of the U.S. government, which hoped that the party's emphasis on moderate reform would steer the country away from communism. While there were still some parties on the far right, including monarchists and fascists, they had, not surprisingly, lost much of their support during the war. The real challenge to the political authority of the Christian Democrats came from the left. Due in no small part to their heroic efforts leading the resistance against Axis occupation, the Communist and Socialist Parties drew massive support from the population—especially in the industrial north and in the central agricultural regions.[2]

While these ideological differences were a major barrier to forging a po-litical consensus, equally divisive was the country's highly uneven "dualistic" economy. Industrial development was concentrated in the northern cities of Milan, Turin, and Genoa, while the southern part of the country was largely agricultural and much poorer. Figures on the territorial distribution of post-war Italy's national income paint a stark picture of this regional divide. Be-tween 1938 and 1955 the per capita income produced in northern Italy ranged from 205 million lire to 276 million lire; in southern Italy, per capita income produced was less than half of that, only between 84 million and 116 million lire in the same period. Northern Italy was industrialized and economically well off; southern Italy remained poor and underdeveloped.[3]

The country was also divided over the issue of international economic integration. Years of fascist rule had kept the Italian economy isolated from the world economy, and even after the fall of the Mussolini government strong protectionist currents continued to raise concerns that the relatively underdeveloped Italian economy would buckle under the pressure of global competition. On the other side of this debate, economic liberals, who only now had a chance to express their antistatist economic views, argued that joining the global economy was the solution, not the threat, to prosperity. To do so the country would need to quickly stabilize its currency and strengthen industries so that they could compete in world markets.[4]

Coming out of the war, the Christian Democrats thus faced a choice as far as which developmental path they would try to lead Italy down. On the one hand, the party could strengthen its ties with the left and pursue a social democratic path, focusing on the problems of unemployment, the low standard of living, and the extreme underdevelopment of the south. On the other hand, rather than addressing internal political and economic divisions, the party could heed the call of the economic liberals and integrate the Italian economy with the American and European economies. This path was the more conservative one as it emphasized boosting incentives for domestic private investment in already-existing sectors of industrial strength and stabilizing the lira by attacking the country's high rate of inflation.

At first, largely due to the popularity of the far left, it appeared that the Christian Democrats would focus on Italy's domestic problems. In the general election of 1946 the Christian Democrats managed to capture only 35 percent of the vote, while the Socialists and Communists together received 40 percent of the vote. As the head of the Christian Democratic party, Alcide De Gasperi reached out to the parties of the left to form a center-left governing coalition. Yet, within two quick years, this center-left coalition completely fell apart. The U.S. government played no small role in this drama as they dangled the carrot of Marshall Plan aid in front of the Christian Democrats, asking for a more moderate government in exchange.[5] Prodded by American officials and aided by growing schisms between radical and reformist elements in the left parties, in May of 1947 De Gasperi formed a new government of Christian Democrats and the more right-wing political parties: Liberals, Social Democrats, and Republicans. When another general election was called in 1948 the Christian Democrats, benefiting enormously from a massive U.S. propaganda effort against the left, managed to get enough of the vote that, when added to the votes for far-right parties, enabled them to completely kick the left out of government and forge a center-right political coalition. To paraphrase Stephen Hellman's perceptive insight, with the main representative parties of the working class excluded from the process of governing, it is hard to see in Italy anything that looks like the oft-described "postwar settlement."[6] Rather, for more than a decade the Christian Democrats held together a center-right political coalition and pushed ahead with a conservative growth agenda built on the tenets of economic liberalism.

Whereas the Americans and the British had, to varying degrees, embraced the Keynesian turn in economic policy, economists in early postwar Italy had no use for state-directed demand management. The influential Italian economists in the 1950s were economic liberals, and the fascist experience had only strengthened their belief that free markets, not the state, were the solution to Italy's economic problems.[7] The Bank of Italy took the first, most aggressive, and perhaps most significant step toward putting the country on a neoclassical growth path. Italy, like other Western European countries, has a tightly controlled system of credit allocation, and at the core of this system sits the central bank, the Bank of Italy. Luigi Einaudi, respected conservative economist and governor of the Bank of Italy, attacked Italy's runaway inflation with a harsh round of monetary tightening in 1947. Known as the "Einaudi line," the measures included an increase in required bank reserves, which reduced the amount of credit available for banks to lend, and an increase in the discount rate from 4 to 5.5 percent, raising the price of credit across the economy. The policy was almost immediately effective in stopping domestic inflation and stabilizing the value of the lira on world markets. Even after Einaudi left his position at the Bank of Italy in 1948 to become president of the republic, his successor, Donato Menichella, held the "Einaudi line" through the 1950s, sticking to the same kind of monetary orthodoxy that, ideally, informed central bank practices during the classical gold standard–monitoring bank reserves and interest rates with a sharp eye on the exchange rate. The Bank's monetary orthodoxy was buttressed by the federal government's fiscal austerity. Under the Christian Democrats, tax receipts increased while public subsidies decreased as part of a larger effort of containing the budget deficit.[8]

It is worth pointing out that even in this broadly deflationary context the government could have taken significant steps to reduce the country's high level of employment by mobilizing its vast network of state-owned enterprises. In 1933 Mussolini had created the Istituto per la Ricostruzione Industriale

(IRI), a state holding company for troubled bank stocks. Over the years, the IRI bought increasing numbers of troubled Italian firms to the extent that, by 1940, somewhere between 20 and 25 percent of all of the capital assets of joint-stock corporations were controlled by the IRI and the Italian state. This placed Italy second behind the Soviet Union in terms of the state's share of total economic activity. The state's control over industry increased again in 1953 when oil and natural gas production was nationalized under the Ente Nazionale Idrocarburi, or ENI.[9]

As Andrew Shonfield observed in his classic study of postwar economic development in Europe, from the standpoint of political expediency the Italian state was in an enviable position to be able to address pressing domestic economic concerns. The country was suffering from a very high rate of unemployment and, through the ENI and IRI, the state was effectively the largest employer in the country. It would have been easy to use this control over industry to cut into the unemployment problem, particularly in the south where unemployment was highest. Instead of going this route, state managers of industry chose instead to modernize existing industries in the north to boost productivity. Moreover, the state had a controlling interest in Italy's most productive and profitable sectors and could have used revenue from dividend payouts to support new social spending or at least to balance the budget without raising taxes on the poor. Here again, the state opted to not take any dividend payments from its shares in ENI or IRI, distributing all dividend payments to the private bondholders who then used these funds to invest in their own firms.[10] In short, state control over industry in Italy did not "crowd out" private capital, nor did it provide a counterweight to an otherwise orthodox, investment-centered growth strategy. Rather, industrial policy fit neatly into the Christian Democrats' larger economic agenda by nurturing the development of private capital.

Looked at in terms of the growth in investment, productivity, and the national income, the Christian Democrat's conservative economic strategy appears to have worked remarkably well. From 1948 through 1961 Italy experienced more than a decade of uninterrupted strong economic growth. In concrete figures, real gross national product per capita more than doubled from 182,000 lire to 370,000 lire,[11] a very rapid rate of growth fueled by the brisk pace of capital investment and sustained by low to moderate levels of price inflation. Significant increases in productivity combined with overall price stability allowed Italian firms to compete on world markets by the time full currency convertibility was achieved in 1958. Writing in the early 1970s, Kevin Allen and Andrew Stevenson could look back over this long postwar decade of growth and call it "the most successful period of economic development in Italy's history."[12]

Although the Christian Democrat's growth model improved the fortunes of the owners of Italy's major industrial firms, from the perspective of workers and consumers the results were not so great. A major reason for Italy's remarkable ability to maintain such a high level of private investment and price stability during a long period of sustained growth was the fact that the country's persistently high rate of unemployment helped to keep labor costs very low. Economic growth was concentrated in a few industrial sectors in the north and, given the capital intensity of those sectors, higher levels of investment did not translate into a higher demand for labor. Moreover, given the rapid pace of industrial and technological change, jobs that did open up required skills that few Italians had—especially not those who hoped to emigrate from the agricultural south. While exact figures are hard to come by, some estimates put the Italian unemployment rate at somewhere between 7 and 9 percent during this period.[13] Data compiled by George Hildebrand show that, between 1946 and 1956, the number of registered unemployed remained unchanged at some 2.1 million people[14]—even though there was a mass emigration of Italians to other countries. Though the unemployment rate did begin to fall in the late 1950s and into the early 1960s, Table 4.1 shows that by comparative standards Italy's unemployment rate remained very high.

TABLE 4.1. Unemployment rates, select OECD countries.

	1960	1961
Belgium	3.4	2.7
France	1.3	1.1
Germany	1	0.7
Italy	**4**	**3.4**
Japan	1.1	1
Norway	1.2	0.9
Sweden	1.8	1.5
United Kingdom	1.5	1.5
United States	5.6	5.7

SOURCE: OECD, Economic Policy Committee, "Economic Growth, 1960-1970: A Mid-Term Review of Progress Towards the O.E.C.D. Growth Target." May 5, 1966, CPE/WP2(66)2, 7.

In short, Italy's economic growth in the early postwar period was firmly rooted in the soil of economic liberalism and fiscal orthodoxy, placing the country in the same company as Germany, the Netherlands, and Switzerland. Faced with a set of contradictory economic and political pressures at the end of World War II, the Christian Democratic party opted to shut the left out of the government and follow a classically liberal growth path that integrated Italy's industrial north with the reemerging global economy. In making this choice, the Christian Democrats largely ignored the problem of unemployment and the low standard of living.

The International Response to Italy's Economic Liberalism

Italy's high rate of unemployment did not escape the notice of the international community. A 1959 report on economic conditions across the OECD area issued by the Economic Policy Committee showed Italy with two to three times the number of unemployed workers as there were in Germany, and ten to twenty times the number of unemployed as in any other Western European country. The figures presented in Table 4.1 come from Working Party 2's midterm report on progress in reaching the OECD ministerial council's growth target, which was first drafted in 1965.[15] There was no avoiding the fact that Italy had a high rate of unemployment. That being said, discussion and analysis of Italy's postwar economic development that took place within the Economic Policy Committee was nearly silent on the subject.

Instead, the discussions that did take place on the subject of Italy's economic development focused almost entirely on the country's strong record of growth and, more important, its impressive record of price stability. As discussed in Chapter 3, one of the major concerns of the Economic Policy Committee in the early 1960s was the rate of wage growth and price inflation in Western Europe. Italy bucked this trend. Between 1955 and 1960, Italy averaged a growth rate of GDP of 5.8 percent and a growth rate of output of 5.1 percent, both of which were second only to Germany.[16] Yet, the average inflation rate in the same period was only 1.8 percent—the lowest in Europe. So while other countries were being cautioned about their growth rates and levels of aggregate demand, the Economic Policy Committee encouraged the Italian government to continue to pursue an expansionary economic program and even to try to increase wage rates.

It is important to note, however, that in supporting a more expansionary economic policy for Italy the international community was not expressing its support for Keynesian demand management but rather wanted Italy to adhere to the principles of global economic liberalism. In the early 1960s the international community grew increasingly concerned with the U.S. balance of payments deficit. One of the consequences of Italy's strong record of growth in the 1950s was that the country began to consistently show a surplus in its international accounts, due to strong export performance and a large inflow of foreign investment. This, in turn, produced a build-up of foreign reserves—mostly dollars—at the Bank of Italy. Italy's balance of payments surplus was thus the flip side of the U.S. deficit. Just over one-third of the U.S. deficit in 1959 was due to imports from and capital flows to Italy; in 1961 that figure rose to just over 40 percent.

Under these circumstances, the Bank for International Settlements viewed the expansionary thrust of the Christian Democrats' economic policies as good international economic practice or, as they more explicitly put it, as "playing by the rules of the game"—letting foreign reserves flow through the banking sector, enter the domestic economy, and provide liquidity to support economic growth at home.[17] Following the same classical-liberal logic, the Economic Policy Committee also encouraged the Italian government to continue to pursue a high level of expansion that would, in theory, bring in more imports and, through this self-adjusting process, restore equilibrium to the country's international account.[18] The build-up of foreign reserves at the Bank of Italy also came up in the discussions of Working Party 3. In early 1962 the German delegates to the Working Party, Gocht and Emminger, called out their Italian colleague, Salvatore Guidotti from the Bank of Italy, on the country's excessively high foreign reserves. Agreeing with the German analysis, S. Posthuma, Managing Director of the Nederlandsche Bank, urged the Italians to continue to pursue a "balanced" growth path, one that would raise wages, which, in turn, would increase imports into the country.[19]

In short, whatever concerns the international community expressed about patterns of economic growth in Italy, they did not come from an embedded liberal or Keynesian framework. Rather, the international community viewed Italian development through the lens of a classically liberal economic paradigm, one that stressed the international rules of the game covering balance of payments adjustment and price stability. The problem of Italian unemployment was absent from these discussions, and although Italian wage rates and living conditions—which were also quite low by European standards—were matters of concern, it was largely because they were seen as a mechanism for achieving a better equilibrium in international payments accounts.

The Opening to the Left

The Christian Democrats' economic policies successfully moved the Italian economy into a position of strength within the postwar global economy. In doing so, however, the party had not only failed to deal with the domestic political and economic tensions that it had confronted in the late 1940s but actually exacerbated those tensions by targeting the country's industrial sectors in the north while ignoring the underdeveloped economy in the south. In 1951 the southern region of Italy was home to 37 percent of the country's population but accounted for only 24 percent of the country's gross domestic product and only 13 percent of industrial investment. By 1960, even as the government directed its state enterprises to channel more investment into the south, these figures had barely changed; the share of population living in the south was more or less the same, and, although the share of investment rose to 15 percent of the national total, the share of national gross domestic product had actually fallen to 23 percent. Foreign direct investment, which had increased from $18 million in 1956 to just over $65 million in 1961 and nearly 80 percent of which flowed to Northern Italy, widened the gap between the two regions.[20]

So, even though the center right was "delivering the goods" in terms of a high rate of overall economic growth, this did not increase the political support for the Christian Democrats or their allies from the Italian people. Rather, given the highly concentrated nature of economic growth, both in regional and sectoral terms, it was only the lucky few who found work in key export industries that were experiencing anything like a postwar prosperity. Most poor and working-class Italians were not benefiting from the Christian Democrat's growth agenda, which contributed to growing popular support for the socialist and communist parties. In the 1946 general election, the Italian Communist Party captured just under 20 percent of the vote; in the 1953 and 1958 elections the party captured around 23 percent of the vote.[21] By 1953 the center right's grip on power was so weak that the ruling coalition was taking desperate measures to stay in power, pushing through the so-called swindle law, which gave the coalition of political parties that won 50 percent of the poplar vote nearly two-thirds of the seats in parliament.[22] While this severely hampered the left's ability to take political power, it was also indicative of the left's growing political strength, particularly the strength of the Italian Socialist Party.

The left, however, was unable to capitalize on its growing relative political power. Existing rifts between the Socialist Party and the Communist Party grew as the former made overtures to the Christian Democrats while the later struggled with its own party platform at a time when Stalinism was undermining support for the communist cause. In addition, the trade union movement also began to splinter as moderate and conservative factions broke away from the main trade union confederation and sought a rapprochement with business leaders.[23]

By the end of the decade even the fractionalization of the left could not stand in the way of the fact that popular support for the center right was plummeting. In addition, trade unions in northern cities like Milan began to capitalize on the fact that, even though unemployment remained relatively high for the country as a whole, labor markets were very tight in these key industrial areas that were so vital for the country's overall level of economic growth and, even more critical, export competitiveness. When it came time to renegotiate labor contracts in 1959 the trade unions pushed employers hard, creating one of the most intense years of labor conflict. In 1959 there were not only more strikes than any year in the previous five years, but those strikes involved more workers and were of much longer duration.[24] By the beginning of the new decade Italy was home to what was perhaps the most active and militant trade union movement in the entire OECD area.[25]

At the same time that labor was growing more active, the Socialist and Communist Parties built on their growing popular support and shifted political tactics, rethinking their abstentionist strategy of doing politics from the outside and starting to engage more directly with the formal political process. The Socialist Party had steadily moderated its more radical positions and become much like the other Socialist Parties of Western Europe: resigned to the reality of capitalism and focused on its most efficient and equitable management. The Communist Party, which, having strongly rejected participation in party politics as a means of achieving its aims for much of the 1950s, began to seek out elected positions. The Socialist Party went even further in this regard, opening a dialogue with the Christian Democrats on the formation of a center-left government.[26]

The Christian Democrats welcomed these overtures from the Socialists as their center-right coalition continued to crumble. Although the Christian Democrats had managed to hold their conservative political coalition together for more than a decade, it was now being ripped apart by internal fractionalization. These internal struggles, combined with the increasing number of votes going to the left parties, brought the Christian Democrat's share of the vote from nearly 49 percent in 1948 to just over 42 percent in 1958. Writing from a perspective of having recently watched these political developments unfold, George Hildebrand summarized the situation as follows: "To the Christian Democrats, the problem was the simple one of how to stay in power despite the continuing erosion of their political base in favor of the parties of the left."[27]

To this simple problem the trajectory of Italian politics over the last decade was providing the Christian Democrats with a clear and simple answer: Move from the center right to the center left. In January of 1962, in what is now referred to as the "opening to the left," the Christian Democrats brought the Socialist Party into the government as the main coalition partner, forming the country's first center-left political coalition since the "grand coalition" of 1946. This move strengthened the Christian Democrats' political position in two ways. First, and most directly, the growing popular support for the Socialists now went to support the ruling government. Less directly, but equally important, the move created a schism between the two left parties as the more radical Communists were excluded from the coalition. In exchange for the support of the Socialists, the Christian Democratic leadership needed to make some changes to its economic policy priorities.

Most visibly, the government quickly met the Socialists' demand to nationalize the electrical industry, but other than this there were no major policy announcements that signaled the "opening to the left." Rather, this shift in the political landscape manifested more in the management of industrial, fiscal, and monetary policy. The government stopped pushing back against the trade unions and their demands for higher wages and became less concerned with balancing the budget instead increasing level of public investment. On the monetary side, the Bank of Italy relaxed its orthodox grip over the money supply and increased the flow of credit to Italy's working-class and middle-class consumers, a change in policy that reflected both the new political situation and the new intellectual climate within the Bank itself. When Donato Manichella, the conservative governor of the Bank of Italy, left his post in

1960, Keynesianism, long criticized by the neoclassical old guard, had become the new orthodoxy among Italy's younger economists.[28] Manichella's successor, Guido Carli, was by no means a left-wing Keynesian, but his approach to monetary policy reflected this break with neoclassical orthodoxy. Between 1962 and 1963 household borrowing from the banking sector increased by some 60 percent—the fastest rate of increase in consumer credit in the postwar period.[29]

The opening to the left was a significant shift in the politics and policies of Italian postwar economic management, yet it was also very brief. Price inflation, long kept under control and a hallmark of the perceived "soundness" of Italy's economic policies, accelerated sharply in 1962 and 1963 to levels that were higher than the country's European peers. Workers' wages, which had also been quite low relative to their European peers throughout the previous decade, jumped by 14 percent in 1962 and then again by 20 percent in 1963. In addition, and partly because of workers' high earnings but also because the Bank of Italy was willing to give easy access to consumer credit, imports into the country increased considerably. In the final months of 1962 Italy recorded its first balance of payments deficit since 1956.[30]

Foreign investors respond to these developments by speculating heavily against the lira, forcing the Bank of Italy to draw down its supply of foreign reserves. Faced with this international economic pressure, both the central government and the Bank of Italy abandoned the domestic economy and once again oriented fiscal and monetary policy around restoring international payments equilibrium. Repeating Einaudi's stance against inflation in 1947, in late 1963 the Bank of Italy reversed its easy monetary policy and clamped down on the supply of credit, which had an almost immediate deflationary impact. The central government followed suit in the early months of 1964 with a round of fiscal restraint, the most significant component of which was an increase in the national sales tax.[31] Through the combined effects of these monetary and fiscal measures, the ranks of the unemployed once again began to swell.

While the "opening to the left" was a response to the changing Italian political landscape, changes that were themselves the product of the Christian Democrats' economic growth strategy of the 1950s, in the end the government's commitment to international economic integration overwhelmed its domestic political concerns. The socialists had found a seat at the table of government, but they were clearly the junior partner to the Christian Democrats and their moderate, internationally oriented policy agenda.

The Center Left in the Eyes of the
International Community

Italy's opening to the left, and the subsequent balance of payments crisis and economic deflation, attracted considerable attention from the international community. Initially, during the entire first year of this new political and economic experiment the international community seemed completely at ease with Italian developments. Data available to the Economic Policy Committee at the time showed only moderate wage pressures in Italy.[32] In fact, given Italy's persistent balance of payments surplus and growing foreign reserves, the Economic Policy Committee went so far as to raise the question of whether countries, like Italy, with strong payments surpluses should be urged to support wage increases as a means of increasing imports.[33]

Whatever international support there was for the opening to the left began to wither in the middle of 1963 as both the Economic Policy Committee and the Bank for International Settlements received more accurate data that painted a very different picture of the movement of wages and prices over the previous year. In its 1963 *Annual Report*, for example, the Bank for International Settlements described 1962 as marking a critical shift in political and economic developments in Italy defined by a more militant trade union movement pushing for higher wages at a time when productivity growth was slowing.[34] Around the same time as the publication of the Bank's report, the Economic Policy Committee lumped Italy in with those other countries of Western Europe where cost inflation was becoming a major concern and where cost inflation was driven by excessive wage increases.[35]

When Working Party 3 began to discuss these developments in the late fall of 1963, the Italian delegation tried to assuage the other members' concerns about mounting inflation. Salvatore Guidotti, one of the more Keynesian members of the Bank of Italy's Research Department, reminded the other delegates that, despite their recent rapid increase, wages in Italy were still among the lowest in Europe and that there were still significant problems of uneven regional development that needed to be attended to. Unfortunately for Mr. Guidotti, these considerations seem to have resonated with only one delegate from Sweden in the room. The general sentiment among the other Working Party members was that, given the new balance of payments figures projecting a deficit for the year on the order of somewhere between $800 million and $1.1 billion, Italy needed to get a handle on wage increases.[36]

Even though the Bank of Italy had acted rather swiftly, and harshly, to deflate the economy by clamping down on the money supply, the international community wanted to see even more restraint. The reason was that both the Economic Policy Committee and the Bank for International Settlements interpreted the balance of payments crisis of 1963 not as a manifestation of short-term contingent factors but rather as a manifestation of a structural imbalance in the Italian economy produced by the political and economic shifts associated with the opening to the left. This helps to explain why, despite the fact that the Italian crisis only really became apparent in the middle of 1963, just a few months later, in February of 1964, the Economic Policy Committee could write that "effective stabilization has already been long delayed," and so monetary action needed to be buttressed by fiscal measures.[37]

While it is unclear whether these sentiments had, by themselves, any substantive effect on policy developments inside the Italian government, soon thereafter the Italian government did announce additional measures of fiscal restraint to support the Bank of Italy's monetary restraint. When this came up for discussion during the first meeting of Working Party 3 in 1964, the other members of the Working Party were generally happy to see that the Italian government was taking its economic problems so seriously, though again some delegates worried that the measures were not enough. Otmar Emminger from the German Bundesbank voiced continuing concern about the rapid pace of wage increases recorded in 1963, while his colleague, Dr. Gocht of the German Ministry of Finance, and Emile Van Lennep, the Working Party chairman, both stated that they wanted to see the Bank of Italy keep a very tight grip over domestic credit markets.[38] The Bank for International Settlements remained pessimistic in its assessment of wage developments in the country that, it argued, needed to be brought "back from the realm of fantasy to something which is in reasonable relation to productivity gains."[39]

The combination of strong deflationary action combined with short-term rescue package arranged with the United States, the United Kingdom, and Germany quickly brought the Italian balance of payments situation under control. By June 1964 Salvatore Guidotti was already reporting to Working Party 3 that the deterioration in the country's current account balance had been stopped.[40] Conditions were so placid that Italy did not even appear in the Working Party's usual roundup of country developments during its September meeting. At the next meeting in October, Guidotti was able to relay some of the damage that the deflationary measures had done to the domestic economy. Growth in gross domestic product and industrial productivity were reduced to 2.5 percent and 1.5 percent respectively and, as a direct result of the deflationary measures, Guidotti estimated that some 200,000 to 300,000 Italians had joined the ranks of the unemployed.[41]

In short, even though Italy had a long track record of maintaining an international payment surplus and ample foreign reserves and, most important, had effectively and immediately halted speculative attacks against the lira with some short-term credit arrangements, the international community was far more concerned with what the deficit augured for Italy's long-term payments deficit than what sharp deflation would do to the domestic economy. For a brief moment, the Christian Democrats had gone off the path of classical liberalism, forced to deal with deepening regional tensions between the north and south that were also pushing the political center of gravity further to the left. However, rather than use the international monetary machinery to support what was really a quite modest reorientation of domestic economic policy to the needs of workers and consumers, the dominant discourse that emerged out of the Economic Policy Committee urged the Italian government to pay full heed to its international obligations and once again become a responsible partner in the cause of international monetary stability.

How the international community responded to this brief, but incredibly tumultuous, period speaks volumes about how far the prevailing norms of adjustment had strayed from Keynes's embedded liberal vision. Indeed, from the perspective of the embedded liberalism thesis, the sequence of events that unfolded in Italy in 1962 and 1963 just should not have happened. The Bretton Woods institutions were supposed to protect national growth experiments from the financial decisions of panicky international investors by providing national governments with short-term financing that they could use to bolster foreign reserves and keep their currency stable. Indeed, Italy in 1963 was the very case for which the Bretton Woods institutions were designed.

The country was not suffering from long-term structural deficits—its payments position was either in balance or in a position of strong surplus for each postwar year preceding the 1963 deficit. Moreover, although the deficit did trigger a speculative run against the currency that reduced the country's foreign reserves, short-term credit assistance was remarkably effective in bringing speculative pressures to an end. The Bank of Italy had made arrangements for a $1 billion rescue package for the lira, consisting of currency swaps and other credit arrangements, primarily with the U.S. Federal Reserve but also with the Bank of England and the German Bundesbank. Once the terms of this package were made public in the spring of 1964 speculation against the lira came to an almost immediate halt.[42] In other words, Italy does not appear to be a case of a country that was inevitably forced to bow to international economic pressure and abandon social democracy; it rather appears to be a case of a country well positioned to use the Bretton Woods institutions to protect and solidify its nascent efforts at political and regional integration. Nevertheless, as Barry Eichengreen has suggested, the deflation of 1963–1964 adhered very closely to the script of classical-liberal balance of payments adjustment orthodoxy: Faced with a deficit, slow the growth of the economy to reduce the inflow of imports and dampen those inflationary developments that scared off foreign investors.[43]

The fact that the ruling center left did not go the path of embedded liberalism and seek to project its new growth experiment no doubt has much to do with the state of domestic politics. The Christian Democrats, after all, were not committed social democrats. Rather, they were a pragmatic political party that had already shown that their political calculus owed more to securing power than to adherence to strong principles. At the same time, international considerations also featured prominently in the Christian Democrats' political strategy. The De Gaspari government abandoned the "Grand Coalition" with the Communists and Socialists in 1948 and forged a center-right coalition in no small part because of their desire to secure the favor of the U.S. government and broader legitimacy in the eyes of the international community. From this standpoint, it is quite significant that the international community did not support a more embedded liberal solution to Italy's payment crisis in 1963. Rather, through 1963 and 1964 the Economic Policy Committee and the Bank for International Settlements supported the deflationary steps that had already been taken and urged the Italian government to continue to contain wages and prices to protect the stability of the international monetary system. When these international bodies did express criticism of Italian economic policy it was that the government needed to do even more to keep inflation in check.

Surplus, Stagnation, and the Limits of Adjustment

Italy's balance of payments position recovered very quickly after the summer of 1964, averaging a $135 million surplus each month for twenty-one months and then remaining in surplus for the rest of the decade.[44] Although this trend spoke well of Italy's return to international economic strength, the flip side of a strong balance of payments performance was a weak domestic economic recovery following the deflation of 1963 and 1964. After dropping sharply in 1964, the rate of private domestic investment remained stagnant, and new investment in manufacturing actually declined at a rate of about 3 percent per year. Despite low rates of new investment, Italian exporters managed to remain competitive in global markets through what Guido Rey characterizes as a "ruthless rationalization on the factory floor." By using the machinery and equipment that had been purchased during the heyday of rapid investment in the beginning of the decade more efficiently, employers were getting more output from fewer workers. As a consequence, unemployment continued to increase, and labor's share of total national income fell.[45]

The country was thus firmly back on a growth path reminiscent of the years when the Christian Democrats ruled from the center right. This is not what the trade unionists and supporters of the Socialist and Communist Parties had envisioned following the ascendancy of the center left. By the end of the decade, the domestic political situation was in chaos as growing domestic frustration with years of broken center-left promises bred mounting agitation from the left, culminating in the "hot autumn" of 1969. In the second half of the 1960s the international community also began to pressure the Italian government to return to a more expansionary policy stance, though from a completely different perspective. Less concerned with the effects that the deflation of 1964 continued to have on the lives of Italy's working class and poor, the international community was much more concerned with the effect that Italian surpluses were having on the stability of the international monetary system.

From 1964 to 1965 the Economic Policy Committee and its member delegates supported Italy's cautious approach to economic growth. In part, this cautious attitude reflected the delays in getting accurate data on the country's balance of payments situation that, despite Salvatore Guidotti's assurance of improvement, was only beginning to manifest in the official statistics. But the more important reason for this cautious attitude was the feeling that Italy, like other Western European countries, had been damaged by the rapid increase of wages over the previous five years, and so governments needed to develop mechanisms to take effective control over future wage developments before growth experiments began anew. For example, in its 1965 *Annual Report*, the

Bank of International Settlements characterized the Italian economy as being in a state of "near stagnation" but went on to argue that growth should not resume until wages were brought under control.[46] Working Party 2, despite its official charge to encourage progrowth economic policies, gave a similar analysis of the Italian situation:

> As a result of the policy of restraint, growth in output has been held down for a period of something like two years; and the pressure of demand has been very materially reduced. If expansion is now resumed, it will be resumed from a lower point; and if future expansion no more than keeps pace with the growth of economic potential, the greater margin of slack will be preserved. *What seems important is that this margin of safety should not be eaten into.*[47]

The Working Party was essentially saying that, through deflationary action, governments had effectively bought themselves some relief from wage-price pressures in the form of economic "slack"—a higher rate of underutilization of economic resources, including higher rates of unemployment. If growth were to resume, it needed to do so under conditions of slack so that a new build up of demand would not lead to price inflation.

This assessment of domestic economic conditions—not just in Italy but also across Western Europe—was tied to the increasing stress being placed on the international monetary system by the persistent and growing balance of payments deficits in the United States and the United Kingdom. Though both of these countries were pressured, often successfully, to take their own adjustment measures, the unavoidable reality was that the flip side of their growing deficits was other countries' large surpluses. The accumulation of reserves in Italy made it patently clear that adjustment had to come from both sides of the payments ledger.

This tension came to a head at the end of 1965 when, in October, both the Working Party 3 secretariat and the Italian delegation issued reports on Italy's balance of payments developments to the working party. Though the balance of payments figures were slightly different across the two reports, they both came to the same conclusion: The country's balance of payments was not just in surplus, it was—in the words of the secretariat's report, an "extraordinarily large surplus."[48] For most of the Working Party members, this was a clear sign that the Italian authorities needed to take strong and immediate steps to raise the level of internal economic demand in the country. Professor Kessler, from the Dutch delegation, "thought the Italian surplus a clear example of deficient demand," which, he argued was a "clear case for stimulatory policies." Several other delegates followed Kessler's line of thinking and suggested specific fiscal measures that could be taken to raise levels of private consumption, such as reducing workers' payments into the social security system or reducing taxes on certain consumption goods.[49]

Publicly, the Italian government committed itself to doing its part to support balance of payments equilibrium, but no significant policy measures were taken to increase private consumption, bring down the rate of unemployment, or reduce the country's buildup of foreign reserves. Rather, economic policy remained investment and export focused. New tax incentives were put in place to encourage private investment, and public investment from state-owned agencies was ramped up considerably. Rather than allow increased public spending to exert an expansionary effect on the economy, the government raised taxes to help keep the budget in balance.[50] By 1967, Italy was enjoying a high rate of economic growth that was the envy of its European peers, but the labor market remained very weak as continued migration from the agricultural south to the industrial north brought an overall decline in employment.[51] Under these economic conditions, Italy's balance of payments surplus remained strong, and the Bank of Italy continued to build up its supply of foreign reserves, even as the international monetary system was lurching from crisis to crisis caused by balance of payments deficits in the United States and the United Kingdom.

At the most obvious level, this was yet another indication of the asymmetrical nature of the balance of payments adjustment process in the Bretton Woods era: Although all countries publicly recognized that adjustment rules worked only if both deficit and surplus countries took measures to move toward balance, the reality was that the Bretton Woods system contained no mechanism to compel surplus countries to adjust, thus placing all of the pressures of adjustment on the shoulders of deficit countries.[52]

More significantly, the fact that the Italian government did not pursue an aggressive expansionary economic policy for balance of payments reasons also points to the way in which understandings about balance of payments adjustment had evolved with the liberalization of capital markets in the 1960s. As shown in Figure 4.1, in the early 1950s Italy had maintained a balanced payments position by supplementing its trade deficit with capital inflows; after 1964 this relationship was reversed. Throughout the rest of the decade Italy

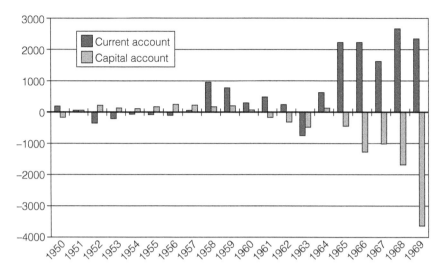

FIGURE 4.1. The structure of Italian balance of payments surpluses and deficits, 1950–1969, in millions of dollars.

SOURCE: Allen and Stevenson, *Introduction to the Italian Economy*, 76–77.

recorded a massive trade surplus but balanced this with substantial capital outflows.

By encouraging capital exports, Italy had found a way to balance its international accounts without having to go through the kind of domestic adjustment process that the Economic Policy Committee wanted. Of course, the international community could register only a weak protest against this means of achieving balance because many of the same people who advocated for firm adjustment rules were also the most vocal advocates for seeing capital flows as an acceptable—indeed for some preferable—means of achieving payments equilibrium.[53] From the standpoint of the evolving international norms around adjustment, Italy could legitimately claim that its accounts were in balance, even if they achieved balance by draining reserves from other OECD countries and then exporting capital around the world. So, even when the Working Party 3 secretariat, in late 1968, tried to characterize Italy as a "straightforward" case of a country that needed "substantially faster internal expansion" to bring down its massive payments surplus, the Italian delegation could respond that, given the country's massive outflow of capital, the case for domestic expansion was not so clear-cut.[54]

In summary, as they had in the late 1950s, the international community once again called on the Italian government to increase the level of internal demand through policies to promote private consumption. And, as in the late 1950s, this policy prescription did not come out an embedded-liberal policy paradigm but rather from classical liberalism's overriding concern with managing the worsening imbalances in the international monetary system. If the international community drew attention to Italy's high rate of unemployment, or its relatively low standard of living, it was not because high employment and the quality of life of the working class were values in their own right but because, as the Working Party 3 secretariat put it, they indicated that Italy could afford to grow, import more goods from other countries, and chip away at its payments surplus.

Embedded Liberalism in Retrospect

In the second half of the 1960s the Christian Democrats had, once again, found a political formula that kept the left in check while bringing the Italian economy back to a position of international strength. At the same time, however, even after more than twenty years at the head of the government, the Christian Democrats never managed to resolve the country's underlying domestic political and economic tensions. Driven by political necessity, the Christian Democrats tried to address the country's domestic economic problems by forming a coalition with the Socialists, but it is clear that economic policy making was always framed by a preeminent concern with the country's international position. The more moderate center-left settlement that followed the balance of payments crisis of 1963 proved to be short lived, as a wave of political unrest and labor militancy erupted in 1968, peaking during the "hot autumn" of 1969.

In this chapter I have used this case of political and economic upheaval in the postwar era to uncover the underlying policy paradigms that informed key segments of the international community's views about the relationship between domestic and international economic developments. Of all the major Western European countries, Italy was a country suffering from what all observers recognized to be a very high rate of unemployment and a very low standard of living. Nevertheless, the central and critical finding of this chapter—a finding that buttresses the analysis given in Chapter 3—is that the international community read the politics and policies of Italian economic growth through the lens of a rather orthodox classical view of international monetary management.

In seeing how the classical liberal paradigm was put into practice, it becomes apparent that common political distinctions between "liberal" and "conservative" do not quite capture classical liberalism's interpretive lens or normative framework. True, the views of the international community typically favored capital over labor, balanced budgets over government spending, tight monetary policy over easy credit. But these more concrete policy views were shaped by a broader classically liberal policy paradigm that favored a balanced, stable international monetary order above all else. The Economic Policy Committee and even the Bank for International Settlements could get behind higher rates of growth, higher wages for workers, easier credit for consumers, and lower rates of unemployment, but only if those things could correct an imbalance in international flows of goods and capital.

Taking this chapter's and the preceding chapter's findings together, the picture that emerges is not one of an international economic order framed by the norms, values, and ideas of embedded liberalism. Rather, it is a picture of an international order still captured by the ideology of the gold standard, yet trying to make room within those classical prescriptions for a new set of postwar concerns, like stimulating economic growth and dealing with the political power of the left. It is a picture, in other words, of embedded liberalism inverted: commitments to growth and full employment defined by a stronger commitment to international economic liberalism and international monetary stability.

5 The Erratic March of Labour

If we are to explain the stagnation or crisis [of the working class], we have to look at the Labour Party and the labour movement itself. The workers, and growing strata outside the manual workers, were looking to it for a lead and a policy. They didn't get it. They got the Wilson years—and many of them lost faith and hope in the mass party of the working people.[1]

WHEN BRITISH HISTORIAN ERIC HOBSBAWM DELIVERED these words as part of the 1978 Marx Memorial Lecture, things looked bleak for those on the left in the United Kingdom. Harold Wilson, who had embodied the hopes of British social democrats in the mid-1960s, had retired from his post as prime minister and head of the Labour Party two years earlier, and the country was mired in an economic recession that would bring the Conservative Party, under the leadership of Margaret Thatcher, back into power. For Hobsbawm, the Wilson years were a lost opportunity, a time in the mid-1960s when the country rallied around the Labour Party's call for an ambitious program of economic modernization on social democratic principles, only to be subjected to tough austerity measures that surpassed anything that the Conservatives had thrown at them in the previous decade. How did the party of social democracy become the party of austerity? This chapter takes up this question by returning to this pivotal period in British politics, a period beginning when the Labour Party first returned to office in 1964 with an ambitious economic agenda that combined efforts to modernize the economy with liberal Keynesian growth policies and ending just three years later when the devaluation of sterling was followed by the harsh economic deflation of 1967–1968.

What makes this case so intriguing is the fact that the Labour government of the mid-1960s began to turn away from social democracy at precisely the same time that popular support for its social democratic agenda was highest. No longer the party representing just the interests of the trade unions or the far-left socialists and communists, under Wilson's leadership Labour had successfully refashioned itself as the party of both the working class and the middle class.[2] Having just squeezed past the Conservatives in the general election of 1964, less than two years later, Labour attracted an additional 800,000 votes in the general election of 1966 and shored up its once-slim parliamentary majority to a solid ninety-seven seats. This was a historic election for Labour, marking the first time since 1951 that the steady decline in the number of people voting for the party had been reversed.

It is at this point, however, that the story of Labour becomes most puzzling because, just as more and more British voters were convinced of the promise of Labour's economic agenda, the liberal Keynesian growth program was brought to a screeching halt. In May of 1966, a mere three months after its decisive electoral victory, the party put forth its budget for 1967 containing tough deflationary economic policies targeted at consumers and workers: reduced access to consumer credit, major cuts in government spending, and a mandatory wage and price freeze.[3] By 1968, after a round of further deflationary measures, the party that promised to push the economy forward had brought the economic engine to a full stop. With voters disillusioned by Labour's broken promises, the 1970 general election brought a Conservative government back into office, headed by Prime Minister Ted Heath. Wilson, and the Labour Party, remained important players in British politics throughout the 1970s, but the end of the 1960s had signaled the end of this experiment in third-way social democracy.

Much as with the previous chapter's account of Italy's "opening to the left," explaining this brief but pivotal moment in British political and economic history necessitates situating the domestic politics of growth within the international politics of balance of payments adjustment. Labour came to power with a long-term vision for modernizing the country's economy that they believed would put an end to both a decade-long economic stagnation and to persistent balance of payments deficits and speculative attacks against the pound sterling. While this vision was grounded in sound economic theory and supported by the British people, it needed time to work, and during that time the Labour government would depend on the financial cooperation of Western European central banks to shore up a weakening currency. This was the undoing of Labour's agenda, as this financial assistance could be secured only if Wilson and his government backed away from their social democratic economic vision and put the economy back on the path of fiscal and monetary orthodoxy that the Conservatives had followed.

Labour's Modernization Agenda

On November 3, 1964, Harold Wilson—head of the Labour Party and the United Kingdom's new prime minister—stood before the British parliament to deliver the Queen's Speech, marking the beginning of a new parliamentary season by laying out the government's agenda for the coming year. For the Labour Party and the United Kingdom as a whole, Wilson's speech signaled a clear turning point in British politics. Out of power since 1951, the Labour Party managed to eke out a slim victory over the long-dominant Conservative Party, taking the parliamentary majority by just five seats. Following through on its campaign promises to carve a new way forward for the country, Wilson laid out an ambitious economic program that would rebuild the country's sputtering economic engine on the principles of social democracy.

Some elements of the new National Plan, such as the nationalization of the iron and steel industries and promises to increase funding to the National Health Service, fell in line with the socialistic principles that had long informed Labour's economic policies. The core of the new National Plan, however, bespoke the emergence of a new Labour Party that, having lost three consecutive general elections, revamped its image from the "party of the trade unions" to the "party of the people."[4]

The National Plan set a target for a rate of economic growth of 3.8 percent, nearly a full percentage point higher than the average rate of growth over the previous decade.[5] To achieve this acceleration in the growth rate, the Labour Party argued that the country needed to go through a process of economic modernization by using the tools of economic policy not simply to redistribute Britain's economic pie but to make that pie substantially larger. To this end, Wilson proposed a new capital gains tax and a new corporations tax. Though both measures were partly framed in terms of economic redistribution from business to labor, the real goal of these proposals was to use the tax code to push British firms into productive, rather than speculative, investments. In addition, the government expanded the state's developmental machinery by creating the Department of Economic Affairs, a Ministry of Technology, and an Industrial Reconstruction Corporation.[6] This was all, as Ilaria Favretto has described it, part of a program built on a "technocratic socialism," a pragmatic, forward-looking recognition that what the country needed was a new long-term growth strategy for a very different national, and global economic context. The economic engine needed more than a tune-up; it needed to be rebuilt.[7]

In addition to being popular with the voters, Labour's economic program enjoyed the support of many British economists. Compared to the profession in the United States, where Keynesianism had to struggle to find a stable place among professional economists, in the United Kingdom Keynesian demand management strategies had become fully entrenched in the field after the publication of the Beveridge Report in 1947. Moreover, whereas American Keynesians tended to be more conservative (and were becoming increasingly so), British Keynesianism had a pronounced left-wing streak, especially in the economics department at Cambridge University. British Keynesians were also more resistant to the highly mathematical versions of the theory that were growing in popularity across the Atlantic. Indeed, rather than seeing themselves as detached technocrats, as mainstream American economists were increasingly wont to do, professional economists in the United Kingdom imbued their work with a sense of social purpose, directly addressing questions of equity and social justice in their research.[8]

To fully appreciate the significance of Labour's 1964 campaign, it needs to be put in the context of a long postwar economic stagnation. Once the world's economic powerhouse, after World War II the United Kingdom's economy experienced a growth rate that fell behind that of its major European competitors. Although the average growth rate of 2.3 percent per year between 1951 and 1964 was actually a marked improvement over the near zero rate of growth of the interwar period, it was the lowest in Western Europe and, most critically, far below the average of the rapidly growing economies of Italy, France, and Germany, who experienced a postwar boom at nearly double the rate of the United Kingdom. While many reasons have been offered to explain the United Kingdom's relatively poor economic performance in the early postwar years—the steam having run out of the country's early industrialization, the lack of a state-directed development program, and the fact that Western Europe was just now enjoying the boom that often comes with the transition from an agricultural to industrial economy—a crucial factor is the legacy of British empire and the successive efforts by both the Labour and Conservative governments in the 1940s and 1950s to protect the value of the pound sterling.

The 1945 general election brought the Labour Party, under the leadership of Clement Attlee, to power in the party's first majority government. Though infused with the ideology and interests of a mobilized and militant trade union movement, the Attlee government was often more concerned with preserving the vestiges of empire by keeping the pound sterling strong than it was with implementing progressive social reforms. The expansion of the welfare state thus came about quite slowly, and workers' take-home pay barely budged. Some industries were nationalized, but they were more often than not weak, noncompetitive industries, resulting in big state payouts to business owners with little gain for British workers and consumers.[9] What the Attlee government was trying to do was to channel as many of the country's resources as possible toward reducing the balance of payments deficit. In the end, however, the government was forced to devalue the pound sterling in 1949, and, although Labour managed to stay in power after the 1950 general election, it lost to the Conservative party in 1951 and would remain in the background of British politics for over a decade.

Like the Attlee government before it, the Conservatives kept a sharp eye on the country's balance of payments position, though they opted for the more market-based practice of subtle demand management rather than the heavy-handed nationalizations and regulations of their predecessors to keep the domestic economy in line with international pressures. When the economy began to grow and the balance of payments deficit worsened, the Bank of England would raise interest rates and induce a recession. In this way, the economy moved through stop–go cycles of economic expansion and contraction timed to the deficits and surpluses in the balance of payments account.

Up to about the middle of the 1950s, the British trade union movement, represented by the Trade Union Council, accepted the reality of balance of payments pressures by moderating their demands for higher wages, a greater say in the workplace, and a more extensive welfare state. With a unionization rate of over 40 percent, the highest in Europe, the Trade Union Council could have pressured Attlee's Labour government to be domestically focused in its economic priorities, but instead it worked to restrain its more militant members through the middle of the 1950s. After 1957, however, the Trade Union Council abandoned its conciliatory position, in part because the trade unions themselves were beginning to take some of the blame for the country's low rate of growth.[10]

Labour's 1964 victory thus came at a time when the postwar settlement had run its course and was not longer economically viable or politically credible. The postwar compromise was ultimately premised on a high rate of economic growth, and neither the Attlee government's attempts at planning nor the Conservative government's market-based cycles of stop–go had been able to deliver an economic environment within which the interests of capital and labor could both be served. In this context it is easy to see why Harold Wilson's pragmatic, growth-centered vision for the British economy would be so resonant.

Labour and Sterling

Not everyone was enamored with Labour's vision of a new way forward. Beneath the more visible eddies and currents of party politics and trade union activism lay a deeper tension between domestic financial institutions—often referred to as the City–Treasury–Bank of England nexus—and the government administration at Whitehall. The country's financial institutions were more concerned with protecting the international value of the pound sterling, an interest that had been well served by thirteen years of Conservative economic policy making that would stomp on the economic breaks any time currency stability was threatened by signs of inflation. Labour, with its commitment to high and steady economic growth and with massive political support from trade unions, threatened these interests.

While the Wilson government prioritized the domestic economy over the international, the balance of payments problem could not be ignored. Britain had long run balance of payments deficits, registering only two years of surplus between 1900 and 1969. In the early years of the twentieth century Britain was still a global power with imperial ambitions. By the middle of the century all of this had changed. Whereas other countries, like Germany, the Netherlands, and Switzerland, had emerged from World War II and quickly became exporting powerhouses, the United Kingdom struggled to compete on world markets.[11] One way to solve this problem would have been to devalue the pound sterling, which would make it easier for the Exchequer to cover its international obligations with instantly higher-valued reserves. In addition, classical trade theory suggested that devaluation would lower the price of British exports relative to imports, improving the country's trade balance and bringing the international accounts closer to equilibrium.

Publicly, the Labour government had come into office swearing that on no uncertain terms would it devalue, hoping to erase fears that the party would repeat itself from its previous term as head of the government when it devalued the pound sterling in 1949, sacrificing some imperial ambition for its domestic agenda. It was this move that many saw as helping to hand the government over to the Conservatives in 1951. In private, however, the Labour government's commitment to sterling was not so solid. Lord Cromer at the Bank of England and Jim Callaghan at the Treasury stood for a strong pound sterling, but Wilson's cabinet also included people like Nicolas Kaldor and Robert Neild who supported an early devaluation. Even more worrisome to those for whom the defense of sterling was paramount, Wilson himself had made clear to Lord Cromer that, if it came down to it, he would take the devaluation question "to the country" and give the voters the choice between Labour's economic program and a devalued pound sterling.[12]

But there was more at stake in protecting the pound sterling than just the pride of the party. Though the sun had long set on the British empire, many national governments that were once part of the empire and many private trading houses and investment firms still used the pound sterling to settle international transactions. Sterling also comprised a significant portion of many countries' stock of foreign reserves. Devaluation would destroy international confidence in the currency and, critically, hurt London's position as an international financial center. Though Wilson seemed to care little about the City and its financiers, he could not help but appreciate the fact that, for decades, a major component on the positive side of the United Kingdom's international accounts ledger was foreign investment inflows. These "invisible" transactions had historically compensated for the trade deficit and for expensive overseas ventures. Letting the pound sterling go may have improved the trade balance, but it would have definitely sent international investment capital fleeing for safer harbors. So, although Wilson was wagging his finger at the City and the Bank, he also needed sterling to stay strong while he tried to right the economic ship.[13]

What made Labour's economic program so ambitious was that it was premised on a different assumption about the relationship between domestic growth and international economic strength. Like the Conservative government before it, Wilson's Labour government was squeezed on both sides by domestic economic stagnation and pressing balance of payments concerns. Unlike the Conservatives, who governed on the belief that the trade-off between domestic and international pressures was a zero-sum game, Labour's economic program was molded by the belief that there was a way forward for the British economy that required neither devaluation nor deflation: that a thorough modernization of the economy would both bring prosperity and equilibrium to the country's international accounts by restoring export competitiveness.[14]

In this effort, Wilson relied on the ideas of Thomas Balogh, a Hungarian-born economist who was taken up by Keynes when Balogh came to England in the 1930s and who served as Wilson's chief economic advisor. Highly skeptical of global economic liberalization and the costs that it imposed on national economies, Balogh argued that only new and innovative productive investment could solve the United Kingdom's balance of payments problems in the long run.[15]

While the logic of Balogh's arguments was sound, it left one critical question unanswered: How would the Labour government finance its payments deficit and ward off speculative attacks in the short run while the long-run changes envisioned by the modernization program worked themselves out? When Labour took office at the end of 1964, the United Kingdom was saddled with a massive balance of payments deficit of some $2.2 billion. Like the Conservative government before it, the Labour government would be forced to turn to the international community to support the pound sterling. However, whereas the Conservatives had largely relied on the International Monetary Fund during times of crisis, by the time Labour came to power the Fund's resources were already being stretched to their limit, forcing the United Kingdom to turn to alternative sources of deficit financing. In addition, whereas the Conservative government subsumed domestic economic priorities to short-term balance of payments management, the Labour government was trying to reverse this relationship and so would essentially be turning to the international community for financial assistance while at the same time, from a classically liberal perspective, abandoning their commitment to short-term international monetary stability. The question, then, was whether the international community would rally around the new British plan and support sterling through this period of economic restructuring.

Just like Italy's opening to the left, which had already come and gone by the time Labour took office, the significance of this period in British economic history is that it laid bare the fundamental question of Bretton Woods: Would countries be provided the balance of payments financing that they needed to

protect their domestic policy agendas, or would national governments be subjected to the kind of adjustment "rules" that had prevailed during the nineteenth century? As already hinted at, and as the rest of this chapter will show
in more detail, Labour's national economic agenda lost out to global economic
pressures. A critical point that emerges from this discussion is that the pressure to abandon social democracy came not from the size of the payments deficits per se but rather from Labour's dependency on the international financial
community to finance that deficit. When Labour came to office, the financing
needs of the balance of payments deficit had forced the United Kingdom to
take on substantial debts with the International Monetary Fund and the central banks of Western Europe. Although the Labour government hoped that
it could continue to draw on the expanding network of short-term balance of
payments financing options while a substantial economic restructuring took
place on the mainland, indebtedness to the international financial community proved to be a substantial barrier to Labour's modernization program.

Time and again, the International Monetary Fund, the Bank for International Settlements, and the representatives of the governments of Western
Europe meeting at the OECD exhorted the Labour government to impose severe domestic restraint to correct the country's balance of payments deficit.
Although the United Kingdom delegates to these international organizations
tried to make the case for Labour's growth program, the pressure of waning
international confidence in the pound sterling proved to be too much, and
third-way social democracy gave way to orthodox austerity. In the end, ever-
harsher rounds of austerity failed to improve the U.K. balance of payments
position, though it did succeed in doubling the ranks of the unemployed.

Stop–Go from the International Perspective

Labour's victory in 1964 may have signaled that British voters were ready for
an end to the Conservative's stop–go economic policies, but whether the international community was ready for such a change is another question. Stop–
go, after all, was simply a putting into practice of classical, gold-standard era
adjustment principles—the same principles that informed the International
Monetary Fund's conditionality agreements and that were being bandied
about by the Group of Ten and in the study of the adjustment process being
conducted by the Economic Policy Committee's Working Party 3.

A case in point is the Bank for International Settlement's evaluation of the Conservatives' handling of the sterling crisis of 1961. In the lead-up to that crisis, the United Kingdom's international payments position had moved rapidly into the red as a $815 million current account surplus in 1958 deteriorated to a $143 million surplus in 1959, becoming a $1.5 billion deficit by the end of 1960. Faced with pressure on its reserves, the Conservative government arranged for a $1.5 billion drawing from the International Monetary Fund in July of 1961.[16] At the same time, the government enacted a series of fiscal and monetary policies to restrain what had been eighteen months of solid economic growth. These measures included a sharp increase in excise taxes, new restrictions on bank lending, and a reduction in government spending. On top of this, the Conservative government instituted a wage and salary pause. As a result, the growth rate of the economy dropped from about 4 percent to a mere 1 percent, and the unemployment rate nearly doubled. The current account balance soon recovered.[17]

Recounting this experience in its 1962 *Annual Report*, the Bank for International Settlement's approvingly noted, "The rescue aspect of this programme worked with classical precision." In addition, the Bank downplayed the effect that the Conservative's austerity measures had on the domestic economy as "some easing of economic activity."[18] Many of the delegates to Working Party 3, particularly those members from Western Europe, shared the Bank for International Settlement's appraisal about the proper role of economic policy for countries facing payments deficits. After the United Kingdom made its intentions clear to draw on the International Monetary Fund, the Working Party secretariat drafted a set of recommendations for the British government to follow. While steering clear of making precise policy statements, the Working Party document emphasized that "internal demand needs to be restrained," noting further that restraint measures "need to be selective and should bear largely on consumption."[19]

When growth resumed in 1963, many Working Party 3 delegates did not welcome the news, instead expressing concern that rising domestic demand would hurt the U.K. trade balance and erode whatever balance of payments gains the country had recently made.[20] Indeed, as the Conservatives themselves grew weary of keeping the British people locked in perpetual movement from stagnation to deflation and began to toy with a new strategy for growth, the Bank for International Settlements joined Working Party 3 in criticizing this move to grow the economy, arguing that anyone who believed in "external balance through expansion" was peddling "dangerous medicine, with many failures and currency devaluations on its record in both industrialized and less developed countries."[21]

This is not to say that there was strict ideological homogeneity on this issue within the postwar organizations of international economic management. The Economic Policy Committee's Working Party 2 came to the conclusion that only a sustained higher rate of economic growth would solve the persistent U.K. payments problems. This is not entirely surprising given that Working Party 2's main task was to come up with policy recommendations that would help the OECD area as a whole grow by 50 percent by 1970. What is interesting is how Working Party 2 understood how economic growth could be compatible with balance of payment stability.

Working Party 2 did share the same concerns that were being raised in the wider discussions of the Economic Policy Committee and other international bodies that excessive price and wage increases would make British exports uncompetitive in global markets. However, what the Working Party recognized was that what made price increases or wage increases excessive was when they exceeded the rate of real economic growth in the economy. Thus, the Working Party reasoned, a higher rate of growth was a potential solution to, not a cause of, the problem of rising prices. As the Working Party observed in its analysis of the prospects for growth in the United Kingdom, "Would the problem of growth not be solved more easily, under better social conditions, if the growth target were set at a higher rate (4 to 4.5 per cent annually, for instance)?"[22] If balance of payments equilibrium demanded stable prices, and stable prices demanded a regulation of wages through incomes policies, then, the Working Party argued, in another analysis published a few months later, that higher rates of growth would serve the cause of payments equilibrium by making workers more willing to accept incomes policies.[23]

Though this argument points to the way in which a strong intellectual case could be made for an aggressive growth program even in the face of a weak international payments position, Working Party 2's assessment of the British situation was not the dominant one within the international community. In the early 1960s British government officials thus found themselves navigating a climate of international opinion where, especially by 1963, the classical adjustment view on the British balance of payments became the dominant one as the progrowth voices in Working Party 2 were more and more confined to the specific question of growth targets.

Labour Turns to Austerity

Given this context, when the Labour government came to power at the end of 1964 it knew that its modernization and growth agenda would not get a warm reception from key segments of the international community. To be sure, it was not an auspicious time to launch such an ambitious program, as it was becoming all too clear that the Labour government was inheriting a balance of payments situation that was going from bad to worse. Figures released by the Working Party 3 secretariat in December of 1964 predicted a deficit of $2.1 billion for the year as a whole—a significant deterioration since the IMF standby arrangement of 1961.[24] Even more worrisome, there was a massive "sterling overhang" as some $12.5 billion in sterling was held overseas as central bank reserves and in private banks and corporations against which the British Treasury held only $2.5 billion in gold and foreign exchange reserves. The British Treasury tried to soften the blow of these figures by releasing its own analysis of economic conditions in the fall of 1964, which suggested that internal demand was a bit high but was also already coming down as consumer spending and industrial production had begun to decrease over the previous summer.[25] Therefore, they tried to argue, there was already reason to believe that pressure on the balance of payments would begin to ease.

Bolstered by this knowledge, Labour officials made their case to the Economic Policy Committee that demand pressures were already easing, meaning that now was the time to launch a growth and modernization program that would solve the country's balance of payments problems. At the December meeting of Working Party 3, the British delegates submitted their own memorandum on the adjustment process. Given that the Working Party had already made plain its skepticism that external balance could be achieved through growth, the British delegation knew that they had to address classical liberalism directly. To this end, the memorandum made two key points. First, contrary to those who had come out in favor of adjustment "rules," the memorandum argued that monetary policy was not an effective means of reducing the balance of payments deficit or of controlling economic demand. Second, the memorandum drew attention to the fact that the Labour government's proposed budget was in fact a deflationary budget whose net impact would be to restrain total economic demand even further.[26]

The British delegates hoped to convince the other members of the Working Party that the Labour government was taking its necessary spoonful of classical adjustment medicine while it tried to carve out a long-term strategy for once and for all fixing the payments problem. Unfortunately for the British delegates, the other members of the Working Party were not impressed. Professor Kessler, speaking for the Dutch delegation, "wondered whether the fiscal programme was adequate to set free that amount of resources which would be necessary to bring about a swing in the current account sufficient to restore equilibrium," a view that was shared by Gabriel Ferras, the Bank for International Settlement's general manager and representative to the Working Party, who thought that the conservative government had been much more "energetic" in its efforts to restrict internal demand during the sterling crisis of 1961.[27] Such skepticism in official circles seems to have been shared by those operating in private currency markets, as there were four significant runs on the pound sterling in the three weeks from November 5 to November 27, totaling nearly $840 million.[28]

The Labour government managed to weather the storm in the currency markets and even began to express some optimism about the country's long-term payments prospects. New data prepared by the Working Party 3 secretariat in the early months of 1965 projected that by the end of the year the United Kingdom could show a moderate balance of payments surplus. Nevertheless, officials at the Economic Policy Committee agreed that the British needed to achieve balance of payments equilibrium more quickly and prescribed a stronger dose of deflationary medicine. For example, in the same report, projecting a moderate payments surplus for the United Kingdom by the end of 1965, the Working Party 3 secretariat also went on to argue that "the balance of payments would stand to be improved if further action were taken to restrain demand."[29] The Economic Policy Committee concurred with this assessment, suggesting that whatever gains were achieved in reducing the balance of payments deficit over the previous few months should be supported by further economic restraint when the new budget was announced in April.[30]

The budget that finally did emerge in April of 1965, the first of the new Labour government, contained many of the things that had been promised during Prime Minister Wilson's speech to parliament the previous November. Most significantly, the government overcame or overlooked opposition from financial circles and imposed the new corporation tax and the capital gains tax, both of which increased the overall amount of revenue collected by the Exchequer. In addition, work on the TSR.2 aircraft—a long-range military aircraft with reconnaissance and nuclear strike capabilities—was canceled, signaling a willingness to sacrifice imperial ambition to protect the pound sterling. But the April budget also contained several measures that had not been initially proposed by the Labour government and that seemed to fall in line with the demands of the international community. Specifically, the budget raised consumption taxes, including taxes on alcohol, tobacco, and motor vehicle purchases, and raised postal charges. In short, the budget that emerged in April was not only more deflationary than the November budget proposals but also achieved this additional deflation on the backs of British consumers.

After the release of the budget, the Working Party 3 secretariat revised its figures on the United Kingdom's balance of payments prospects and estimated that the additional restraint contained in the April budget would reduce total effective demand by $420 million, or just under one-half of one percent of total final expenditure for the year, generating some further improvement in the U.K. payments account by increasing exports, reducing imports, and reducing the outflow of long-term capital.[31]

Yet, even with these additional measures and their projected impact on the balance of payments, those who had expressed the most concern about Labour's economic program were not satisfied. Wanting to see a much more rapid improvement in the country's balance of payments position, the Bank for International Settlements argued that the budget measures failed to adequately restrain demand because they did not reduce the level of public spending or effectively control wage increases, the latter of which were creating an inflationary situation.[32] The Economic Policy Committee concurred with this appraisal, citing a "real danger" that wage increases would outstrip productivity increases and thus lead to price increases that would hurt British firms' ability to compete in global markets.[33]

In the face of these criticisms, the Labour government continued to argue that the standard, classical adjustment formula would not provide real, long-term relief to what was now nearly two decades of persistent payments imbalances. In a report prepared for Working Party 2's midterm assessment of progress toward reaching the OECD's 50 percent growth target for 1970, the United Kingdom delegation had the following to say about what was essentially a desire to see a return to the days of stop–go:

At the same time it has become clear that structural imbalance in the balance of payments cannot be corrected by short period regulation of the level of demand—the disinflationary action required to bring about the necessary improvement in the balance of payments tends to have self-deflating effects on business confidence and industrial investment.[34]

To support their case the British only needed to remind their colleagues of recent experiments with economic restraint and their lack of success in bringing the country toward balance of payments equilibrium. One Economic Policy Committee analysis found that the austerity measures put in place during the sterling crisis of 1961 did soften domestic demand and did slow the pace of wage growth but did not produce the anticipated growth in exports.[35] The secretariat of Working Party 3 reached the same conclusion in a report on economic conditions in the United Kingdom: "On previous occasions when demand has been checked, this does not appear to have provoked an acceleration in exports, at least to any marked degree. *It would seem unlikely to do so now.*"[36]

Moreover, it was not even clear that the underlying conditions that many in the international community were citing as causing the payments imbalance—rapid wage increases leading to price increases that made British exports uncompetitive in world markets—even existed. A review of academic and policy institute studies of the competitiveness of British industry, published in June of 1968, found that, beginning in 1960, wage increases in Western Europe had been significantly greater than those in the United Kingdom; by 1965 hourly earnings in Italy, West Germany, and France were 21 percent, 17 percent and 7 percent higher, respectively, than those in the United Kingdom. Where the British were losing out was in the area of industrial productivity.[37] Working Party 2 had likewise reported data to the broader Economic Policy Committee in 1966 showing that the United Kingdom lagged behind many Western European countries in capital investment and productivity.[38] In addition, the Economic Policy Committee published its own data showing that average hourly earning increases in the United Kingdom from 1960 through 1964 were lower than those in all other OECD countries except for the United States and Canada.[39]

At the very least, all of this would seem to suggest that there was something far more complex going on inside the British economy than a simple wage-push story of excess demand. Nevertheless, the official rhetoric coming out of the Economic Policy Committee and the Bank for International Settlements continued to call for austerity, falling back on the argument that if deflation had not worked in the past it was not because the basic tenets of classical liberalism were wrong but rather because the British had not deflated enough. Perhaps the clearest example of this awkward reasoning is found in an Economic Policy Committee assessment of the British economy in early 1966. On the one hand, the Committee's report acknowledged that "the growth of demand has already been restricted quite severely." Yet, when it came time to offer its policy recommendations, the report called for additional fiscal and monetary measures to slow the British economy.[40] Specifically, as the European delegates to Working Party 3 made clear to their British colleagues, the Labour government needed to do more to impose a strict incomes policy and to reduce the level of public spending.[41]

Despite its decisive electoral victory in March of 1966, and despite accumulating econometric evidence that classical adjustment prescriptions were not working, beginning in May of 1966 the Labour government continued to try to appease the international community by making the national budget more and more austere, a process culminating in the "July measures." In addition to sharply restricting the supply of bank credit, especially bank credit for consumer purchases, and reducing public spending by some $1.4 billion, most controversially the July measures imposed a price and wage freeze for six months to be followed by future months of severe restraint.[42]

The July measures represented a critical turning point in Labour's economic policy program. Elected into office less then two years earlier, and recently reelected in an even greater showing of public support, the July measures marked the end of Labour's growth experiment. As shown in Figure 5.1, whereas unemployment had fluctuated between 1 and 2 percent during the era of stop–go and had been brought back down during Labour's first two years in office, the July measures brought about a doubling of the unemployment rate in the next year, which continued to grow in the years to come. The party of modernization, of third-way social democracy, had become the party of austerity.

For classical liberals in the international community, it was about time. As the Bank for International Settlements put it, the July measures brought about the end of a failed experiment to show that a concerted government effort to expand the economy could produce a long-term solution to the country's balance of payments problems.[43]

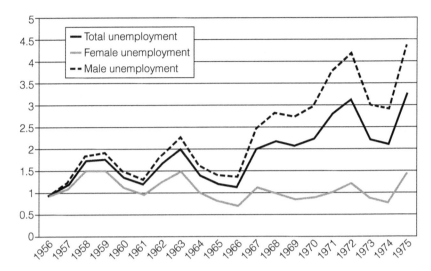

FIGURE 5.1. Unemployment rates in the United Kingdom, 1956–1975.
SOURCE: OECD, Annual Labour Force Statistics, summary tables.

Why Austerity?

Taking a wide-angle view on the political and economic context in the United
Kingdom in the 1960s, a perspective common in the international relations
literature that emphasizes the structural constraints that political leaders face,
there appears to be no real mystery as to why Harold Wilson's government
subjected the British economy to the harsh austerity of the July measures. His
government, despite high-minded intentions, was ultimately unable to overcome the pressures of the balance of payments deficit and the recurring crises
of the pound sterling.

Yet, having zoomed into the debates and discussions that took place
around the brief, but critical, year and a half of economic policy making that
led up to the July measures, it becomes clear that the wide-angle picture does
not really capture the story of how, or why, things unfolded in the way that
they did. For one, despite the Bank for International Settlement's pronounce-
ment of the failure of the Labour experiment it is clear that, at best, Labour
was able to make only a halfhearted attempt at its modernization program.
After all, its very first budget contained new levels of restraint not envisioned
in Wilson's November speech to Parliament, and over the course of the next
fifteen months the Labour government time and time again tried to quench,
rather than fuel, the fires of economic growth.

If there was one experiment that did seem to have failed it was, ironically, the classical adjustment experiment, the idea that imposing economic restraint could bring about a balance of payments surplus. It was this experiment that had informed the stop–go policies of the Conservative government during the 1950s, the failure of which was so apparent that even that party had abandoned it in favor of a new growth agenda. Moreover, the classical adjustment program failed to generate success during Labour's time in office—a fact that groups like the Bank for International Settlements and the Economic Policy Committee recognized.

Looking deep within these policy debates makes apparent a puzzle where once there was certainty: Why did the classical adjustment view win out? Why did the embedded liberal machinery fail to protect Labour's domestic agenda from international pressure? The reason has to do with the other side of Labour's modernization program, the problem of short-term balance of payments financing. Harold Wilson and the Labour government understood that their long-term program for dealing with the deep, structural issues keeping the United Kingdom in perpetual payments deficit required substantial short-term balance of payments financing from the international community. Unfortunately for the Wilson government, although this financing was available, it increasingly came from state and private actors who did not share Labour's view that there was a social democratic path to international monetary stability.

Through much of the 1950s and up to the balance of payments crisis of 1961, the United Kingdom relied on the International Monetary Fund to provide short-term financing to shore up the pound sterling against speculative attacks. However, while the International Monetary Fund is a key player in the story of British austerity in the 1960s, by the time Harold Wilson took office as prime minister the mechanisms of balance of payments financing had shifted away from the International Monetary Fund, and the United Kingdom became increasingly dependent on new financial arrangements to hold the speculators at bay.

These new financial relationships began to really take shape in the summer of 1964. The balance of payments figures for the first half of that year had not been promising, and, for each of the three months of April, May, and June, the trade balance had recorded an average deficit of some $126 million. In this context, the United Kingdom went back to the International Monetary Fund and asked for an extension of a standby credit arrangement that had been negotiated during the previous year.[44] The United Kingdom intended this standby arrangement to be largely symbolic, a show of force demonstrating the capacity of the International Monetary Fund to mobilize resources to defend currencies against speculative attack. Both the Fund and the British government expected that these funds would not actually be drawn on.

By the summer of 1964, however, the United Kingdom's balance of payments situation had become much worse, and it was clear that an actual drawing on the Fund would need to take place. In principle, this was precisely the kind of use that the Fund's resources were designed for. Unfortunately for British government officials, their need for financing came at the same time that the United States, still struggling with its own balance of payments deficit, had announced that it too would need to draw on its standby arrangement with the International Monetary Fund to the tune of $500 million.

In this new context, the United Kingdom's financing needs now exceeded the financial resources of the Fund, forcing it to turn to the newly created General Arrangements to Borrow to supplement its own reserves with contributions from the Group of Ten central banks. However, whereas recourse to the Fund was automatic for member countries, the Fund itself did not have automatic recourse to the General Arrangements to Borrow. Rather, as part of the original negotiation creating this arrangement, participating governments retained the right to review each case before agreeing to contribute to the Fund's reserves, and the monetary authorities participating in the General Arrangements to Borrow were not willing to contribute resources without some assurance that they would be used appropriately. As André de Lattre, from the French Ministry of Finance, put it: "The Group of Ten should not be deprived of its chance to examine the borrowing countries' requests in its own right."[45]

When it came time to discuss the Fund's activation of the General Arrangements to Borrow to shore up the pound sterling, some members of Working Party 3 made it clear that cooperation to help the beleaguered British was contingent on evidence that the government was going to take the responsible road and restrain the economy. For example, in explaining why he did not think that the International Monetary Fund should be given an automatic standby arrangement with the General Arrangements to Borrow, S. Posthuma, Managing Director of the Nederlandsche Bank, observed:

> In the past the United Kingdom appeared to need a standby without actually having to draw upon it, but now it seemed likely that it will have to draw in the near future. *This deterioration justified demands by other countries that the United Kingdom undertakings should be more precise.*[46]

Similarly, the Chairman of the Working Party went so far as to explicitly call on the British government to take measures to restrain the economy even as they were facing an election in a short four months. "Even if such measures might not become immediately effective," he argued, "they would constitute a commitment for action later on."[47] The language here is striking because it shows that classical liberals like the Working Party chairman were more interested in seeing the British play by the rules than they were in the actual outcome.

In summary, this time when the British turned to the Fund they became financially dependent on the monetary authorities of the Group of Ten participating in the General Arrangements to Borrow. At the same time, the British authorities expanded their existing swap network from an arrangement that had been made with the U.S. Federal Reserve to include the Bank of Canada and the central banks of six unspecified European countries. The German delegation to Working Party 3 took this chance to link the issue of British payments financing to what they perceived to be a domestic economic policy that was not effectively restraining internal demand. "For how long did the United Kingdom authorities expect to march through the 'valley of horrors,'" asked Dr. Gocht of the German Ministry of Economics, "and by whom was this excursion to be financed?"[48] Even as Wilson occasionally let slip that he might be willing to let the pound sterling go, European monetary authorities would not give their financial support to the British with no strings attached. Rather, what is critical to understand is that when Harold Wilson's government took office in October of 1964 the international context that greeted them was not just one where balance of payments was in steep deficit, but, more important, one where the system of financing those deficits was spreading out from the insular, bureaucratic halls of the International Monetary Fund and into the hands of North America's and Western Europe's central banks. In concrete material terms, when the Labour government took office the United Kingdom was $1 billion in debt to the International Monetary Fund, but it was also another $600 million in debt to various national monetary authorities.

Balance of Payments Financing, Dependency, and the Problem of Confidence

When Working Party 3 reconvened in February of 1965, the British delegation made clear that the scale of the balance payments deficit would require further drawings on the network of credit swaps established with foreign central banks over the previous year and a further extension of credit from the International Monetary Fund (to be announced later in the spring), in addition to the $1 billion that had already been borrowed. Naturally, this request for additional financing from the international community brought with it considerable discussion from the other Working Party members, many of whom wanted to see more austerity in the British budget. In this discussion it was the Working Party chairman, Emile van Lennep, who once again placed the issue precisely and squarely in front of the British. It was not that the money did not exist to finance the British deficit, he argued, but rather that "it would be necessary to convince lending countries that solid improvement had been achieved."[49]

The time to do that convincing was in the lead-up to the announcement of the first budget, and, although Labour did incorporate further deflationary measures into the final outcome, many members of the Economic Policy Committee were not impressed. This sentiment came out clearly in the Working Party 3 meeting of May 1965. Commenting on the new budget, Dr. Gocht stated: "It was his opinion that the present measures were not sufficient to restore equilibrium in the reasonably near future." More pointedly, he then drew an explicit connection between the future course of British economic policy and Germany's, and perhaps other countries', willingness to continue financing the British balance of payments deficit. "Sometime during 1965, the governments of the countries around the table would have to give an answer when they were asked for money. Under present conditions, he would have to advise his Government that the prerequisites for continued assistance had not been fulfilled."[50]

Dr. Gocht did not have to wait long for such a situation to emerge. On May 12, private investors began to sell off their sterling holdings at a furious pace, betting that both the size of the payments deficit and the new government's commitment to the domestic economy would force a devaluation of the currency. The United Kingdom once again went to the International Monetary Fund for financial support, bringing the United Kingdom's total indebtedness to the Fund to $2.4 billion—the highest level that it would reach for the rest of the decade.

The money owed to the International Monetary Fund was the public face of British indebtedness. In the background, the British government was also becoming increasingly indebted to foreign monetary authorities and the Bank for International Settlements. By the time of the May drawing on the Fund,

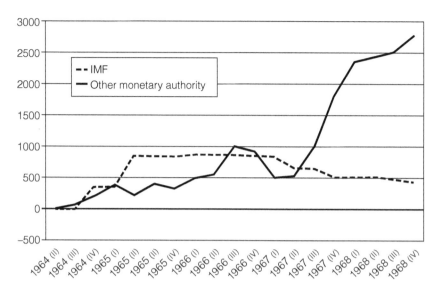

FIGURE 5.2. Cumulative official financing of the U.K. balance of payments deficit, millions of dollars, select years and quarters.
SOURCE: Cairncross and Eichengreen, *Sterling in Decline*, 172.

U.K. indebtedness to the monetary authorities of other countries and to the Bank for International Settlements had grown to $940 million dollars—increasing by $230 million just between February and May. Even more significantly, the composition of foreign financing of the British payments deficit had changed. In the early 1960s the British had largely relied on the United States for balance of payments financing beyond what it received from the International Monetary Fund. By May of 1965 the United States was still extending some $320 million in credit to the United Kingdom, but total financing from Western Europe had grown to $530 million, a large portion of which came from Germany.[51]

Looking at the changing composition of British payments financing over the long term shows that the spring of 1965 was, in fact, a critical turning point in the structure of international financing for the U.K. balance of payments deficit. As shown in Figure 5.2, although total debt to the International Monetary Fund did not increase any further after the 1965 drawing, total debt owed to foreign monetary authorities continued to grow, first surpassing the total debt owed to the Fund in the fall of 1966 and then increasing dramatically in 1967 and 1968. This growing level of public indebtedness was closely linked to the extremely high level of "private indebtedness"—the large holdings of sterling by private financial institutions. Credit arrangements with foreign monetary authorities helped to paper over the drains on British reserves every time the pound sterling came under attack, throwing up a façade of strength in front of a currency that, if further weakness showed, would surely crumble.[52]

This short-term financial relief came at a cost. As its debts grew, the United Kingdom was placed in a position where it was no longer sufficient to achieve balance of payments equilibrium to restore the stability of the pound sterling. Rather, it became necessary for the United Kingdom to achieve a significant balance of payments surplus to convince foreign monetary authorities that the British would make good on their debts. This new dynamic gave additional weight to those voices calling for austerity as the discourse of confidence was intertwined with the issue of growing British debt. An example of this can be seen in an Economic Policy Committee report summarizing its assessment of the U.K. economic prospects for the year in early 1966: "Both in order to maintain confidence and to prepare for the debt repayment required in subsequent years, it is important that measures taken should now err on the side of doing too much rather than doing too little."[53]

This growing indebtedness to foreign monetary authorities helps to explain why, even as the U.K. payments balance showed some improvement in the later months of 1965, the international community was unsatisfied with the rate with which the British government was moving toward balance of payments equilibrium. Most vexing was the Labour government's admission in early 1966 that its previously stated goal of achieving balance by the end of 1966 was now very unlikely to occur. Expressing deep concern over this development, Otmar Emminger emphasized that "the present was an occasion for restraint," adding, "Keeping in step was not enough, some of the ground lost must be won back, if outstanding indebtedness were to be repaid."[54] In addition, Emminger's colleague from the Economics Ministry, Dr. Gocht, drew attention to the fact that delaying the return to balance would require further short-term financing, which was something that should only be given under the strictest of criteria: "It would be most undesirable if the $500 million now available under the increased United Kingdom [IMF] quota were to be granted except with full respect for the normally stringent terms for a drawing in the final credit tranche."[55]

The level of concern expressed over debt repayment underscores how far the Bretton Woods international monetary system was from the one Keynes had envisioned in the early 1940s. Had Keynes's plan for an International Clearing Union been put into effect, countries like Italy, Germany, the Netherlands, and Switzerland that tended to run a significant balance of payments surplus would have been required to contribute to the Clearing Union's accounts, and the United Kingdom would have been able to draw freely from those funds without having to worry about short-term repayment. The Bretton Woods system, however, never contained a mechanism to compel surplus countries to move toward balance. Rather, balance of payments surpluses were *lent* to deficit countries with the expectation that such debts would be repaid to the lending country in a timely fashion. The expectation of repayment thus added a new layer of constraint on deficit countries' economic policy goals; such countries were pushed toward austerity not only by the elusive specter of private financial market confidence in the stability of their currency but also by the demands of foreign monetary authorities that borrowing countries achieve an extra-large surplus to not only cover existing deficits but to quickly pay off accumulated debts.

From the July Measures to Devaluation

As the deflationary impact of the July measures worked their way through the British economy, the balance of payments began to improve, earning the Labour government a respite from the constant criticism coming from the classical liberals in the international community. In the early months of 1967 the Working Party 3 secretariat reported that the United Kingdom had recorded $232 million nonmonetary balance of payments surplus and had rebuilt some of its foreign currency reserves. Looking forward, the secretariat forecasted continuous improvement in the U.K. balance of payments—assuming the government could maintain a depressed level of internal demand. The Bank for International Settlements also lauded the positive effect that the July measures had had on the payments balance, though it qualified its assessment by pointing out that the U.K. payments position had benefited greatly from lower interest rates in North America and Western Europe that drove funds into London through the Eurodollar market.[56]

Despite this promising start, the reality was that for the Labour government achieving balance of payments equilibrium, or even a moderate surplus, was simply no longer enough to satisfy the foreign skeptics. At the March meeting of Working Party 3, Sir Dennis Rickett of the British Treasury saw the new balance of payments figures as evidence of a "decisive break" with past patterns and marking the beginning of what he hoped would be several years of surplus. Sir Dennis's optimism did not win over the Working Party chairman, who thought that the degree of improvement seemed "very small" when put up against the $900 million that the United Kingdom would soon have to repay to the International Monetary Fund.[57]

By the summer of 1967, even this fragile veneer of optimism began to give way to clear signs that whatever balance of payments improvement had occurred in late 1966 and early 1967 was not going to be sustained. At the July 1967 meeting of Working Party 3, Sir Dennis Rickett admitted that some favorable balance of payments forecasts for the year as a whole were "far too rosy," in part because of the very puzzling phenomenon of a continuing rise in imports in the face of deflationary measures but also because of a bad string of international events, notably a crisis in the Middle East that was driving up oil prices and an economic slowdown in the United States and Western Europe, which combined to boost the price of imports and lower the demand for British exports.[58]

For the Labour government, these developments were particularly troubling as state officials were hoping to be able to put in place some mildly reflationary policy measures to bring down an unemployment rate that had climbed to 2.3 percent since the July measures. Within Working Party 3, however, the view was that this clear deterioration in the United Kingdom's international position meant that domestic policy still needed to be attentive to international, not domestic, considerations.[59] Such official concerns were backed by turbulence in the exchange markets and a new run on sterling that drained the British Treasury of some $1.4 billion in currency reserves just in the third quarter of 1967.

Sterling was once again in crisis, and despite some halfhearted efforts to support the currency—including around $300 million in credits from Swiss bankers and the Bank for International Settlements as well as a half percent increase in the Bank of England's bank rate to try to draw more funds to London[60]—by November the conclusion seemed inevitable: The pound sterling needed to be devalued.

Devaluation, Deflation, and the Fall of Labour

The devaluation of the pound sterling came on November 18, 1967, when the exchange rate was changed from £1 = $2.80 to £1 = $2.40, a 14 percent reduction in the value of the British currency. In his memoirs, Harold Wilson recounted that, in the week leading up to the decision to devalue, the International Monetary Fund and the Group of Ten were willing to consider a massive financial support operation to prevent devaluation, but it came with too heavy a price tag. According to Wilson, agreeing to the terms of further financial assistance would

> . . . lead to the most searching intrusions not only into our privacy, but even into our economic independence, not least from the French. And all this would be against the background of unacceptably high unemployment, and the play that would be made in Parliament about sacrificing the unemployed to the bankers.[61]

As Wilson's saw it, devaluation was the best means to protect the country from further austerity at a time when the unemployment rate was nearly double what it had been when he had taken office.

Unfortunately for Wilson, and for whatever hopes he harbored that devaluation would afford him some breathing room to advance his economic agenda, devaluation did not spare the United Kingdom from financial dependency on the European central banks. The devaluation of the pound sterling sent a shock wave through foreign exchange markets, threatening to destabilize an already fragile situation. This, in turn, required substantial financial assistance from not so much the International Monetary Fund as from the central bankers of the Group of Ten to shore up the pound sterling.

The logic behind the devaluation, as it is behind all currency devaluations, is that by lowering the value of a currency the price of exports from the devaluing country will drop relative to the price of imports and the trade balance will improve. In reality, to the extent that these dynamics ever work themselves out in this way, it is only in the long run. In the short run, countries that devalue often see their trade balance worsen because the flip side of less expensive exports is more expensive imports. This was particularly problematic for the United Kingdom, which, year after year, footed a quite hefty import bill even during periods of economic contraction. Moreover, devaluation shattered whatever confidence foreign investors retained in the pound sterling, exacerbating a capital outflow.

Given these two contradictory pressures, the devaluation of the pound sterling did not eliminate calls for austerity; rather it heightened them. After all, devaluation was a major blow to the entire international monetary system—it had to work. Part of ensuring that the devaluation of sterling did have its intended effect, the Working Party 3 secretariat argued in an analysis published just five days after the devaluation announcement, was to reduce internal demand for British goods so that firms would be encouraged to sell abroad. This meant that consumer incomes, wages, would need to be kept low—policies that would be especially punishing during a time when rising import prices would increase the cost of living for most Britons.[62]

The other members of the Working Party, who also expressed a general skepticism of the Labour government's economic program, largely shared the Working Party 3 secretariat's assessment. Moreover, several members of the Working Party reminded the U.K. delegation of two pressing concerns: first, that the country still owed substantial short-term debts to European central banks and the Bank for International Settlements; and, second, that despite the optimism expressed by the U.K. delegation, it was quite likely that they would be back in front of the International Monetary Fund and the central bankers of the Group of Ten seeking financial assistance in 1968.[63]

Faced with more of what had now become a common refrain from the Economic Policy Committee, the Labour government struggled to gain support for even a modest effort to take some of the deflationary sting out of the economy. In January of 1968 economic advisor to the Treasury Michael Posner presented the Labour government's economic targets for the rest of the year and through 1969 to Working Party 3. The government was hoping to bring the economy back up to a 4 percent growth rate in output to reduce the unemployment rate to somewhere between 1.5 and 2 percent. Although Posner tried to present this economic program as one that was still "extremely hard" and one that the government would not be willing to make any harsher,[64] at that same meeting the Working Party secretariat presented its own analysis of the British situation, one that suggested, contrary to Posner's claims, that unemployment had in fact been falling too much and needed to be stabilized before it went below 2 percent. To do this, the United Kingdom needed to aim for a lower growth target of 3 percent.[65]

Over the next four months leading up to the announcement of the new budget in April of 1969, this 3 percent growth target became the new rallying point of the Economic Policy Committee's call for continued austerity for the United Kingdom. At the March meeting of the Working Party, Richard Goode, representing the International Monetary Fund, summarized the Fund's view that "the growth of GDP should be reduced to 3 per cent as soon as possible." In an unusual turn, the Working Party chairman officially polled the other delegates on their position on the 3 percent question, achieving a general Working Party view that the new budget needed to slow the rate of growth of the economy.[66]

While resistant to this assessment, the Labour government's ability to argue for a faster rate of economic expansion was being undermined by turbulence in the foreign exchange markets. Facing its own balance of payments crisis, the United States said that it would no longer be able to commit any of its gold reserves to the London Gold Pool, leading to the suspension of that financial arrangement, which in turn triggered a new round of speculation against sterling. Just as had been anticipated after devaluation, the United Kingdom went back to the central bankers of the Group of Ten for financial assistance, this time to the tune of $1.5 billion.

In the end, the three percenters got their way. When Wilson announced the government's new budget, it included the largest overall tax increase in British history. Furthermore, while the new budget did deliver on a promised increase in the corporation tax, the vast majority of the measures targeted private consumption. Economic historian Jim Tomlinson called the Labour government's 1968 budget "the most deflationary budget since the war," a view shared by Wilson himself who, in his memoirs, called it "the most punishing Budget in Britain's peacetime history."[67]

Although Wilson and his government were clearly dismayed by their inability to deliver on the promise of social democracy, on the other side of the table the international community seemed to be satisfied. Meeting in April after the budget announcement, the members of Working Party 3, for the first time in several months, had little to say about the United Kingdom's economic situation. The Working Party chairman did remark, however, that he felt the group would be "generally satisfied" with the measures taken.[68]

Although it took some time, and another round of tax increases in February of 1969, the balance of payments did eventually recover. The Labour government had come into office facing a deficit of some $2.2 billion, but by the end of 1969 was able to record a surplus of $717 million and an even stronger surplus of $1.6 billion the year after. The United Kingdom could now afford to pay down its short-term debts owed to the International Monetary Fund and foreign central banks. Yet achieving this success on the international front came with real political costs. Labour had foisted the burdens of balance of payments adjustment onto the shoulders of British workers and consumers, and their support for the party plummeted in the next election.

Conclusion: The International Politics of Growth and Employment

It is worth lingering over this debate over a seemingly trivial 1 percent difference in what was seen as an acceptable growth rate as it was a manifestation of the underlying politics of growth as much as it was a manifestation of two different understandings about the relationship among growth, prices, and the balance of payments. There was really no disagreement between the British delegation to the OECD and those members representing other governments or other international bodies over the question of whether a higher level of wages, all else being equal, tended to result in a higher level of prices—though certainly some believed that the connection was stronger than others did. In addition, as was discussed in Chapter 3, by the early 1960s there had emerged a broadly shared view that income policies were the best way to manage wage growth.

The real question was how to manage the inevitable politics of growth that came with governments' efforts to control wages and prices through incomes policies. Countries like Germany, the Netherlands, and Switzerland had managed to achieve high rates of growth with relative price stability because their weak trade union movements and corporatist bargaining structures kept workers from being able to effectively push for higher wages. These domestic political conditions did not exist in the United Kingdom, and so the Labour government's push for a 4 percent growth rate was based in its position that, given the political context, incomes policies could be made to work only in an environment of high economic growth. British trade unions, they correctly believed, would be more willing to sign onto an income policy if it meant that their wages could still grow at a reasonable rate. From this perspective, growth took some of the pressure off income policies by creating space for a slightly higher rate of wage growth that would not result in price inflation.

The Economic Policy Committee, along with those who operated within a more orthodox policy paradigm, came to the exact opposite conclusion. Yes, they conceded, income policies inevitably raised political problems. But these problems emerged not because workers were being treated unfairly but because they *felt* that they were being treated unfairly and, most importantly, were capitalizing on the political leverage afforded them by a tight labor market to make unreasonable wage demands. If the British government could not build the kind of corporatist institutions that would keep the trade unions in check, then the only other solution was to drive down the rate of growth so that unemployment would rise and trade unions would have less structural power to push for higher wages.

6   Global Finance and the U.S. Growth Agenda

F OR THOSE WHO ARE ATTUNED TO THE HISTORY OF "GREAT
power politics," the fact that the Labour government's growth and
modernization agenda would fall victim to the orthodoxy of the international
financial community may not seem all that surprising. By 1964 the age of British global hegemony had long since passed, leaving the postwar governments
struggling to salvage whatever vestiges of imperial privilege that they could
out of a world system where the center of political power had shifted to the
United States. Yet, even the postwar hegemon, the country that had not only
written the rules of the Bretton Woods order but also, with the dollar anchor-
ing the entire system, was in the best position to break those rules to its own
advantage, fell under the sway of an increasingly empowered international
financial community.

Just as Harold Wilson had come into office promising a new way forward,
John F. Kennedy was elected in 1960 largely on the promise that he would
guide the United States into the "New Frontier" by revitalizing the stagnant
economy. Like Wilson, Kennedy was compelled to compromise his domestic
agenda in the face of international pressure, specifically pressure from other
OECD governments and their central banks, to moderate the pace of domestic expansion to control the balance of payments outflow. The fact that these
two cases are so strikingly similar belies the conventional understanding of
U.S. global dominance in the postwar era. Whereas Wilson was struggling to
protect the vestiges of an empire held together by a weak currency, Kennedy's

domestic ambitions should have been protected by the dollar's pride of place in the Bretton Woods system.[1]

This was not what happened. As the U.S. balance of payments position worsened, the Kennedy administration, like the Wilson administration, became dependent on short-term financing from Western European central banks to hold off international speculation against the dollar. In particular, the United States was most dependent on financing from Germany and Switzerland, both of which were trying to keep a tight rein on domestic price stability and thus were not happy with the massive inflow of dollars coming across their borders. While Kennedy's economic advisors pushed hard for the domestic growth program, in the end the ties of financial dependency proved too strong, pulling the Kennedy administration's economic program in a classically liberal direction.

Politics and Policy in the Kennedy Years

The early 1960s was a watershed in American economic policy. Immediately on taking office, newly elected President Kennedy was confronted with the problem of how to reduce unemployment, fight poverty, and restore the productivity and competitiveness of American industry. During the presidential campaign Kennedy had criticized the Eisenhower administration for being too cautious in its attempts to combat what had become a long recession, and now it was time for the new administration to make good on Kennedy's pledge that he would mobilize all of the government's fiscal and monetary tools to turn the economy around. The Kennedy administration abandoned the fiscal passivity that had characterized the economic policies of the Eisenhower administration and launched an ambitious program of fiscal activism and economic management that has come to be known as "commercial Keynesianism."

That commercial Keynesianism would come to define economic policy making in first the Kennedy and then the Johnson White Houses was not only quite surprising at the time but remains puzzling for scholars of U.S. politics and policy making. On the campaign trail, Kennedy portrayed himself as the flag bearer of New Deal liberalism, drawing attention to the plight of the poor and unemployed. Organized labor threw its weight behind Kennedy, calling for more spending on public works and, quite controversially, for a workweek shortened to thirty-five hours to tackle the problem of unemployment. Once in office, however, the administration failed to live up to its liberal promise. For some, this was simply a product of an inhospitable political climate. Labor was fairly moderate and weak, and there was the legacy of the New Deal political settlement defined by a fracturing of the Democratic party between the liberal North and the conservative South.[2]

Kennedy's victory over his Republican challenger, former Vice President Richard Nixon, was the closest that any election had seen since 1916. Kennedy had managed to capture just over 56 percent of the electoral vote but had managed to eke out only slightly over 100,000 popular votes more than Nixon (around two-tenths of 1 percent more than Nixon's popular vote count). The situation did not bode much better in the legislature, where the Democratic Party held a 263 to 174 majority in the House and a 65 to 35 majority in the Senate. These numbers belie social progressivism's much more precarious position given the number of conservative, southern Democratic legislators who were unsympathetic to the social and economic agenda of the liberals.[3]

While these political factors were real, the problem with placing too much stock in domestic political constraints is that it presumes that the administration tried to push a progressive social agenda. In reality, Kennedy was both a hesitant liberal and a hesitant Keynesian. The first signs of Kennedy's economic inclinations manifested during his confrontation with Khrushchev over West Berlin in June of 1961. Kennedy called for supplemental defense appropriations totaling nearly $3.5 billion and, at least initially, wanted to pay for the extra defense spending by raising taxes. It was only the persistent pleading of his Council of Economic Advisors, who worried that tax increases would dash any hopes for economic recovery, that finally dissuaded him from raising taxes. It was not until the middle of 1962 that Kennedy publicly came out as a Keynesian, famously telling an audience at Yale University that the country needed to get past the "old mythology" that budget deficits necessarily came with inflation. Thus, at least through the first year of Kennedy's term in office, there was still a powerful inertia around fiscal conservatism and the fight against inflation.[4]

This shift in Kennedy's position on fiscal policy has led some scholars to argue that the commercial Keynesian agenda was not a response to domestic political constraints but instead was a successful case of political entrepreneurship on the part of the Council of Economic Advisors and its chairman, Walter Heller, and, more generally, shows how economic ideas can have a powerful influence over the policy-making process. According to this view, when Kennedy entered office the American economy was stagnant, and, more importantly, existing methods of achieving economic growth no longer seemed to work. The professional economists staffing the Council of Economic Advisors stepped into this policy void and effectively framed the Kennedy and Johnson administrations' understanding of economic problems such that they were able to articulate a new kind of economic policy agenda— commercial Keynesianism.[5]

To be sure, there is much to this argument, and the importance of Heller and his Council for crafting, and then pushing, tax cuts as the centerpiece of the administration's fiscal policy agenda cannot be ignored. But ideas and political entrepreneurship do not tell the whole story here. While Heller was successful in seeing his ideas about fiscal policy make it into the administration's policy agenda, he was unsuccessful when it came to the question of monetary policy.

In the end, the full shape of the fiscal and monetary policies that comprised the Kennedy administration's policy program was a strange amalgam of activist fiscal policy defined by the "new economics" of the commercial Keynesians combined with a new experiment in monetary policy that sought to keep credit markets simultaneously easy and tight. Neither domestic politics nor the power of ideas can account for the complete story of economic policy making in the Kennedy years. Rather, the lines of causality become clear only when the administration's domestic economic agenda is contextualized within the politics of international monetary management.

The Commercial Keynesian Agenda

The Kennedy administration's commercial Keynesianism was both distinctly American, in that it retained some of the core features of the kind of Keynesian economic management that both the Truman and Eisenhower administrations had institutionalized in the early postwar period, and a major departure from the basic policy paradigm of the 1950s, in that it emphasized growth over stability. Commercial Keynesianism was not the Keynesianism of popular lore, the New Deal, or even of Lord Keynes himself. These Keynesianisms are better understood as liberal Keynesianism, the central tenet of which is that when the economy falls into recession the government needs to prop up demand by substituting public spending for private investment and by bolstering the purchasing power of the poor and middle class. To follow a liberal Keynesian paradigm means that, if private employers will not hire workers, then the state will employ them through public works programs; if wages in private labor markets are too low, then the state will boost them with transfer payments. In short, liberal Keynesian policies correct for, or supplement, failures of capital accumulation and private market activity.

Commercial Keynesianism, on the other hand, uses the tools of Keynesian demand management to boost private economic activity, rather than substitute for it. In practice, whereas both liberal and commercial versions of Keynesianism stress the role of fiscal policy for mitigating the effects of recession, liberal Keynesians believe that such fiscal action should take the form of increased spending, whereas commercial Keynesians prefer tax reduction.[6] The driving force behind getting commercial Keynesianism accepted as the framework for Kennedy's economic program was Walter Heller, an economics professor from the University of Minnesota whom Kennedy appointed as chairman of the Council of Economic Advisors. Heller was staunchly committed to the "new economics," a movement in the field of academic economics pioneered by Paul Samuelson and Robert Solow to integrate neoclassical and Keynesian economic theory. One of Keynes's great insights was that markets frequently diverge from neoclassical equilibrium because economic activity is intimately bound up with cultural practices and political processes. While the "new economists" maintained the importance of Keynes's rejection of the classical claim that markets automatically tend toward equilibrium, they downplayed the cultural and political sources of these market imperfections, attributing them instead to technical problems of asymmetric information flows and exogenous forces. Once chair of Kennedy's Council of Economic Advisors, Heller set to work trying to apply the insights of the neoclassical synthesis to forge a new path for economic policy. In this fight, Heller was not alone. Samuelson and Solow were appointed to an important economic task force at the beginning of Kennedy's term. In addition, Heller staffed the Council of Economic Advisors with strong advocates of the neoclassical synthesis, notably James Tobin, who, along with Samuelson and Solow, was one of its intellectual architects.[7] So, while Walter Salant is no doubt right in observing that "the 1960s represented a high point in the acceptance of Keynesian doctrines by government and private concerns,"[8] it is also true that American Keynesianism in the 1960s was a new kind of intellectual animal.

Heller was relentless in pushing an initially cautious Kennedy to take firm action on tax reduction, and his efforts bore fruit in the form of two major tax cuts that formed the heart of the administration's economic program. The first, the Revenue Act of 1962, simplified corporate depreciation schedules and made it easier for firms to write off past investments and also granted a flat 7 percent tax credit on new private investment. Second, and much more ambitious, was the Revenue Act of 1964, which cut individual and corporate income taxes across the board. The effects of these two tax measures were substantial. Before the provisions of the 1964 Act were passed, individual income tax rates had ranged from a low of 20 percent to a high of 92 percent. The legislation revised these rates downward to a range of 14 percent to 70 percent. Not only were the reductions in the average tax rate greater for those in high income brackets than those in low income brackets, but those making over $200,000 a year actually saw their marginal tax rates decline. For businesses, the combined effect of the Investment Tax Credit, accelerated depreciation, and the cuts embodied in the 1964 Revenue Act yielded a collective reduction on corporate tax rates of 9 percent.[9]

The story that is often told of postwar American capitalism tends to gloss over this subtle shift in postwar economic policy, focusing instead on the much more dramatic oil shock and stagflation of the 1970s and the "Reagan Revolution" of the 1980s, which, for many scholars, was the death knell of Keynesian demand management and the beginning of a neoliberal era of monetarist and supply-side economic policies. Looking back, however, it is clear that commercial Keynesianism was a transition period between postwar Keynesianism and contemporary neoliberalism. First, this was a very technocratic Keynesianism, one that had little use for Keynes's own preoccupation with the social, cultural, and political sources of economic dynamics. Even more critically, it was a much more conservative model of economic growth than one might assume, given its roots in both the ideas of Keynes and the social democratic rhetoric of the Kennedy White House. Like the supply-side economic policies that would define the Reagan administration twenty years later, commercial Keynesianism tried to stimulate economic growth by channeling economic resources away from the working class, the poor, and consumers and toward private businesses.[10] Walter Heller himself captured the similarities between these two seemingly disparate economic approaches when, after leaving his post as Council Chairman and returning to the University of Minnesota, he wrote: "Comparing economists of today with those of twenty-five years ago I am sure it is fair to say that there is more of both Keynesian and conservative in us all."[11]

The sudden rise and success of the commercial Keynesians is puzzling and begs for further investigation. Few observing American politics in 1960 could have predicted that in just a few short years the country's economic fortunes would be tied to the commercial Keynesian experiment in growth policy. Labor unions never supported the administration's tax policies, pushing instead for a liberal Keynesian jobs program or, at the very least, a program of tax cuts targeted more at the lower rungs of the income ladder. The legislature remained locked in a traditional debate between Eisenhower-era fiscal conservatives and New Deal–style liberal Keynesians. Even business leaders were initially skeptical of the administration's tax plans and came around to them only after the proposed bills were stripped of tax reform measures.[12]

Adding to the puzzle is that, although Heller and his staff were remarkably successful in pushing through their ideas about fiscal policy, they had a very hard time influencing monetary policy, which they argued was crucial for the success of the commercial Keynesian program. Although the tax cuts were the centerpiece of the fiscal program of the Council of Economic Advisors, for the tax cuts to succeed they needed to be supported by an easy monetary climate of abundant credit offered at low interest rates. On this front, the commercial Keynesians lost the battle over economic policy as monetary policy was steadily tightened over the decade. Although the story of monetary policy is often downplayed in the larger tale of the commercial Keynesian ascendancy, including it forces a careful reconsideration of the far too simple image of a small group of intellectual renegades toiling away in the White House to remake American economic policy.

To try to get at this puzzle, this chapter focuses on the years 1961 to 1963, when the commercial Keynesian economic program was fighting for a space to define a new policy agenda for growth. Where the existing scholarship on this period has debated the roles of party politics, business interests, and the changing face of economic expertise in shaping the Kennedy administration's economic program, this is a debate that focuses entirely on the domestic forces shaping the policy-making process to the neglect of the way in which economic policy making is embedded within a set of international constraints. Indeed, as the next section will take up in more detail, given both the centrality of the dollar to the Bretton Woods system and the emerging weakness of the dollar, American economic policy decisions were of major international interests. Indeed, while the policy settlement that ultimately emerged by

1963—steep tax cuts combined with tight money—maps imperfectly onto the objectives of the Kennedy administration, it fits quite neatly with the views of classical liberals in the international community.

A Confluence of Crises

The commercial Keynesian revolution can be understood only in the context of a confluence of domestic and international pressures that confronted the Kennedy administration in early 1961. Domestically, the American capitalist machinery was sputtering, hardly producing the kind of results that one might associate with the conventional wisdom that the country was moving through a postwar "golden age" of economic activity. The U.S. economy had grown rapidly between 1938 and 1952, largely as a result of the mobilizations for World War II and the Korean War. After the end of hostilities in Korea, the economy did continue to grow, but it was a weak and sluggish growth characterized by declining rates of corporate profit and private investment that, in turn, led to a steady decline in manufacturing output. The drop-off in economic activity was quite severe in the second half of the decade as the growth rate of the economy, and of manufacturing output more specifically, fell from an average of 5 percent from 1950 to 1955 to an average of about 2 percent.[13]

Economic stagnation hit the working class especially hard as the ranks of the unemployed began to swell. After falling to a record low of 2.9 percent in 1953 following the Korean War economic boom, the unemployment rate thereafter began to increase steadily. By 1958 it had reached a postwar high of 6.8 percent and lingered at this level. When President Kennedy took office in 1961, some 4.7 million Americans were unable to find work.[14]

As the domestic economy languished in a postwar stagnation, major transformations in the international economy were placing additional strain on the country. In the first decade following the end of World War II, the United States ran a substantial international payments deficit, the result of military transfers, grants, and loans from the federal government to Western Europe and of private foreign direct investment. These transfers were seen as vitally necessary for revitalizing the global economy and, critically, were balanced by a significant trades surplus in favor of the United States. While this system of public and private capital transfers balanced by the trade account worked to stabilize the global economy for about a decade, by 1958 the U.S.

balance of payments deficit was becoming a burden not just on the United States but on the larger postwar international monetary order.

The reason was the rapid economic recovery of Western European economies to the extent that they could now compete on world markets, eroding the U.S. trade position. Although the overall trade balance remained positive throughout most of the period—with the notable exception of a sudden $261 million trade deficit in 1959—the most dramatic shift occurred in the trade balance on consumer goods. After 1959 this item in the overall trade balance went into deficit, and as the decade wore on the degree of imbalance on trade in consumer goods accelerated. Between 1959 and 1970 the deficit on consumer goods trade increased from $261 million to $4.8 billion. While the trade balance weakened, private and public overseas investments remained large. Private investors were drawn to the high rate of return promised by rapid growth in Western Europe, and the U.S. Cold War posture sent billions of dollars abroad in the form of developmental aid and military expenditure.[15]

That the United States was facing a severe balance of payments problem became clear in 1958 when the country experienced its largest ever drain on its gold reserves: $2.2 billion. Large gold losses were also recorded in 1959 and 1960. These movements could have been written off as yet another one of those sharp swings in international monetary movements that characterized the postwar global economy if it had not also been becoming increasingly clear that these gold losses were tied to declining U.S. trade competitiveness and, even more critically, a growing feeling that the United States might no longer have had the economic strength to support the international monetary order.

This last point is key because it points to the way in which the balance of payments deficit was becoming a threat to the U.S. hegemonic position in the postwar global political and economic order. In the early postwar years, Western European governments consented to U.S. global leadership in exchange for reconstruction assistance and a stable international economic environment anchored on the dollar. While some states, like France, resented American hegemony, for the most part the Western Europeans consented to this arrangement because they extracted real benefits from it.[16] However, by the late 1950s the benefits to be gained from U.S. leadership were diminishing. Western Europe was growing rapidly and claiming a larger share of world markets. The U.S. payments deficit, once vital to European recovery, was now a threat to many countries' growth models. And, although most still agreed that a strong dollar was necessary for international monetary stability, Western European governments had already had experience settling their international accounts through regional payments unions and, most important, were beginning to rethink the process of international monetary adjustment.

What the Kennedy administration needed, therefore, was not just a plan to revitalize the domestic economy but an economic growth program that would at the very least not aggravate the balance of payments situation and, ideally, would in fact help to correct it. From the perspective of Walter Heller and the other members of the Council of Economic Advisors, a commercial Keynesian growth program was the best way to meet these interconnected domestic and international challenges. The Council reasoned that its program of tax cuts targeted at private industry in a context of easy money would restore economic growth at home by encouraging private investment, which, in turn, would increase the demand for labor. At the same time, as firms invested in new plants and equipment, their production costs would go down, allowing them to once again compete in the world market, turning around the trade deficit and thus enabling the country to balance its international payments accounts without having to sacrifice its global ambitions.

The Puzzling Course of Monetary Policy

Although the core of the commercial Keynesian strategy was the fiscal program of tax cuts, the Council of Economic Advisors believed that, by themselves, tax cuts would be insufficient for creating the kind of growth that the country needed to bring itself back from the brink. To work, tax cuts required the active support of an easy monetary policy. If firms were going to take advantage of the new fiscal environment, they needed access to cheap and plentiful credit, something that had been lacking during the Eisenhower administration when interest rates for business loans increased from 3.1 percent to 5.2 percent.[17] This situation did not sit well with the growth-minded members of the Council of Economic Advisors. In the January 1961 issue of *Challenge* magazine, Yale economist and member of the incoming Kennedy administration's Council of Economic Advisors James Tobin gave the following analysis of economic growth:

> The basic requirement of a growth policy is a shift in the composition of national output, so that a larger proportion goes into uses that enlarge productive

capacity ... The federal government can engineer such a shift by following a relatively "easy" monetary policy—using low interest rates and abundant credit to
encourage investment by business firms and by state and local governments.[18]

Tobin was not only laying out the kind of monetary posture that he, and
other commercial Keynesians, believed was essential for economic growth,
he was also openly taking the Federal Reserve and the chairman of its Open
Market Committee, William McChesney Martin, to task for restricting the
country's growth potential by following an overly restrictive monetary policy
during the Eisenhower years. Over the next three years, in addition to fighting
for tax cuts, the Council of Economic Advisors tried to get the administration to push the Federal Reserve over to the side of monetary ease. Walter
Heller was especially frustrated by the Federal Reserve's unwillingness to
actively lower long-term interest rates, telling President Kennedy during his
first months in office that "the Federal Reserve must be petted, pressured, or
pushed into firm resistance of rising interest rates."[19]

Despite these efforts, and despite their success on the fiscal front, Heller
and the Council of Economic Advisors were unable to get the monetary policy
that they desired. Instead, the administration and the Federal Reserve began a
new experiment in monetary policy that became known as "operation twist."
The "twist" was essentially an exercise in monetary micromanagement with
the goal of distorting the typical market relationship between short-term interest rates and long-term interest rates. In the past, the standard practice of
the Federal Reserve was to maintain a gap between higher long-term interest
rates and lower short-term interest rates. From the end of 1961 through 1963
the Federal Reserve actively manipulated this structure by restricting supplies
of short-term interbank credit, which raised short-term interest rates while
at the same time keeping long-term interest rates from rising by aggressively
operating in the market for government debt.

The effects of this "twist" on the structure of the United States credit market are shown in Figures 6.1 and 6.2. Figure 6.1 charts the steady decline in
the supply of free banking reserves in the financial system. Free reserves are
reserves held by financial institutions that are in excess of the reserves required by the Federal Reserve, net of any borrowed reserves. Put simply, they
are cash or cashlike assets that are sitting around, earning no interest for the
bank. Banks with a large stock of free reserves will lend them to other financial institutions that may be temporarily short in reserves through the federal

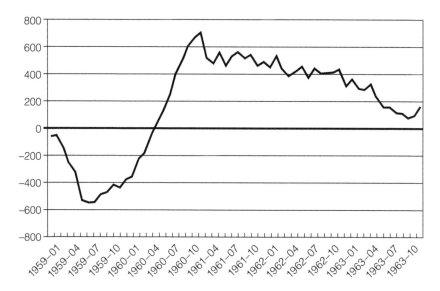

FIGURE 6.1. Free reserves of depository institutions, millions of dollars, 1959–1963, year and month.
SOURCE: Board of Governors of the Federal Reserve, H.3 Statistical Release.

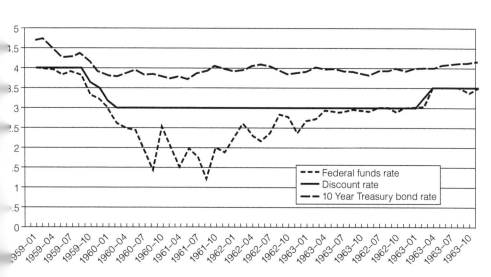

FIGURE 6.2. Select U.S. interest rates, 1960–1963, year and month.
SOURCE: Board of Governors of the Federal Reserve, H.15 "Selected Interest Rates."

funds market, earning a rate of interest known as the federal funds rate. The level of free reserves is thus a good indication of how liquid credit markets are: When banks are holding large amounts of free reserves, it is easier for firms to borrow, and to borrow at low interest rates. However, when there are fewer free reserves in the banking system, banks running low on reserves will compete for the limited supply by bidding up the federal funds rate, raising rates across the short-term credit market. Controlling the supply of free reserves is thus one of the Federal Reserve's major mechanisms for influencing credit markets.

The impact of the shrinking supply of free bank reserves on the structure of interest rates is shown in Figure 6.2. The federal funds rate began to steadily increase in the middle of 1961, pressing up against the discount rate the following year. Banks running short on free reserves have the option of borrowing reserves from the Federal Reserve directly from the "discount window." However, the Fed prefers that reserve transactions take place in the private federal funds market rather than having banks rely on the central monetary authority for short-term credit needs. Thus, to discourage discount window borrowing, the Federal Reserve tries to keep the federal funds rate below the discount rate. When the federal funds rate begins to press up against the discount rate, the Federal Reserve faces the choice of either taking measures to increase the supply of free reserves and easing pressure on the federal funds market or raising the discount rate and letting private, short-term rates continue to rise. The former option is called "monetary easing," while the later is "monetary tightening," reflecting their effects on the supply and cost of credit.

When faced with this scenario in 1963, the Federal Reserve opted for a course of monetary tightening, raising the discount rate to accommodate upward pressure in the federal funds market. While the initial discount rate increase was modest, over the next three years a combination of tight credit markets and high rates of economic growth pushed the economy into a major "credit crunch" in the summer of 1966 which, as Gretta Krippner has documented, set the stage for a deeper financialization of the U.S. economy.[20]

It was precisely for fear of this scenario that operation twist never sat well with Heller and his Council of Economic Advisors. In principle, the twist was supposed to resolve competing domestic and international pressures. Higher short-term rates were supposed to slow the outflow of short-term investment capital seeking higher rates of return in Europe, while keeping long-term rates stable supported the administration's aggressive growth program. The

Council, however, was not convinced that the Federal Reserve could maintain a tight short-term credit market without the effects spilling over into the long-term market.[21] Of particular concern to the Council was the stability of the discount rate, arguing that any increase would undermine the president's economic growth program because it would both make it more expensive for firms to borrow in the short run and, in the long run, create more upward pressure on rates as financial markets expected to be operating in a tight monetary environment.[22] Why was the Council of Economic Advisors, seemingly so capable of using commercial Keynesian ideas to push their fiscal program, unable to convince policy makers of the need for an easy monetary climate?

The answer lies not with domestic politics but with changing distribution of international monetary power in the Bretton Woods system. Faced with a severe balance of payments deficit that was increasingly being financed by Western European central banks, policy makers in the Kennedy administration were forced to contend with the fact that securing international financial cooperation depended on how foreign financial institutions reacted to the way in which the administration dealt with domestic economic stagnation. For the commercial Keynesian agenda, the country's dependency on foreign monetary authorities was a mixed blessing. On the one hand, Heller and the Council of Economic Advisors were able to mobilize international opinion to support their commercial Keynesian fiscal policies. On the other hand, international opinion worked against their monetary agenda, instead bolstering the views of monetary conservatives in the White House and Federal Reserve. The rest of this chapter looks at the debates over U.S. economic policy that took place in the Economic Policy Committee, the way those debates were framed by the problems of dependency and confidence, and, critically, how these international discussions filtered into the sites of U.S. economic policy making.

The International Push for Commercial Keynesianism

When seated among the other members of Kennedy's cabinet and executive staff, Walter Heller likely felt like a lone voice crying in the wilderness, trying to convince his cautious colleagues and an even more cautious president to embark on a bold, activist growth program. Yet, when seated among their international peers in the meetings of the Economic Policy Committee, Heller and the other members of the Council of Economic Advisors found themselves surrounded by intellectual allies, state officials and policy experts from Western Europe who often seemed even more frustrated than Heller himself at the timidity with which the Eisenhower and newly arrived Kennedy administrations pulled at the fiscal levers.

The European members of the OECD were very concerned about the American economic recession. For one, even though by 1960 Western Europe had recovered significantly from the devastation of World War II, the American economy still made up a major share of the world's economy; any stagnation in the American economy was felt globally and thus hurt other countries' growth prospects—especially those small, open economies whose own economic vitality was dependent on robust export markets. In addition, weakness in the American economy suggested weakness in the American dollar, the anchor of the entire Bretton Woods system and the source of postwar monetary stability.

When the newly constituted Economic Policy Committee held its first meetings in early 1961 the problem of slow growth in the United States was treated with cautious optimism. Some data indicated that the recession might soon be ending, especially given that some modest fiscal measures proposed by the Kennedy administration had yet to be implemented.[23] However, as the American economy remained stagnant into 1962, the Economic Policy Committee began to make the same case that Walter Heller had been making at cabinet meetings: Without a substantial fiscal stimulus, the economy would remain mired in recession. Reviewing the economic situation of the OECD members in late 1962 the Economic Policy Committee detected a growing stagnation in the American economy and argued that any future economic growth would likely need to come from some form of public stimulus.[24] Raising Cold War fears, the Bank for International Settlements struck a similar tone, lamenting that without a flexible fiscal policy "the United States will risk continuing to have a rate of growth well below that of Europe—east and west."[25]

These concerns about the lack of economic growth in the United States were tied to the deeper problem of declining confidence in the dollar. This is how Dr. Gocht of the German Ministry of Finance framed the issue when he observed: "A small [balance of payments] deficit under conditions of rapidly growing U.S. activity was more favourable to confidence than equilibrium at the expense of slow growth and high unemployment."[26] A growth program that inspired confidence abroad was one that favored private investment and capital accumulation, not increased expenditure on social programs or public works projects.

For example, after returning from a meeting of European Central bankers held in Basel in early July 1962, Alfred Hayes of the Federal Reserve Bank of New York conveyed the bankers' sentiments regarding American fiscal policy to Treasury Secretary Douglas Dillon. "If there is to be a tax cut," Hayes wrote, "it should be oriented toward improved business incentives; should be of a permanent and reform character; reductions centered on lower bracket personal income would be regarded as fiscally loose 'bread and circuses,' although some companion action in this sector would be understandable."[27] Walter Heller offered a similar interpretation. In a memorandum to President Kennedy, Heller claimed that "tax-cut induced deficits are also far more acceptable to the world financial community than expenditure-induced deficits, i.e. far less likely to touch off new gold outflows."[28] In other words, commercial Keynesianism wasn't just good for the domestic economy, it was also good for protecting the U.S. international position. While it certainly cannot be said, based on the previously discussed historical evidence alone, that international opinion was the decisive factor that pushed American fiscal policy in a commercial Keynesian direction, it is certainly the case that the balance of payments crisis added considerable weight to international opinion that, in turn, lent support to the commercial Keynesian agenda.

The commercial Keynesians could not, however, count on the members of the Economic Policy Committee or the central bankers who met in Basel to support all of their policy goals. While the Kennedy growth program is most remembered for its tax cuts, a necessary adjunct to these fiscal measures, at least in the eyes of the Council of Economic Advisors, was an easy monetary policy. On this issue, however, the commercial Keynesian growth program faced stiff opposition from a vocal contingent within the international organizations of international monetary management who urged the Kennedy administration to essentially follow the prescriptions of classical liberalism and let interest rates rise to slow the outflow of private capital.

The Balance of Payments and Monetary Policy Debates

From a purely ideational standpoint, both commercial Keynesianism and classical liberalism can make a perfectly logical case, built on solid economic principles, for why lower or higher interest rates will correct a balance of payments deficit. The commercial Keynesian argument is that low interest rates and plentiful credit make it easier for firms to invest, which would provide a long-run solution to the country's payments deficit by increasing the level of exports. Classical liberals, on the other hand, argued that higher interest rates would restore balance of payments equilibrium in the short run by making it more attractive for investors, both domestic and foreign, to put their money in the United States. The problem with the commercial Keynesian strategy was that it took the long view on the balance of payments deficit and left open the problem of how to deal with the ramifications of payments deficit in the short run.

In an attempt to receive cooperation from OECD members in working through short-term payments difficulties while the long-term benefits of the commercial Keynesian program worked their way through the economy, in April of 1961 the United States submitted a paper to Working Party 3 of the Economic Policy Committee calling attention to the spread that had developed over the last three years between low American interest rates and high European interest rates. While the early Bretton Woods architects may have seen this as evidence of the need to place stronger controls on short-term capital flows, by the early 1960s the predominant view was that short-term capital flows were not only not harmful to the international monetary system but, as the U.S. paper noted, "are essential elements in the mechanism of international adjustment."[29] This paper began a long debate within Working Party 3 over the relationship among capital flows, interest rate differentials, and the process of balance of payments adjustment. While few disagreed with the idea that capital outflows were creating serious problems for the American payment deficit, American and European delegates to Working Party 3 disagreed over the causes of capital outflows and the potential effects of different remedies to correct it.

For many of the European delegates the answer was simple: Capital flowed to where returns were higher. Therefore, American interest rates needed to be raised. In the early meetings of the Working Party, calls for the United States to tighten its monetary policy for external reasons were somewhat equivocal. Salvatore Guidotti, who came to the Working Party from the Bank of Italy's research department, commented at the Working Party 3 meeting of October 26: "It would be helpful if interest rates in the U.S. went up somewhat."[30] His rather lax appraisal of American monetary policy in 1961 was characteristic of most of the other delegates' sentiments. Over the course of the following year, however, calls for the United States to raise interest rates to stop its capital outflow became more frequent and more direct. In April of 1962, the OECD secretariat released a new set of figures painting a grim picture of the U.S. international position: Gold reserves had fallen considerably due to a worsening of the current account balance, a large part of which was attributed to short-term capital flows and other speculative flows that were difficult to measure.[31] The new figures renewed concern that low American interest rates were creating a structural imbalance in the American international account.

A consensus quickly emerged among the European delegates to the Working Party that interest rates in the United States needed to be increased to combat the capital outflow. The problem, as argued by Otmar Emminger, who sat on the Board of Directors of the German Bundesbank, was that "interest rate differentials contributed to speculative fears in the sense that investors were worried that the United States was not taking the necessary measures to correct the outflow."[32] The Working Party chairman added his support to this view, as did Mr. Stevens of the British delegation, who "thought that present holders of dollars were looking for a clear indication from the United States Government about the prospects for the budget deficit and for a rise in interest rates."[33] The Dutch, Swedish, and Swiss representatives also voiced their concerns about low American interest rates, the latter arguing that "external considerations should be given priority in the shaping of United States economic policy, especially in the field of interest rates."[34]

During this time, the United States was also getting pressure from other intergovernmental organizations to do something about interest rates. The Bank for International Settlements, in its *Annual Report of 1961*, stated: "It would seem most appropriate to direct monetary measures to the external problem by keeping the gap in money-market rates as narrow as required and to secure the stimulus to the economy through either a cut in the tax rates or an increase in government expenditure."[35] The following year, when the American payment deficit worsened, the Bank for International Settlements took an even stronger position, arguing that even domestic economic expansion needed to take a backseat to reestablishing payments equilibrium.[36]

The United States responded to these arguments in two ways, first by making the commercial Keynesian case that the only long-term solution to the payments deficit was to get the American economy out of recession, which in turn required low interest rates.[37] Other working party members, however, did not agree with the basic premise of this argument. S. Posthuma, Managing Director of the Nederlandsche Bank, "questioned the belief that high interest rates had an important impact on capital investment plans," a doubt that was supported by a British delegate who argued that "of the two ways of influencing the economy, i.e., the budget and the interest rate level, the latter had the more important influence on international capital movements."[38]

Second, the American delegation attempted to offer an alternative explanation of the excessive capital outflow from the United States, namely that the cause was not that American interest rates were too low but rather that the Europeans had inefficient capital markets, making it difficult for their firms to borrow at home and forcing them to borrow from Wall Street. Undersecretary of the Treasury Robert Roosa first raised this argument at the April 1962 meeting of Working Party 3 during a discussion of the problem of capital outflows.[39] While the European delegates were pushing the United States to raise interest rates, Roosa was trying to get the question of capital market structures on the Working Party's agenda.[40]

This part of the story is at first glance a bit puzzling. Why would U.S. Treasury officials urge Europeans to borrow in their own capital markets rather than in New York? It would seem to serve the U.S. global hegemonic ambitions if European firms were dependent on the United States for investment capital. As David Calleo has insightfully pointed out, only some components of the overall payments deficits, what he called the "imperial deficit," furthered the U.S. global ambitions. These are military spending, foreign aid, and foreign direct investment.[41] Lending to private European firms, however, was not and only threatened the stability of the larger Bretton Woods system, which was vital to American global interests. On the other side of the table, countries like Germany, the Netherlands, Switzerland, and Italy were interested in seeing an end to economic stagnation in the United States if it meant a larger market for their exports, but they were not interested in the revitalization of the United States as an export competitor. This debate over seemingly minute and inconsequential details of American monetary policy was thus part of a much deeper set of conflicts over the distribution of power within the Western-led postwar global economic order.

Calls for the United States to adopt a tighter monetary policy to alleviate balance of payments pressures continued into 1963. Robert Roosa attributed the problem to a poor trade performance and tried to use this to argue that economic policy, including monetary policy, should be oriented toward promoting economic growth and export competitiveness. Representatives from Germany, Canada, Sweden, and the Netherlands continued to call this reasoning into question.[42]

Finally, at the July 12 meeting of the Working Party, the debate reached a temporary resolution as Robert Roosa announced that the Kennedy administration was going to be taking substantial steps to correct the payments deficit. In addition to a new interest equalization tax to reduce the incentives for Americans to invest in high-yield European securities, the president's balance of payments program included an increase in the Federal Reserve discount rate from 3 percent to 3.5 percent. While the magnitude of this change may appear rather small, bearing in mind that since joining the OECD in 1961 the U.S. delegates had consistently argued that tightening monetary policy would have no effect on capital outflows and that monetary policy would be structured around domestic, not international, concerns, Roosa's announcement becomes quite significant. It represented nothing short of a concession to the "tight money crowd," as Walter Heller had called them, without any real progress on the issue of European capital market liberalization.

Crises of Confidence and Relations of Dependency

Scholars who take a constructivist approach to explaining policy making argue that during moments of political and economic uncertainty experts will play a decisive role in the policy-making process. In this case, however, the evidence is clear that the Kennedy administration did not adopt the views of the "tight money crowd" because of the technical or factual merits of the experts. For one, there was little consensus among the representatives to the working party as to the precise macroeconomic effects of interest rate differentials on capital movements. In fact, studies conducted by the OECD secretariat on European capital market structures seemed to bear out the claims made by Robert Roosa: Capital would continue to flow from the United States to Europe so long as inefficiencies in European capital markets failed to supply adequate credit to domestic investors. Commenting on the results of the secretariat's study, M. M. Perouse—Roosa's counterpart in the French Treasury—conceded that "an increase in the United States interest rates would only have a marginal influence on international capital movements."[43]

So, if the technical merits of adjusting monetary policy were so shaky, even to the point where the Europeans themselves were not convinced, why did it form the cornerstone of their demands on American officials? The answer has to do with the nature of the American payment deficit and the problems associated with trying to finance that deficit. As noted earlier, the problem for the United States was not that too many dollars were going overseas but rather that foreign investors and financial institutions were no longer holding onto their excess dollars but were instead cashing them in for gold. In this context, what American officials needed was to find a way to convince international holders of dollars that the currency was strong and a good investment so that they would not cash them in for gold. Moreover, American officials recognized that they needed to do more than convince vague, unspecified private financial market actors of the strength of the dollar but, more critically, needed to convince European monetary officials to aid in the defense of the dollar.

Walter Heller spelled this out to President Kennedy in May of 1962. Balance of payments deficits, Heller explained, were problematic because "a U.S. balance of payments deficit adds to the dollars in foreign hands, private or official. If foreign private banks and individuals get more dollars than they want, they sell them to their own central banks for their local currencies. If the central banks thus acquire more dollars than they want, they use them to buy gold from us." The United States was in a difficult position because even if the balance of payments deficit was ended immediately there were still billions of dollars of dollar liabilities in the hands of foreign central banks and private investors. As Heller further explained,

> It is this overhang which places us at the mercy of the "confidence" which foreign central bankers, private bankers, and financial pundits have in the dollar. *So long as we have to worry about "confidence," we are not masters in our own house.* Domestic policy is perpetually inhibited by what this or that measure may do—or by what someone thinks it may do—to confidence in the dollar. In particular, measures to stimulate employment and growth are inhibited—even though in the long run unemployment and economic stagnation also weaken confidence.[44]

Heller recognized the close connection between private confidence in the dollar and official confidence in the dollar and also recognized that a loss of either could prove to be a constraint on policy making.

As the U.S. balance of payments deficit worsened without any substantial action on monetary policy, some of the European delegates to Working Party 3 questioned whether the United States could continue to expect help from foreign central banks to finance its deficit. Commenting on the growing size of the American payments deficit at the February 1963 meeting, the Working Party chairman "thought it was unrealistic to hope that financing would become available for central banks while waiting for market forces to redress the situation."[45] A Swiss delegate put it more bluntly: "Cooperation of central banks in financing the deficit could not go on indefinitely and a substantial reduction in the payments deficit was necessary if cooperation was to be maintained."[46] The chairman of the Working Party, speaking as a representative of the Netherlands, followed suit by stating, "Financing of United States external deficits by the Central Banks of surplus countries could continue only so long as these countries were convinced that all necessary steps had been taken to correct the United States deficit."[47] What the "necessary steps" would be had been made all too clear: Raise interest rates and reduce credit market liquidity.

These thinly veiled threats that European monetary authorities would no longer cooperate to help prop up the dollar in foreign exchange markets were backed by the material reality of the U.S. financial dependency. Over the three years that these discussions took place, the United States had become increasingly reliant on short-term credit arrangements to support the dollar's value in the exchange markets. By early 1963 the Federal Reserve's holdings of foreign currencies had increased to $1.3 billion. The size of the swap arrangements with the Italian, Swiss, and German central banks had been increased to $150 million each. Swap arrangements had been established with the Austrian central bank and the Bank for International Settlements, and negotiations were underway to extend the network of currency swaps to Sweden and Japan.[48] In short, the currency swap system had become both broader and deeper.

Particularly problematic, from the standpoint of gaining support for the administration's growth agenda, was that the two countries playing the most vital role in propping up the dollar—Germany and Switzerland—had little interest in these kinds of growth experiments. During the 1960s, Germany held between $3.5 billion and $2.5 billion in its foreign reserves—more than any other country in the world.[49] Even more importantly, unlike the French, who converted their dollar reserves into gold almost as quickly as they got them, the German central bank held a much higher portion of its reserves as dollars rather than exchanging them for gold. Because the U.S. balance of payments deficit became a significant issue only when dollars held abroad were converted into gold, American officials had an incentive to try to ensure that central banks would keep their reserves in the form of dollars. In some instance, like France, this was a lost cause. The French government made it abundantly clear that they resented the "special position" of the dollar in the postwar international monetary system. Germany, however, seemed willing to hold dollars, but this willingness could never be taken for granted.

At the same time that American officials were trying to maintain German interest in keeping their foreign exchange holdings of dollars, they were also relying heavily on their swap arrangements with the Swiss National Bank to defend the gold stock from speculation against the dollar. While the U.S. swap network had expanded over the course of the decade to include over a dozen countries, nearly one-third of all swap transactions were conducted with the Swiss National Bank in Swiss francs. Switzerland had become an important international money market that, due to its strong currency and relatively high interest rates, attracted capital from all over the world. Although this was a sign of financial strength, the scale of these capital inflows was very problematic as they not only made it more difficult for the Swiss National Bank to manage the domestic money supply but also drove up the Swiss franc in international currency markets, which only increased opportunities for currency speculation that threatened the Bretton Woods fixed exchange rate system. From 1962 to 1964 the Federal Reserve Bank worked aggressively in the market for francs, swapping francs that it did not have to both the National Bank of Switzerland and the Bank for International Settlements for dollars that it was desperate to see returned to the United States. By 1964 the Federal Reserve owed $220 million worth of francs to both institutions.[50]

The problem of confidence was thus structured by a set of material relationships that redistributed international monetary power within the evolving Bretton Woods institutional framework. Maintaining confidence in the dollar was critical because it anchored the entire system of postwar stable exchange rates. Once the American balance of payments deficit threatened to undermine this role for the dollar, the United States increasingly relied on cooperation from foreign central banks—particularly those central banks that were holding a balance of payments surplus—to help prop up the dollar's value in foreign exchange markets, thus providing incentives for private investors to hold onto their dollar-based financial assets.

By the end of 1963 the American delegation to Working Party 3 was beginning to reap some of the benefits of having bolstered the confidence of the Europeans by making modest concessions to their demands for a tighter monetary policy. Presenting figures on the U.S. balance of payments deficit for the year, Ralph Young projected a total deficit of somewhere around $3 billion—a figure that, earlier in the year, Robert Roosa had projected as a possible "worst-case scenario." Yet, despite this dramatic worsening of the American balance of payments situation, Alexander Hay, director of the Swiss National Bank and normally a harsh critic of the American payments deficit, "considered the news from the United States very encouraging."[51]

International Confidence and Policy Conflict at the Federal Reserve

The ties of financial dependency between the United States and Western European central banks, the clear articulation of those ties of dependency, and the conditional nature of balance of payments financing explain why the Kennedy administration ended up in the contradictory position of having a classically liberal monetary policy to go along with its commercial Keynesian fiscal policies. That being said, this story is not complete without an examination of how international pressures found their way into the Federal Reserve, the institution that plays a key role in setting monetary policy. On the surface, this may seem to be a fairly straightforward story. As the central bank, the Federal Reserve, like other central banks, prefers monetary stability to growth.

At the same time, however, the Federal Reserve is also conservative in that it prefers to nudge credit markets rather to embark on bold credit market experiments like operation twist. Indeed, the fact that domestic and international economic pressures called for competing policy moves—monetary easing to help get the economy out of its stupor and monetary tightening to protect the balance of payments—only heightened this conservatism as members followed a strategy of non–decision making, trying to maintain the current policy course while waiting for some change in the macroeconomic picture to force them into action.

In addition, even though there were those within the Federal Reserve's Federal Open Market Committee (the body charged with managing the federal funds market and where most control over monetary policy is vested) who would have gladly heeded the Europeans' call for tighter money, including Federal Reserve Chairman William McChesney Martin and President of the New York Federal Reserve Alfred Hayes, they had to contend with more liberal committee members like J. L. Robertson, who had been appointed to the Board of Governors of the Federal Reserve in the early 1950s, and George

W. Mitchell, who had been appointed to the board by President Kennedy in 1961. More than any other members, Robertson and Mitchell were concerned with the sluggishness of the economic recovery.

Finally, most of the FOMC members approached monetary policy discussions emphasizing domestic, rather than international, economic conditions. This bias emerged from the way in which FOMC meetings were structured, whereby each member first commented on the economic conditions of their particular district before giving their policy views. Thus, much of the concrete "data" that the FOMC members brought to the policy table were about the domestic economic situation. For the most part, international developments appeared only in reports presented by FOMC staff analysts.

Despite these obstacles Martin and Hayes were able to effectively mobilize the specter of waning international confidence in the dollar to sway their colleagues to tighten monetary policy four times between 1962 and 1963, the most significant tightening occurring in July of 1963, which set the stage for the Board of Governors to raise the discount rate from 3 percent to 3.5 percent.

The first move to tighten monetary policy occurred on June 19, 1962, in the context of two interrelated domestic economic developments. First, stock market prices had fallen precipitously beginning in April, the Standard and Poor's index losing nearly 20 percent of its value in just two months. Second, and partly in response to the stock market crash, the Kennedy administration released its plans for a major fiscal stimulus in the form of tax credits and tax cuts. As vice chairman of the FOMC, Alfred Hayes was given first opportunity to speak at this meeting. Hayes was the governor of the New York Federal Reserve, which was not only where the Fed's international economic analyses were performed but, even more important, was where much of the world's gold reserves were held. For this reason, Hayes was one of the few Committee members who came to the meetings with a heightened appreciation of the international implications of American economic policy.

In his opening comments Hayes made the case that this change in the administration's domestic economic policy increased the need to tighten monetary policy to protect the dollar. The reason, Hayes argued, was the effect of these policy measures on foreign confidence in the dollar: "To put it another way, foreign confidence in the dollar could be seriously hurt if the impression were to gain ground abroad that a more expansionary fiscal policy was likely to be accompanied by an unchanging policy of monetary ease."[52]

By the time each of the other committee members had a chance to speak, five (including Hayes) had come out in favor of monetary tightening in light of the international situation. This was a substantial departure from the four previous meetings, when no committee members had taken this position. Of course, Hayes's reasoning did not convince everyone at the meeting, but what Hayes's formulation of the problem did do was to frame the ensuing discussion such that all of the committee members had to take the balance of payments situation seriously when stating their policy preferences. In addition, with Mitchell absent from this meeting, Martin was able to swing the decision to the side of monetary tightening.

The adjustment was modest and tenuous. The FOMC voted to raise the target minimum for the federal funds rate, the key interest rate setting short-term interest rates, from 2.5 percent to 2.75 percent. However, over the next few months there was a renewed push among many of the committee members to return to a position of greater ease, particularly after the administration announced in August that there would be no tax cut until 1963, undercutting Hayes's original argument for the need for tightening. In addition, while the problem of confidence had worked well in advancing Hayes's call for tightening in June, by October the question of confidence seemed to be working in favor of the advocates for ease. The report given on money market conditions by the manager of the System Open Market Account at the October 2 meeting noted that "reports from the [International Monetary] Fund and the [World] Bank meetings have suggested to the market that confidence in the dollar may have improved sufficiently so that greater weight might be given to the domestic side in the formulation of policy."[53]

Hayes challenged this interpretation, arguing: "The grave question is whether confidence in the dollar as a reserve currency can be maintained while balance is gradually being attained."[54] Mr. Deming, representing the ninth district of the Federal Reserve System, offered a different view, noting that "it seemed to him there had been a worsening of the balance of payments problem recently, but at the same time some increase in the confidence of the dollar."[55] The question of confidence was thus a highly contested one and was mobilized by the advocates for both monetary ease and monetary tightening. While Martin was able to hold on to the degree of tightening that had been achieved at the June meeting, something would have to be done to tip the scales toward a new round of tightening.

At the November 13, 1962, meeting of the FOMC two subtle but important changes to the standard conduct of the Committee's meetings were enacted that would bring international affairs to the forefront of the committee's discussions. The first change was moving the report of Federal Reserve foreign currency operations from the end of the meeting, after the vote on the new policy directive had already been taken, to the beginning of the meeting, following the presentation by the manager for the System Open Market Account on the domestic money markets.

The second change was giving Ralph Young, Committee secretary and delegate to Working Party 3, the opportunity to comment on the tone and tenor of the Working Party's discussions early in the meeting, before the expression of policy views. Both of these changes put international concerns directly in front of the other Committee members and thus served to frame the ensuing policy discussions around international issues.

As the minutes of the December 18 meeting clearly show, one of the major effects of this procedural shift was providing a link between the policy preferences of the Europeans and the decision making of the other Committee members. In his comments, Young summarized the views of the European delegates to Working Party 3 who "may have felt that they had failed, through inadvertence, to exact a compensating U.S. commitment that its monetary policy now begin to carry a larger burden in combating the persisting balance of payments deficit."[56] In the ensuing discussion, Young essentially served as the European proxy to the Committee, responding to inquiries from members Mills, Mitchell, and Robertson from the European perspective and distributing documents prepared by the Working Party secretariat to the FOMC.

By having Young give his comments before the committee members gave their usual views on policy, the discussion was effectively oriented toward the balance of payments problem. For example, committee member Deming, while generally favoring no change in policy at the December 18 meeting, did note that any latitude afforded to the System Open Market manager should tilt toward a slight increase of short-term interest rates. His reasoning for this emerged from Young's presentation and his articulation of the problem of confidence: "From Mr. Young's comments, and others he had heard, he thought he detected a feeling that the problem with respect to capital flows and interest rates involved more a question of confidence than a question of real movements of funds." While skeptical that the committee could do much

to reverse capital outflows, he did believe that "it might be of more importance than he had thought two weeks ago to insure that the short-term rate
did not drop appreciably."[57] By the end of the discussion, Martin was able to
count seven members of the committee (including himself) who favored a
further tightening of interest rates.

This was a significant shift in views. Since the June tightening, open market interbank lending rates had already crept up to the discount rate offered
by the Federal Reserve. By voting to further tighten monetary policy, the
committee was essentially voting to keep open market rates pushed up against
the discount rate while also reducing levels of free bank reserves. This monetary policy posture was not sustainable; either the discount rate would need
to be increased, or the committee would have to back down from its tighter
position.

The resolution of this dilemma came in the middle of the following year.
At the meeting of March 5, 1963, Ralph Young once again gave an extended
report on his most recent trip to the Working Party 3 meetings, noting that
"the tone of the meeting was highly critical of American financial policy." He
told the committee members that the Europeans felt that there was too much
liquidity in American financial markets, with the excess spilling over into foreign markets.[58] Two months later at the May meeting of the FOMC, Young
once again brought the sentiments of Working Party 3 to the other Committee members. Young reported that the Working Party felt that "U.S. expansion
and prosperity were essential to a strong U.S. payments position" but also that
"there was urgent need to supplement such expansion by an active monetary
policy to reduce excessive internal liquidity."[59] Young's assessment was supported by data on recent Federal Reserve foreign exchange operations showing that higher interest rates in the Netherlands and Germany were placing
strong pressure on the dollar.

Building on this momentum, Alfred Hayes took the opportunity at the
June 18 meeting to make the first explicit call for an increase in the discount
rate, drawing the committee's attention to a memo prepared by Charles
Coombs (who managed the committee's foreign exchange operations) "expressing the judgment that we have reached a critical phase and that the
dollar has become vulnerable to a break in confidence which might occur
almost without warning."[60] Though few other committee members were willing to follow Hayes's call for a discount rate increase at this point, the problem of confidence in the dollar raised in Coombs's memo loomed large. As

committee member Irons stated, "If a substantial loss of confidence in the dollar was imminent . . . he would favor such an action."[61]

The proponents of monetary ease, who remained concerned about the sluggish pace of domestic economic recovery, did not let this issue of confidence go uncontested. Reporting on his recent trip to the Bank for International Settlements in Switzerland at the July 7 meeting, J. L. Robertson noted that the central bankers at the meeting "seemed satisfied that the best course was to push for improving business activity by maintaining monetary ease and making efforts to get the supplemental stimulus of a tax cut as soon as possible."[62] Unfortunately for Robertson and the cause of monetary ease, the work of the previous year of bringing the lack of European confidence in the dollar into the committee's discussions was not going to be outdone by this single impression.[63]

By July, Martin was ready to call the other Committee members to action. Describing a recent meeting between himself and key cabinet officials in the White House, Martin reported that he had effectively agreed to a discount rate increase to 3.5 percent as part of a broader package of reforms aimed at curbing the dollar outflow. The question, as he put it to the rest of the committee members, was whether they wanted to come out as team players or sabotage the Kennedy administration's efforts. Although the FOMC itself does not vote on changes to the discount rate (this is done by the Board of Governors), the choice that the committee faced was whether to maintain the existing level of firmness in the money markets, which would effectively call for a discount rate increase, or to ease up. By a vote of ten to three the members passed a policy directive "to accommodate moderate growth in bank credit, while putting increased emphasis on money market conditions that would contribute to an improvement in the capital account of the U.S. balance of payments."[64] Shortly after this meeting, the Board of Governors voted to raise the discount rate to 3.5 percent.

The Global Politics of Commercial Keynesianism

In the final months of 1963 the Kennedy administration's economic growth program had taken a clear shape. Significant tax cuts were working their way through the Congress, wage-price guideposts were being used to exert pressure on labor unions, and credit markets were being restructured to deal with competing international and domestic demands. While many important pieces of this program bore the indelible stamp of Walter Heller and the commercial Keynesians, taken as a whole this package of policies reflects the policy goals of the international organizations of postwar economic governance. With some issues, like cutting taxes and restricting wage growth, there was an easy harmony between the views of international forums of policy discussion and the views of domestic policy-making experts. In the case of monetary policy, harmony gave way to discord, and in the end international pressure proved to be decisive.

Though the policy adjustments that were made in the face of international pressure may seem minor, particularly when compared to the much more dramatic shift in policy that the Labour government was compelled to undertake in the latter half of the decade, the fact that the Kennedy administration was compelled to compromise its growth agenda for balance of payments purposes challenges the conventional wisdom about the dominant position of the United States in the postwar international order. According to the prevailing wisdom, the fact that the dollar anchored the Bretton Woods order should have allowed the United States to exert control over the other OECD members, particularly over the content of their domestic macroeconomic policies. As Arthur MacEwan has argued, the centrality of the dollar in the Bretton Woods system "assured that the U.S. government would have the power to force macroeconomic policies on other governments: the United States could act as it saw fit, and other governments, committed to maintaining fixed exchange rates, would have to adjust."[65]

According to this interpretation, it was the Western European nations who should have been forced to make adjustments to their national economies to maintain balance of payments equilibrium, and the United States should have been able to avoid balance of payments constraints by sending its excess dollars into hungry global markets and thus "exporting" domestic inflation. This "privileged and comparatively invulnerable position of dollar domination,"[66] as Susan Strange put it, both protected American policies markers from international economic constraints on the domestic agenda and provided one of the key mechanisms allowing the United States to coerce the OECD partners into accepting its global agenda.

This is not what happened. Many governments, notably those of Germany, Switzerland, and the Netherlands were not happy about excessive dollar inflows, and, most critically, their central banks were now the first line of defense against rampant speculation against the dollar in an increasingly liberal global economy. U.S. hegemony depended on a strong dollar, and the strength of the dollar was dependent on foreign central bank cooperation. Critically, it was not the size of the American balance of payments deficit in and of itself that placed pressure on American officials but rather the new power that the European financial community—both private and public—to affect the integrity of the international monetary system that was key. This power was the result of the historically contingent nature of the American balance of payments deficit in the late 1950s and early 1960s and the evolving institutions of postwar international monetary management, which both made it vital that the United States maintain international confidence in its currency and made active cooperation between central banks and finance ministries essential for preventing speculative runs on currencies.

As the next chapter will show, this episode also proves to be very significant for understanding not only the beginning of the end of the commercial Keynesian experiment but also the rise of systemic fragility in the American banking sector. "Operation twist" was a dramatic new experiment in monetary policy, restricting access to credit at a time when the economy was rebounding. This forced banks to find new, innovative ways to take in deposits and lend money and made speculative dealings in short-term markets more lucrative relative to the stagnant returns offered in the long-term credit markets. Over subsequent years these innovations would put the American financial sector on an increasingly fragile footing, threatening the commercial Keynesian growth program and the social democratic goals of Lyndon Johnson's Great Society.

7 Guns, Butter, and Gold

THE YEAR 1965 SAW THE HALCYON DAYS OF COMMERCIAL Keynesianism. Whereas the Kennedy administration had faced stiff political opposition to its economic program from all sides, Lyndon Johnson's decisive victory over Barry Goldwater in the 1964 presidential election, combined with Democratic gains in the legislature, bespoke an acceptance of Kennedy's economic and social agenda. Most importantly, as 1965 drew to a close it appeared that the commercial Keynesian experiment in economic policy making, begun in earnest just three years earlier, had accomplished its domestic and international economic goals. There were clear signs of significant improvement in the domestic economy as real gross domestic product grew by 5.8 percent and then 6.4 percent in 1964 and 1965, more than double the near-2.5 percent growth rates of 1960 and 1961. Private investment, which had been stagnant and even declined slightly in 1960 and 1961, grew by 8.2 percent in 1964 and then 14 percent in 1965—the highest rate in nearly a decade.[1] The unemployment rate, which had remained vexingly high even through 1964, finally fell below 5 percent, reaching 4.5 percent in 1965. In addition, price inflation was staying in check as the consumer price index increased only 1.7 percent in 1965, well within the norm for the first half of the decade, and the producer price index increased by a moderate 2.2 percent. Overall, the national economic picture looked promising.

In addition, the commercial Keynesian agenda had yielded positive results on the international front, though looking just at the balance of payments figures belies this conclusion. The trade balance waffled between improvement and worsening deficit in 1964 and 1965, and levels of foreign direct investment and other long-term capital investments remained high though, at the same time, 1965 did record the most positive (or, perhaps one should say, the least negative) level in the gross liquidity balance since 1957. The real improvement came from the fact that the commercial Keynesian agenda had instilled some confidence among international investors and foreign central banks that the United States was serious about addressing its balance of payments concerns. The balance of payments problem was by no means solved, but it was also no longer in a constant state of crisis. In fact, the administration was so confident that the country would begin to register strong balance of payments surpluses that in June of 1965 a study group was formed under the directorship of the Treasury Department to explore new mechanisms for providing sufficient liquidity to the international economy when the American balance of payments deficit was erased.[2]

The promise of the New Frontier and the Great Society had been held at bay by the domestic economic stagnation and international economic crises of the first half of the decade, but now it was time to fulfill that promise, and no one had to look far to find unfinished business that needed attending to. The commercial Keynesians had always argued that once the country began to reap the fruits of a higher level of economic activity then the government would be free to make good on the social democratic promises that had informed Kennedy's rhetoric about the New Frontier and that featured even more prominently in Johnson's call for the creation of a Great Society. Many programs and key pieces of legislation had been forced to wait for the Kennedy tax cuts to make their way through the legislature, but, once these were passed, the Johnson administration quickly set about dealing with its social priorities. Two Civil Rights Acts were passed in 1964 and 1965, outlawing discrimination in employment, housing, and voting; the Social Security Amendments of 1965 brought public health care coverage to the aged and the poor; and the administration declared unconditional war against poverty.

This combination of successes in the areas of economic growth, the international payments situation, and the country's social needs signaled to many that the promises contained in the Democratic Party's return to power in 1961 were finally being fulfilled. However, as most people familiar with American postwar history already know, in the end 1965 did not mark the beginning of a new era of shared prosperity but was rather a brief calm before the storm that would produce the most enduring images of a country in the midst of deep political and social unrest: protests on college campuses, clashes between militant trade unions and management, attacks on civil rights groups, deep political divides over the war in Vietnam, riots in the cities, and the assassination of major political figures. By 1968 the cities were burning, Vietnam was out of control, and the Democratic Party was in disarray.

This new crisis, the breakdown of whatever consensus had been forged by Lyndon Johnson in 1964, did not just play out in the streets but also found its way into the secluded, often dryly technocratic realm of White House economic policy making. For most scholars and interpreters of postwar American history, the failure of the commercial Keynesianism and the Great Society was the necessary, even inevitable, result of a government trying to do too much: too much spending on social programs and too much spending on Vietnam. The economy, already running hot, could not handle the injection of "guns and butter." Growth gave way to a decade of dizzying price inflation and economic stagnation, setting the stage for the Republican revival of the 1980s.

At stake, then, in telling the story of American economic policy making in the late 1960s is much more than just historical precision; at stake is the story of the politics of today, the account of how the postwar Keynesian consensus was transformed into the post-Reagan neoliberal era. One of the central goals of this chapter is to challenge this handed-down wisdom that emphasizes the role of "guns and butter" in the historical narrative.

Though there are some fairly straightforward economic data that pose real questions for the "guns and butter" story, the more fundamental point that this chapter seeks to make is that the story of the breakdown of the commercial Keynesianism in the late 1960s is not so much one of excessive demand but rather one of institutional and policy incongruity, specifically the growing divide between fiscal expansion and monetary restraint, between a national government pushing hard for expansion and an international institutional environment scared of rapid growth.

In *Capitalizing on Crisis*, Gretta Krippner shows how the 1960s was a pivotal moment in the transformation of credit markets in the United States when government regulation of the credit supply steadily gave way to the market regulation of the credit supply, resulting in the dramatic run-up of interest rates in the 1970s and 1980s. Krippner's analysis builds on that of economist Hyman Minsky, who, in the 1980s, was perhaps the first to draw attention to the unstable financial system that emerged out of this era of "financial innovation." One of the key contributions of Krippner's work is that she traces how the financial innovations of the 1960s were the beginning of a deeper financialization of the U.S. economy, a shifting of the center of economic gravity from the cycle of production, consumption, and reinvestment to profit making through speculative investments in financial instruments that culminated in the global financial crisis of 2008.[3]

Through Krippner convincingly ties together the politics of credit in the 1960s to today's politics of finance and financial crisis, what is not entirely clear in her account is why, rather suddenly, in the 1960s credit markets in the United States became so tight. To understand this, it is necessary to bring the international politics of growth, and its effects on United States economic policy making, to bear on the story. As Chapter 6 showed, this tension in American economic policy first emerged with "operation twist," itself a concession to the international pressures brought on by the U.S. balance of payments deficit. Over the course of the rest of the decade this tension was never resolved but only became worse as credit markets became tighter and tighter while the economy grew more rapidly. A central tenet of this chapter is that the commercial Keynesian growth agenda broke down in 1968 because the conditions for sustainable growth had never been put into place.

By 1966 it was becoming apparent to some observers that tight credit markets could not abide the high levels of growth brought on by the Johnson administration's domestic and international policies. Members of the Economic Policy Committee in particular made clear their concerns that the U.S. economy was overheating and urged the Johnson administration to reverse its growth-oriented policy posture and pass an across-the-board tax increase to slow things down. Rather than entertain this suggestion, Johnson instead followed the advice of his own economic advisors and, even as credit markets were being crunched in 1966, pressed ahead with a growth-oriented budget.

Why, in this case, was the Johnson administration able to largely ignore international opinion about American economic policy when, just three years earlier, the international community had been much more effective at restraining the Kennedy administration's growth ambitions? The answer, as this chapter will show, is connected to the weakening ties of financial dependency between the United States and foreign monetary authorities. Having achieved a balance of payments surplus for a couple of years, the United States was able to pay off a significant portion of its short-term foreign debts. Because of this, classical liberals in the international community lost much of their capacity to effectively tie its concerns about, and prescriptions for, American economic policy to the problem of foreign confidence in the dollar because the problem of confidence had lost much of its material bite.

In the end, however, this was an all too brief respite from international pressures. The return of balance of payments deficits in the latter half of 1966 came at a time when the pound sterling was under heavy pressure, which once again made the problem of confidence in the dollar extremely salient. Through the later part of 1967 and through 1968 the Johnson administration beat a hasty retreat from its expansionary position and tried to apply the fiscal brakes. By this point, however, the divide between the fiscal and monetary sides of the economy had grown too great and had been given too much time to wreak havoc on domestic credit markets. The fiscal clamps were put on in 1968, but it was already too late to salvage an economy that, for too many years, had been driven in different directions by opposing forces.

A Promising Start

By 1964 a tenuous consensus had emerged both within the government agencies responsible for economic policy making (the Office of the President, the Council of Economic Advisors, the Treasury, and the Federal Reserve), and between U.S. policy makers and the international community that commercial Keynesianism was working. Encouraged by signs of success, the Johnson administration continued to frame its economic policy program around a growth agenda. Indeed, the only real concern that Johnson's advisors had was that economic growth would peter out by the middle of the decade if further steps were not taken to drive it forward. In the summer of 1964, Walter Heller spelled out these concerns and some steps that could be taken to alleviate them:

> We—you—have said that with continued moderation by business and labor, there's expansion ahead "as far ahead as the trained eye can see" into 1965. That means, roughly, to mid-1965. But stretching our vision beyond that, we don't see where the steam needed for further expansion in late 1965 and 1966 is going to come from.[4]

Heller located two sources of steam for the growth engine. First, the administration would cut excise taxes in late 1965. Second, an additional push would come from the spending side by expanding existing programs, specifically the payment of social security benefits.

The "troika" of agencies responsible for producing the budget and assessing domestic economic developments—the Council of Economic Advisors, the Department of the Treasury, and the Bureau of the Budget—shared Heller's views. Summarizing their assessment of the economic prospects for 1966, the heads of these three agencies signed off on a report, noting:

> Unless there is significant tightening of monetary policy (coupled with an increase in the discount rate) or an unexpected deterioration of private demand, *present programs should hold the fort against any downturn* until mid-1966. *But prospects of increased slack and rising unemployment in early 1966 are not pleasant.* They suggest the *economic desirability of a larger fiscal stimulus*, including a more generous excise tax cut, a smaller rise in payroll taxes, and a Federal pay increase.[5]

Perhaps even more important, for once the administration's own assessment of the country's economic prospects were shared by the international community.

The Bank for International Settlements, for example, struck a very positive note in its analysis of U.S. economic developments in 1964, citing an improved balance of payments position and strong economic growth that, perhaps most importantly, did not show signs of price inflation.[6] The Economic Policy Committee's assessment was quite similar and, like the Council of Economic Advisors, was more concerned with the possibility that the impressive U.S. growth record would weaken without further fiscal measures to expand the economy than they were with the prospects of economic overheating.[7]

This is not to say that the views of the international community did not diverge at all from that of the Johnson administration. Staff at the International Monetary Fund, for example, felt that American policy makers had already achieved an appropriate mix of fiscal expansion and monetary tightness and did not need to move either in the direction of further expansion or tightening. In addition, both the Bank for International Settlements and the Economic Policy Committee did warn that American economic successes could be quickly undone if wage and price pressures reemerged. As a final sour note on an otherwise strong score of successes, at the end of 1964 the United States recorded some rather disastrous balance of payments figures, putting what was supposed to be a moderate annual deficit of $1.5 to $2 billion into the $3 billion range, leading to some concern within Working Party 3, mostly expressed by the German delegates, that American credit markets were still too liquid.[8]

Overall, however, the international community shared the Johnson administration's view that keeping the growth engine humming along should be priority number one. As a result, calls for tight money and other restrictive measures that had been the hallmark of the international community's policy prescriptions in previous years were muted.[9]

Trouble Reemerges

The year 1965, however, would prove not to be the beginning on a new period of sustained growth and social democratic policy change but rather the apex of a rather short-lived moment of calm and optimism. True, the economy would continue to expand through the end of the decade, but already by the end of 1965 signs pointed to significant shifts in the domestic and international economy that threatened to undermine the commercial Keynesian growth agenda and, ultimately, bring the Bretton Woods system of international monetary relations to an end.

Much of the scholarship on the conditions contributing to the downfall of Lyndon Johnson and his Great Society have emphasized the over ambitiousness of his simultaneous pursuit of guns and butter—an increasingly costly war in Vietnam and the rapid expansion of the welfare state at home. However, while spending for warfare and welfare are certainly important factors for helping us understand why economic growth accelerated, the real source of pressure on the American economy was the rapid pace of private business investment in a context of increasingly tight credit.

Figure 7.1 shows the annual growth rate of gross domestic product and the annual growth rates of the three major components of gross domestic product (federal government consumption and expenditure, consumer spending, and gross private investment) for the years 1961 to 1968. As the figure shows, the years from 1961 to 1966 were characterized by rapid economic growth, greater than 4 percent per year. During these years of rapid growth, private fixed investment was growing even more rapidly than the overall pace of expansion of the economy. It was only during two years, 1961 and again in 1965,

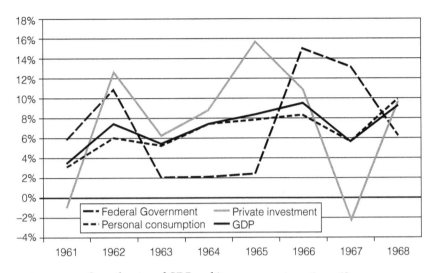

FIGURE 7.1. Growth rates of GDP and its components, 1961–1968.
SOURCE: Bureau of Economic Analysis, National Income and Product Accounts, Table 1.1.5.
Gross Domestic Product.

that federal spending, which includes both defense spending and nondefense spending, grew more quickly.

On the one hand, this rapid advance in the rate of growth of private investment was precisely the scenario that the commercial Keynesian economic program was designed to bring about. On the other hand, commercial Keynesianism had always argued that robust, sustained economic growth needed the support of an easy monetary posture, a condition that had been substantially compromised by "operation twist." Over the course of 1964 and 1965, monetary policy continued to be strongly guided by the basic principle embodied in the twist: The Federal Reserve steadily reduced levels of free banking reserves to reduce supplies of credit and keep short term interest rates high while at the same time taking steps to prevent these tight credit market conditions from pushing up long-term interest rates.

Figure 7.2 documents the increasingly twisted structure of American credit markets. Levels of free bank reserve had fallen so much that, by May of 1965, free reserves were actually at a negative $100 million. Banks were borrowing reserves from each other just to meet their federally mandated reserve requirements. This points to the incredible demand for credit that was coming from the rapid pace of private investment. Even though it cost banks to borrow reserves, it was worth it. Under normal market conditions such a strong

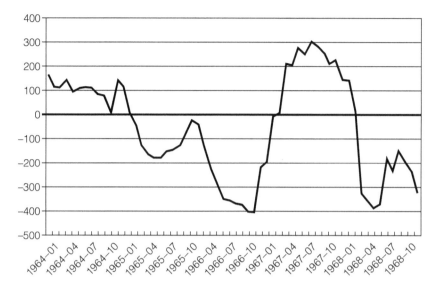

FIGURE 7.2. Free reserves of depository institutions, millions of dollars, 1964–1968, year and month.

SOURCE: Board of Governors of the Federal Reserve, H.3 Statistical Release.

demand for credit under conditions of limited credit availability would lead to a general run-up in interest rates.

This is indeed what happened in the market for short-term credit, particularly interbank credit, but "twist" operations in long-term credit markets tended to keep long-term interest rates from rising as quickly, especially the rate on long-term government debt. The result was that from, 1964 to 1966, American credit markets became twisted beyond recognition. As discussed in Chapter 6, during the first years of the "twist" short-term interest rates were constantly pressing up against the Federal Reserve discount rate and were edging closer and closer to long-term interest rates. Although these rates were clearly not traditional market rates, the structure was still, in some sense, normal: Rates were highest on long-term debt, lower at the discount window, and lower still in the federal funds market.

As Figure 7.3 shows, from 1964 to 1966 the interest rate structure lost even this thin veil of normalcy. Competition for bank reserves pushed the federal funds rate higher and higher to the point where it exceeded not only the rate on offer at the discount window but even the rate on long-term Treasury bonds. The Federal Reserve tried to maintain order in the credit markets,

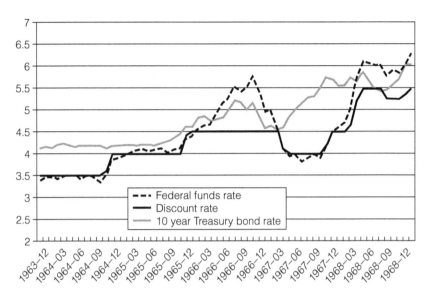

FIGURE 7.3. Select U.S. interest rates, 1964–1968, year and month.
SOURCE: Board of Governors of the Federal Reserve, H.15 "Selected Interest Rates."

raising the discount rate from 3.5 percent to 4 percent in November of 1964 and then from 4 percent to 4.5 percent in December of 1965, but was hesitant to do more to control credit markets through the discount rate, lest they put pressure on long-term rates.

Tight credit markets combined with a strong demand for credit pushed American credit markets into a "crunch" in the summer of 1966. The 1966 credit crunch, and its long-term effects on the American economy, has received serious attention in scholarly circles, beginning with Hyman Minsky's study of the emergence of financial market instability and, most recently, in Gretta Krippner's study of the origins of the American financial crisis of 2008.[10] What these studies show is that while the credit crunch was fairly brief, coming to a head in the summer of 1966 and ending a few months later, its deeper significance was that it manifested some of the perverse consequences of processes of financial innovation that had been unfolding in American credit markets as banks tried to find ways to meet their reserve requirements while still satisfying the intensifying demand for loans from their business customers.

As a means of increasing their deposits banks began to tap into new financial instruments, like certificates of deposit, that drew in the savings of middle class households. Although now a familiar part of the financial landscape, before the 1960s certificates of deposit were issued only in denominations of a million dollars or more, limiting them to wealthy investors. As credit demands rose, however, banks began to experiment with issuing certificates of deposit in smaller denominations. For middle-class savers, these new "low-denomination" certificates of deposit were a real boon, offering a nice rate of return with almost no risk. Over time, certificates of deposit grew increasingly attractive as banks competed with each other for new deposits by offering higher and higher rates. In January of 1966 certificates of deposit with a three-month maturity earned 4.93 percent interest on the New York market; by September that rate had been bid up to 5.88 percent.[11] The downside of this development was the strain that ever-escalating interest rates were placing on state and local governments and on savings and loan banks (or "thrifts"), which were strictly regulated in terms of the interest rates that they could offer. With better returns being offered elsewhere, savers began to pull their money out of the thrifts, and investors stopped purchasing state and local government bonds, as they were attracted by the better rates that they could get on the loosely regulated certificates of deposit. As the credit crunch wore on, savings and loan institutions found it harder and harder to finance mortgages, and states and cities found it harder and harder to fund public works projects, investments in infrastructure, and new public housing.

By distorting the structure of interest rates and unleashing a wave of financial innovation, the credit crunch was becoming an impediment to the goals of the Great Society. The Great Society was premised on sustained high rates of economic growth, but during the crunch businesses found supplies of credit limited and expensive. The Great Society promised new public investment to address pressing social needs, but state and local governments were having a hard time getting investors for their various projects.

The credit crunch was a clear indication that economic growth in the United States was becoming unstable, but it was not the only sign. As already discussed, the big success of the commercial Keynesian growth program was not just that it got the economy moving again but that it got the economy moving again without triggering price inflation. Indeed, it was this aspect of the U.S. economic growth that the international community was so enamored with. Price stability in the early 1960s had not only lent support to the commercial Keynesians' claim that growth did not need to be accompanied by inflation but it had also given a real boost to the international payments account. Whereas prices were stable in the United States, in Western Europe they were increasing much more rapidly, which tipped the scales of global trade in favor of the United States.

In 1965 and 1966, however, this stability showed signs of erosion. Between 1961 and 1964, the U.S. consumer price index had barely increased at an annual rate of around 1 percent. The producer price index was even more stable, fluctuating between a negative 0.3 percent and positive 0.3 percent annual rate of change. In 1965 and 1966 this picture was very different. The consumer price index increased 1.7 percent and 2.9 percent in those years, and, even more dramatically, the producer price index increased 2.2 percent and 3.1 percent.[12]

Prices began to rise in the United States at the same time that countries in Western Europe began to get their inflationary situations under control. The effect was a distinct narrowing—or in some cases eliminating—of the competitive advantage for American firms, which cast a shadow over the U.S. balance of payments position.

Renewed Concerns about Growth

Just as the Kennedy administration had come into office faced with a conflicting set of domestic and international economic pressures, by the middle of the decade the Johnson administration was trying to navigate among stability, growth, and international confidence in the American economy. Despite the tight credit markets and some signs of inflation, the prevailing view within the White House was that all signs pointed toward an economic slowdown and possible recession. Johnson's advisors predicted that growth rates would fall to 3 percent in 1967 and then again to 2.5 percent in 1968. Walter Heller had left his post as chairman of the Council of Economic Advisors in 1964, but its new chairman, Gardner Ackley, picked up the mantle of the commercial Keynesian growth agenda and urged President Johnson to resist calls for economic restraint. Writing on behalf the Council, Ackley gave the following assessment of economic conditions at the end of the year 1966:

> In our view, the worst of the risks to be considered is of a recession. Our "most probable outcome" for 1967 is a fairly weak advance, one that would involve rising unemployment, falling capacity utilization, and declining profit margins. If some element of private demand turns out a bit weaker than our forecast, we could easily slip into recession.[13]

Ackley wanted an economic program tuned to fighting off stagnation. Other voices, both domestic and international, read the same tea leaves but divined a different fate: The economy was showing early signs of overheating, and it was time to apply the economic brakes.

The domestic voice of restraint was the Federal Reserve, which, beginning in 1966, increasingly called on the Johnson administration to restrain the economy through fiscal measures, either by raising taxes, by reducing spending, or both. Unlike the Council of Economic Advisors, who saw signs of potential economic stagnation when they looked at the macroeconomic data, the Federal Open Market Committee saw signs of imminent economic overheating, potentially leading to an inflationary spiral. For the first few months of the year the FOMC tried to deal with these concerns through what had by now become fairly routine practice in the era of the "twist": restricting access to credit by holding a tight reign on free reserves.

By the spring, however, it was becoming clear that the Fed was not going to be able to twist itself out of mounting demand pressures. At the April meeting of the FOMC Alfred Hayes, governor of the Federal Reserve Bank of New York, laid out a prescription for policy that would become a recurring refrain: Tight monetary policy had done a good job at holding back the boom, but monetary policy was now being asked to do too much. The Johnson administration needed to impose some fiscal restraint to get the economy under control.[14] As summer rolled around, the economic data became increasingly difficult to read. Some trends, like the rate of business capacity utilization and levels of private investment, pointed to excessively strong demand, while other data points, like declining home sales and construction, suggested that maybe the peak had been passed.

Despite this ambiguity on the domestic front, the FOMC remained committed to tight money and once again called on the Johnson administration to impose some fiscal restraint. The reason was that, although the domestic situation was uncertain, the international situation was not. The Committee's analyses of balance of payments developments drew attention to the rising level of imports, data that signaled a fundamental weakness in the U.S. global trade position. In addition, meetings between FOMC members and European central bankers revealed that the Fed's foreign counterparts were becoming increasingly dissatisfied with the Johnson administration's lack of a strong fiscal program.[15] Even as credit markets calmed down in the early fall, and even after the administration announced a batch of modest restraint measures, the FOMC argued that more needed to be done on the fiscal side.[16]

These conflicting views were placed right in the president's lap. On the same day that Gardner Ackley sent a memo to President Johnson making the case for keeping the economy on an expansionary path, Federal Reserve Chairman William McChesney Martin sent his own memo to the president calling for fiscal restraint. Martin argued that a tax increase was needed both to show the American people and international observers that the administration was serious about being fiscally responsible at a time when Vietnam War costs were escalating and to help take some of the pressure off of monetary policy. True, things were uncertain, but, from Martin's perspective, given the weight of international and domestic factors, it would be better to err on the side of restraint:

> Indeed, in these circumstances, I would be far more concerned about the effects at home and abroad of a failure to propose an increase in taxes than I would be about the effects of proposing one, with a candid presentation of the facts, giving full weight to the costs of our efforts in Vietnam.[17]

Classical liberals in the international community joined the Federal Reserve in calling on the Johnson administration to apply the fiscal brakes. Initially, members of the Economic Policy Committee greeted the first signs of overheating in the American economy with their standard refrain: Tighten monetary policy to ease demand pressures. Citing a weakening in the U.S. balance of payments position from its strong performance in 1965 due to a growing trade imbalance and signs that government expenditure and private business investment would continue to place pressure on the country's economic resources, in early 1966 the Economic Policy Committee suggested that "in these circumstances there would seem to be scope for a substantial tightening of monetary conditions without adversely affecting levels of activity."[18]

Calls for the United States to tighten monetary policy also became a subject of debate at the Working Party 3 meetings. Although recognizing that the data coming in about the state of the American economy did not point to an inflationary crisis, several delegates made the case that the Johnson administration would be better off responding sooner, rather than later, to what appeared to be signs of overheating. For example, Dr. Gocht of the German Economic Ministry agreed that it was "difficult to show an immediate need for additional measures in the United States at the present time" but nevertheless urged fiscal restraint on the grounds that "governments tended to take such measures much too late."[19] The Working Party chairman agree with this assessment and added to Dr. Gocht's argument by noting not only that were there significant lags between the time that policies of restraint were enacted and the time that they took effect, but also that, as a political matter, governments often needed time to persuade legislators and voters of the need for restraint.[20]

While the main focus in these first few months was on monetary policy, it was also already becoming clear to international observers that the scope for monetary action was limited in the United States given existing tightness in credit markets. As the Bank for International Settlements observed in its 1966 *Annual Report*, interest rates were already high by historical standards, and, if they were raised further, monetary policy would lose its flexibility. For this reason, the Bank argued, the United States needed to be ready to adopt fiscal measures to slow the pace of growth of aggregate demand.[21]

By June, international concern over the American domestic economic situation had grown considerably. Demand pressures remained high, prices were increasing, the trade balance had not improved and, perhaps most critically, domestic credit markets were completely disorganized as a result of the rapid run-up of interest rates. Under these conditions the international community became more and more focused on pushing the United States to adopt some strong fiscal restraint measures. In particular, discussion focused on a policy idea that had been floated by the Johnson administration but not yet acted on: a 6 percent income tax surcharge.

Jim Duesenberry, member of Johnson's Council of Economic Advisors, conveyed this sentiment to the president after returning from an Economic Policy Committee meeting in July:

> The OECD Secretariat and the European delegation—particularly the Dutch and Germans—expressed *concern about our balance of payments and about the dangers that a wage-price spiral may be getting underway*. They wanted a U.S. tax increase to help solve both problems.[22]

Throughout the discussions with the international community that took place in the first half of the year, the American delegates tried to stress that the Johnson administration stood ready to apply the fiscal brakes to the economy should the need arise. They also made sure that the other members of these organizations were aware that the administration had already adopted some (admittedly moderate) fiscal measures to try to take some of the steam out of the economy: eliminating excise tax credits, accelerating the collection of some income taxes, and increasing payments into the social security system. In addition, coming into the July meeting of Working Party 3, Fred Deming, serving as undersecretary of the U.S. Treasury, stressed that the Johnson administration was committed to holding down the growth of government spending.[23]

The other members of the Working Party were not impressed. Professor Kessler, speaking for the Dutch delegation, felt that the United States was risking putting its balance of payments into serious jeopardy by not taking stronger fiscal action to reduce economic demand. Professor Kessler's views were shared by many of the other Working Party delegates: Domestic demand was too high, causing imports to flow into the country at too high a rate, but monetary policy had done all that it could at this point. Any additional tightening would not only further disrupt American credit markets but would create real imbalances in international capital flows that would cause problems for other countries' payments accounts.[24]

By the end of the year, the international community had grown even more pessimistic about the U.S. economic prospects. Concern with the fate of sterling and the British economy kept the United States from being the focal point of international discussions, but more data were coming in, showing a significant deterioration in the trade balance over the last year, and some analyses suggested that the United States was entering a wage-price inflationary spiral.[25] Through these latter months, Johnson administration officials continued to try to assure their European colleagues that appropriate steps had been taken, or would be taken, to restrain the economy and put it back onto a noninflationary growth path. Nevertheless, European delegates to the OECD remained seriously concerned about American inflationary pressures and what they augured for the balance of payments and called on the United States to adopt an immediate tax surcharge.[26]

Yet, despite all of this pressure to raise taxes coming from the Federal Reserve and the international community, the administration held off on taking fiscal action. Superficially, the Johnson administration's management of economic policy in 1966 and its budgetary plans for 1967 appeared to heed the call for fiscal restraint in the same way that the Kennedy administration had sacrificed core features of the commercial Keynesian growth program to satisfy international pressures. The day after Ackley and Martin sent President

Johnson their conflicting views on fiscal policy, the representatives from the administration's troika outlined the following course of action: a 5 percent tax surcharge to help cover the budget deficit and restrain inflationary pressures, a substantial easing of monetary policy (driven, as Martin originally hoped, by the restraining effects of the tax increase) to both offset the deflationary impact of the tax increase and to restore order to credit markets and, finally, a substantial increase in Social Security benefits to boost consumer purchasing power to stave off a recession.[27]

Publicly, the Johnson administration gave the appearance of appeasing those voices calling for restraint while still making good on its pledge to increase Social Security benefits. In reality, however, the administration's policy priorities were oriented toward warding off any possible economic slowdown and downplayed the need for fiscal restraint. True, the budget message of January 10, 1967, referenced a tax surcharge on all corporate and individual incomes in addition to major increases in both the minimum and overall social security payments,[28] but it is also true that the tax surcharge received the lowest priority of these two measures.

What the administration was really hoping was that it could achieve quick success on increasing Social Security benefits while delaying discussion of the tax surcharge until the end of the following year, hoping that the economy would cool off on its own and make it unnecessary.[29] In other words, the administration never intended to enact the tax surcharge, which was the budget's only measure of fiscal restraint. Moreover, by March of 1967 the president was back in front of Congress asking for a reinstatement of both the investment tax credit and accelerated depreciation, and by July the administration was looking forward to the House Ways and Means Committee reporting on a Social Security bill that, as Acting Secretary of Health, Education, and Welfare Wilbur Cohen pointed out, contained "the biggest annual dollar annual increase in social security *cash* benefits ever enacted."[30]

In short, the Johnson administration's 1967 budget priorities were clearly guided by the Council of Economic Advisors' concerns about the country's long-term growth prospects and gave only minor consideration to those voices expressing concern about an imminent economic overheating. This is not to say that the administration, or its economic advisory staff, did not recognize the potential for economic overheating and that fiscal measures would need to be adopted if such a situation arose. But what is key about this episode is that the administration's approach to policy was guided by its own internal assessments of economic dynamics, which placed greater weight on domestic economic concerns than on international ones. Why was the Johnson administration able to operate with such domestic policy autonomy in this instance, privileging the domestic growth agenda over international payments concerns?

Growth and the Evolution of Financial Dependency

As in other cases when competing economic policy proposals become the subject of heated debate, looking at which side gave the more accurate analysis of present economic dynamics and future economic prospects provides few clues as to why the cause of economic growth won out over the cause of economic restraint. From a purely technical econometric standpoint, the Council of Economic Advisors' arguments are the least convincing compared to those of the Federal Reserve, the Bank for International Settlements, or the Economic Policy Committee. Although Gardner Ackley could only estimate the likelihood of future economic developments, those arguing for monetary restraint could point to the very real, very present signs of crisis already developing in the American economy: Credit markets were too tight, and prices were rising. True, no one knew the future with certainty, but Ackley's and the Council's only weapon against this uncertainty was future probability; the Federal Reserve and the international community could easily fight back with present reality.

Moreover, by the latter months of 1966 it was becoming increasingly clear that whatever hopes that American officials had harbored that the country's balance of payments deficit could be eliminated, or even significantly reduced, were going to be dashed. The deficit recorded in 1966 was as bad as, if not worse than, those recorded in the crisis years in the beginning of the decade, and this was after two years of solid performance. This not only cast further doubt on the Johnson administration's view that the real problem facing the American economy in 1966 was a potential slowdown; it also raises another question: If the United States payments deficit was growing, why was the international community unable to leverage this to pressure the Johnson administration to make the tax surcharge central to its 1967 budget?

The answer to this question is that, although the overall balance of payments deficit was growing, it was not growing in such a way as to force administration officials to turn to foreign monetary authorities for assistance in financing the deficit. During 1964 and 1965 both the Treasury department and the Federal Reserve capitalized on the shrinking payments deficit to reduce their holdings of foreign currencies, pay back short-term debts accumulated through swap transactions, and restore the U.S. reserve position with the International Monetary Fund. These actions weakened the ties of financial dependency between the United States and foreign monetary authorities.

Somewhat paradoxically, the United States achieved this greater level of international financial independence not according to the commercial Keynesian formula—exporting its way into a massive trade surplus—but rather by benefiting from those same liberalized global capital markets that, in 1962 and 1963, had been wrecking havoc on the dollar. Signs that something had changed in global capital markets first emerged as officials from the United States and the international community tried to make sense of conflicting accounts of the U.S. balance of payments deficit, the measurement of which had become much more complicated in the middle of the decade.

To understand this, it is necessary to take a detour into the technocratic world of balance of payments accounting. Coming up with a single statistic, the "balance of payments," is notoriously difficult. This difficulty emerges, in part, from the need to coordinate accounting systems across countries. It also emerges from the fact that the balance of payments statistic is an aggregation of a wide range of economic transactions, all of which factor into the total figure but not all of which may be relevant for trying to understand critical economic dynamics. For example, a balance of payments deficit that grows because more tourists are traveling abroad is different from a balance of payments that grows because exporters are having a hard time competing in global markets.

To deal with the growing complexity of balance of payments accounting in an increasingly liberal global economy, national governments and international organizations developed multiple measures of a country's international account balance, each measure incorporating more international transactions than the last. In the early postwar years, discussion focused on the "current account balance." This is the simplest measure of balance of payments flows and includes trade in goods and services, government transactions like foreign aid and military spending, and long-term capital flows, such as foreign direct investment. In the early postwar years, when these items were the major components of global economic flows, the current account balance gave a reasonably good picture of overall payments balance between countries.

As capital controls were relaxed and short-term capital flows became a much larger component of global economic transactions, national and international agencies increasingly turned to the study of the "liquidity balance." In addition to the items contained in the current account transactions, the liquidity balance includes liquid long-term capital flows and, somewhat confusingly, nonliquid short-term capital flows. The liquidity balance therefore captures not just the value of goods and services but also flows of money tied to nonspeculative investments. In a global economy where capital flows are relaxed or nonexistent, the liquidity balance gives a better sense of a country's overall balance of payments position.

Finally, beyond the liquidity balance, payments accounts can be measured on an "official" basis. In addition to the elements captured by the liquidity balance, the official balance includes liquid short-term capital flows and the movement of reserve assets—gold, International Monetary Fund drawings, and other liabilities and assets—between official monetary authorities.[31]

Tracking these three measures can provide clues as to how international transactions are flowing across different global economic actors. In the middle of the 1960s balance of payments data on the United States began to show a sharp divergence from earlier patterns. On the one hand, when measured on a liquidity basis, the balance of payments figures showed a steep deficit, reflecting the weakening trade balance and increased spending on the war in Vietnam. On the other hand, when measured on an official basis, the U.S. payments accounts appeared to be nearly in balance.[32]

These technocratic minutiae carried a real significance, as they gave clear evidence of shifting patterns of financial strength and dependency in the global economy. Specifically, the growing gap between the American payments deficit measured on a liquidity basis and the deficit measured on an official basis suggested a dramatic strengthening of the dollar in international exchange markets. As discussed in Chapter 6, the problem that Kennedy administration officials faced with respect to the balance of payments in the early part of the decade was that private and public holders of dollars were exchanging them for either domestic currency (for private holders) or gold (for official monetary authorities). These transactions manifested in the payments accounts as a close relationship between the liquidity balance and the official balance: The drain of dollars through trade imbalances and capital outflows was translating into a drain of reserves from American to foreign monetary authorities.

By the middle of the decade, the global financial environment had changed in ways that made it attractive for holders of all those dollars flowing out of the United States to keep them rather than deposit them in their central banks or, if they were the central bank, exchange them for gold. First and foremost, with high short-term interest rates in the United States, and high interest rates being offered on the offshore "Eurodollar" currency markets, dollars were now a smart investment. In addition, other currencies were losing some of their luster, most notably the pound sterling (which had not had any luster for quite some time), but also once-strong European currencies, like the French and Belgian francs, which were beginning to face some speculative pressure of their own.[33]

One effect of this was that many dollars that left the United States in one form actually returned as liquid short-term investments as private banks in the United States, trying to maintain their own reserves during the credit crunch, repatriated dollars through the Eurodollar market. Between 1965 and 1969 many banks actively conducted business through the offshore Eurodollar market to work around both a growing system of domestic capital controls and the tight credit market conditions. By the end of these four years U.S. banks held nearly one-half of all claims on Eurodollar deposits, replacing the London mercantile banks as the dominant players in the offshore markets.[34]

Even more important, Johnson administration officials did not have to worry about financing those remaining dollar balances that were not repatriated back to the United States. So long as dollars were a more lucrative asset than gold or other national currencies, they were far less likely to show up in the foreign currency reserves of European central banks. This is because commercial banks with dollar surpluses were less likely to send them off to their national central banks and more likely to make their own investments in the Eurodollar market. Strong private confidence in the dollar made public confidence in the dollar a nonissue.

Having received this respite from private and public international pressure on the dollar, the Federal Reserve began to wean itself off the short-term debts that it owed to foreign central banks. Chapter 6 discussed how the Federal Reserve Bank had negotiated an ever-expanding network of swap arrangements with foreign monetary authorities in the early 1960s and, in 1962 and 1963, made significant drawings on these swaps to help support the dollar against currency speculation. While neither the Federal Reserve nor the Treasury Department maintains systematic data on these swap transactions, Michael

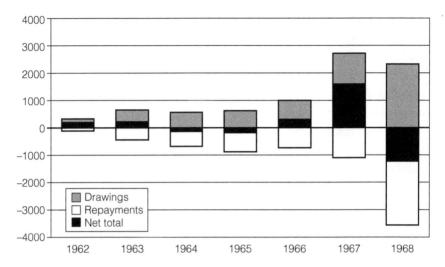

FIGURE 7.4. U.S. swap network transactions, 1962–1968, millions of dollars. Transactions with Belgium, France, Italy, Germany, the Netherlands, and Switzerland.

SOURCE: Bordo, Humpage, and Schwartz, "Bretton Woods, Swap Lines."

Bordo and his colleagues have sifted through records from the Federal Reserve Bank of New York to paint a picture of the U.S. foreign exchange operations from 1961 through 1997. Drawing on this data, Figure 7.4 shows that in 1964 and 1965 the Federal Reserve not only stopped drawing on its swap network but actually began to pay back some of these short-term debts. Even the swap arrangements with the Swiss National Bank, the most heavily used swap line in 1962 and 1963, went into standby status as funds flowed out of Switzerland and into the Eurodollar market, forcing the Swiss National Bank itself to draw on the swap arrangement and sell francs and gold to the U.S. Treasury to maintain its dollar reserves.[35]

In other words, even as the network of swap agreements persisted and grew ever larger over the decade, during 1964 and 1965 the United States became much less reliant on it. These developments were not lost on the international community. At the July 1965 meeting of Working Party 3, Gabriel Ferras, representing the Bank for International Settlements, reported on the official settlement of international payments positions over the first five months of the year. Each month, Ferras reported, the United States had reduced its liquid liabilities owed to monetary authorities in Western Europe by selling down its gold reserves.[36]

This pattern of transactions continued well into 1966. The fact that American monetary authorities were paying off their short-term debts with reserves—the gold stock and the U.S. first line of nonconditional reserves with the IMF—to make official balance of payments settlements deserves special attention.[37] In the past, drawing down these reserves would have been taken as a sign of weakness by private investors and foreign monetary authorities. Now, however, they were transactions conducted from a position of strength, signaling to the world that the United States was so confident in the renewed strength of the dollar that the country could move back into the original liquidity constraints established by the Bretton Woods settlements.

Astute observers will note, however, that Figure 7.4 also shows the United States drawing heavily on its swap network in 1966 and 1967. Why did this not renew foreign monetary authorities' capacity to press the Johnson administration to adopt a tighter fiscal stance leading into 1967? The answer is that although the swap network was expanded and used much more heavily in 1966, it was not for the purpose of protecting the dollar but rather for protecting the pound sterling. This is the final piece of the puzzle of the loosening of American ties of financial dependency in the middle of the decade. In 1962 and 1963, the dollar was the weakest pillar of the international monetary system; from 1965 through 1967, the pound sterling took over that unenviable position. In this context the American payments deficit operated as it had in the early postwar period, as a means of shoring up the international monetary system by financing the payments deficits of other countries.

This discussion highlights the critical distinction between a balance of payments deficit and financial dependency—a distinction too often glossed over in the international political economy literature. In the early 1960s the United States was beset by two interrelated international confidence problems: Private investors were losing confidence in the dollar, which meant they were placing more of those dollars on deposit with their central banks, who in turn were being asked to take up some of the work in financing American payments deficits. In the middle of the decade, however, private confidence was restored, which in turn eliminated the need for foreign financing of the still-massive payments deficit. This meant that foreign official confidence in the dollar was a nonissue. In both cases there was substantial disagreement between American officials and the international community over the causes of, severity of, and solution to the American payments deficit, but it was only in the early part of the decade that the international community had material leverage on American policy makers. Dependency, not just deficit, was the decisive factor.

From Calm to Crisis

The Johnson administration resisted calls for strong fiscal restraint at the height of the economic overheating of the fall of 1966 and economic indicators in early 1967 seemed to suggest that this had been the right decision. Growth had slowed, inflationary pressures were subsiding, and, afforded this breathing room, the Federal Reserve actively worked to restore liquidity to the financial markets. However, even as the drop off in price pressures and worries over recession in early 1967 undermined those who were calling for fiscal restraint, the real legacies of the 1966 credit crunch were making fiscal restraint all the more urgent, as indicated by the growing discord between Federal Reserve policy and the behavior of the financial markets.

Interest rates for both private and public securities had fallen substantially in the closing months of 1966. By early 1967, private market rates were beginning to creep back up despite the Federal Reserve's best efforts to ease credit markets by lowering the discount rate and releasing more reserves to the banks. The first sign of trouble came in the market for long-term Treasury bonds. Between September 1966 and January 1967 the interest rate on Treasury bonds fell from 4.8 percent to 4 percent. Starting in February, however, rates began to sharply increase again and, by May, had returned to levels seen during the previous year's crunch. The trend prompted a meeting among Gardner Ackley, Arthur Okun (a member of the Council of Economic Advisors), and seven governors of the regional Federal Reserve banks. The results of the meeting were troubling. Ackley had called the meeting to ask the Federal Reserve to do more to lower interest rates; however, after talking to the governors, it became clear that the Federal Reserve was losing its ability to control credit markets. As Ackley recalled in a memo to the president:

> We were prepared to push them hard on why they weren't buying long-term bonds instead of bills, and whether they shouldn't consider reducing the discount rate. We learned that, in fact, they have been buying substantial amounts of long-terms (which shows up in their weekly statement today), and that they are going to continue to do so (highly confidential). We also learned that they have been at least discussing a cut in the discount rate. However, they are very

pessimistic about their ability to affect long-term interest rates. They feel that the market is convinced that a boom is coming and that no tax action will be taken.[38]

By July of 1967, rising interest rates were the trend across the board, though only in the long-term Treasury bond market did rates actually begin to exceed those from the previous fall's crunch.

These developments pointed to the need for a strong stance on fiscal policy. "The market is still strongly influenced by doubts about tax policy," Gardner Ackley wrote to the president. "The big deficit figures being tossed about have frightened financial people."[39] Facing increasing pressures on the Treasury to finance the war in Vietnam, and fearing that this could crowd out an already-tight credit market, Treasury Secretary Henry Fowler pushed for more aggressive fiscal restraint than had been contained in the president's original economic message, calling for a 10 percent, rather than a 6 percent, tax surcharge.[40] Even Walter Heller, writing from his office at the University of Minnesota, counseled the president to apply the fiscal brakes. He agreed that the expansionary push of the early part of the year had been the right policy choice. "But, unless a lot of us are wrong on our GNP forecasts for next winter, we should soon ease up on the accelerator: A 6 to 10% surtax (with a somewhat higher rate on corporations than individuals) to take effect on January 1 ought to be just about right."[41]

This chorus of voices calling for restraint brought an abrupt end to the expansionary thrust of the administration's domestic policy in the first months of 1967. In early March President Johnson had stood before Congress asking the legislature to reinstate the investment tax credit and accelerated depreciation (both of which had been suspended during the crunch of 1966). Just five months later he was back, though this time calling for a 10 percent tax surcharge to take effect on July first of the following year.

Renewed concerns about economic overheating, and the inflationary pressures that would no doubt follow, were driven in part by signs of further erosion in the U.S. trade competitiveness relative to the Europeans. Between 1966 and 1967 the United States had enjoyed mild to nonexistent inflationary pressures. Inflation in the producer price index dropped from just over 3 percent to just over 1 percent over the course of the year. The problem, however, was that European producers had also gotten their inflationary pressures under control, in some cases even better than the United States had. France was the most dramatic case of the latter phenomenon. Over the course of the same year the rate of growth in its producer prices plummeted to just shy of *negative* 1 percent. As the economy moved through 1967, the disparity between American and European producers on the price front only worsened. By the middle of 1967 producer prices once again began to climb in the United States after briefly stabilizing in the early part of the year. In contrast, French producer prices continued to fall at an even faster rate, and German producer prices also began to fall.

The result, not surprisingly, was a further deterioration of the American trade balance with deleterious effects on a balance of payments situation that was already precarious, given the increased overseas expenditures tied to the Vietnam War. Whereas the overall trade balance had stood at a surplus of nearly $2 billion in 1965, in 1966 it had dropped precipitously to $665 million, and to $277 million in 1967—the last year of surplus before systemic deficits would characterize American trade patterns.[42]

Moreover, the crisis in sterling was spilling over to the dollar. While the United States had been able to rely on inflows of short-term capital to finance its balance of payments deficit in 1965 and 1966, the United Kingdom was relying on this same pool of dollars flowing through the London-based Eurodollar market to help finance its deficit; having the two reserve currency countries competing for the same pool of speculative capital was less than ideal. So although the United States may have enjoyed a temporary boost to foreign confidence from short-term capital inflows, it was becoming increasingly clear to international investors and foreign monetary authorities that this was not a long-term solution to the country's payments imbalance. Even more fundamentally, although the international community had accepted that the United States was temporarily financing its payments imbalances through capital inflows, it was still the case that long-term confidence in the dollar rested on the country's performance in the real economy. To be seen as strong, the United States needed to be a net capital exporter with a substantial trade surplus.

Restoration of sanity in domestic credit markets and the maintenance of European confidence in the dollar depended on the Johnson administration being able to achieve some real degree of fiscal restraint in the form of the tax surcharge. Unfortunately for the administration, the measure languished in the Congress. Fiscal conservatives like House Ways and Means Committee

Chairman Wilbur Mills were holding up the bill in exchange for promises from the Johnson administration to severely cut back on spending for Great Society programs; liberal Democrats did not support the bill because they feared that the measure would plunge the economy into recession and because they were unwilling to raise taxes to fund a war that they did not support. In the end, the tax surcharge never even made it to the floor of the House of Representatives for a vote in 1967 as Wilbur Mills led his House Ways and Means Committee to table the measure.[43]

The failure of the tax bill forced the administration to abruptly change its budget plans for 1968, specifically its plans for Social Security. Rather than use the Social Security bill, as originally outlined in the State of the Union address, to boost expenditures and consumer demand by significantly increasing benefits over revenues, by the middle of October administration officials were reworking their proposals to achieve the opposite effect. The strategy, as outlined by Undersecretary of Health, Education, and Welfare Wilbur Cohen, was to keep the administration's State of the Union promise to raise overall benefits by 20 percent while at the same time sharply increasing Social Security taxes to yield a massive surplus.[44] The hope was that this measure, which was effectively a backdoor tax increase, would drain purchasing power out of the economy and combat inflation.

By November the administration's plan was moving through the legislature with the Senate Finance Committee approving a version of the Social Security legislation that would yield a $6 billion surplus in the trust fund in 1968. Once again, the administration received pressure from congressional liberals who were loath to let the administration finance its Vietnam War–induced budget deficits with the Social Security system after it failed to get the tax surcharge through.[45]

Ultimately, the administration achieved some success on the Social Security front in its efforts to restrain the economy, but its international economic objectives still depended on the successful passage of a tax surcharge. The administration's capital controls program had done much to reduce the country's outflow of foreign investment but, as the December report of the Cabinet Committee on Balance of Payments made clear, this was not the ideal solution to the problem:

> To achieve a sustainable equilibrium which will permit us to forego these constraints, a greater trade surplus must be achieved. This surplus must be achieved

through expanding exports rather than employing any restrictive measures on imports.

The principle measure through which this surplus would be achieved was a more effective management of the domestic economy. More effective management meant fiscal restraint through a tax surcharge. As the Committee's report went on to state:

> A program of fiscal restraint to check inflation, to promote balanced economic growth at home, and protect and enlarge our trade surplus, which is under renewed pressure. To this end reduction of our current government expenditures for fiscal 1968, an austere budget for fiscal 1969, and Congressional passage in early 1968 of the bill before the House Ways and Means Committee—calling for temporary tax increases—is of transcendent importance.[46]

In 1966 much of the discussion around the tax surcharge had centered on the domestic monetary crisis and the idea that domestic economic policy needed a better mix in its fiscal and monetary measures for economic growth. By the end of 1967 and through 1968 the question of the tax surcharge was now firmly located in the distinct possibility of a major collapse in world confidence in the dollar and the end of the Bretton Woods system, a point that the international community was quick to stress to administration officials.

In February of 1968 the State Department received word of a meeting among Fred Deming, Eugene Rostow, and the director of the German Federal Bank, the latter of whom warned that failure to pass the tax surcharge in the next month would yield "a massive, new wave of speculation against the dollar which we would be unable to withstand."[47] These sentiments were echoed by Federal Reserve Chairman William Martin, who found that, after meeting with European central bankers, the passage of the tax bill was essential to maintaining cooperation with the United States in seeking to stabilize the international monetary system.[48] In the same week as Martin's meeting, the European delegates to the Economic Policy Committee expressed their deep concern over the deteriorating U.S. trade balance and urged a healthy dose of fiscal restraint to push economic growth back under 4 percent.[49]

While the U.S. balance of payments situation worsened, and international confidence in the dollar grew weaker, the tax surcharge legislation remained tied up in the legislature. In March of 1968 the United States experienced a massive drain on its already limited gold supply driven primarily by the British devaluation of the pound sterling but also by the overall decline in world gold liquidity (as gold supplies moved into industrial uses and new mining turned out decreasing returns) and by speculative activity on the part of investors who were betting that these pressures would precipitate a rise in the dollar price of gold.[50] The March crisis passed, but even this major threat against the dollar was not enough to get the tax surcharge bill out of the House Ways and Means Committee.

Unlike in previous years, when the international community had needed to actively mobilize the threat of confidence to get the Kennedy administration to change policy course, in this instance the Johnson administration and the international community were on the same page. The problem now was mobilizing the problem of confidence to get the legislature to abandon its resistance to the tax surcharge. This was no easy task, as recognized by new Council of Economic Advisors Chairman Arthur Okun. Writing to the president in May of 1968, Okun noted that "the notion of an international financial crisis is vague and not very meaningful to most Americans." What the administration needed to do, he argued, was to spell out how the failure of the tax bill could trigger a global economic crisis, and why this would be detrimental to American national interests:

> One immediate result would be a major world political defeat for the United States. Our inability to meet our solemn pledge to convert dollars into gold would be the equivalent of a bank failure or bankruptcy by the nation. There would be an immediate body blow to international trade. Merchants could not know how the value of the dollar would fluctuate in terms of marks, francs, etc. Thus, they would not know how much foreign goods would really cost them. This uncertainty could paralyze world trade. There could be immediate cutbacks in employment and in plant and equipment spending by firms with big export operations. Management would follow very conservative business policies, waiting for things to settle down.[51]

Reforming the international monetary system had begun in 1965, and by 1968 the United States and the international community came increasingly close to agreement on the creation of a new international currency called Special Drawing Rights. This would reduce the Bretton Woods system's dependence on the dollar while simultaneously maintaining sufficient liquidity in world markets. The problem, as President Johnson told the American people in

March of 1968, was that these reforms still depended on the United States restoring order to its international accounts, which in turn depended on swift action at home to restrain the economy. Speaking on the recent progress made on the Special Drawing Rights, Johnson cautioned:

> But to make this system work the United States just must bring its balance of payments to—or very close to—equilibrium. We must have a responsible fiscal policy in this country. The passage of a tax bill now, together with expenditure control that the Congress may desire and dictate, is absolutely necessary to protect this Nation's security, to continue our prosperity, and to meet the needs of our people.[52]

It surely pained Lyndon Johnson to speak these words conceding his Great Society programs in exchange for Wilbur Mills's and the Republican Party's support for the tax surcharge. When the bill came up for a vote in June of 1968 it passed easily in both the House and Senate. Though the measure still received stiff opposition from antiwar Democrats, Johnson's pledge to cut social welfare spending brought over enough Republicans to push the measure through.

Johnson signed the Revenue and Expenditure Control Act on June 28, 1968. The administration got its much-needed 10 percent tax surcharge but at the expense of $6 billion in immediate budget cuts for 1969 as well as other reductions in expenditures. Just four years after being ushered in with a flurry of legislation, the largest expansion of the American welfare state since the New Deal came to an end.

What followed was tragedy layered on tragedy. Despite all of the controversy that it had raised and political costs that it had incurred, the tax surcharge proved to be too little, too late, to save the Bretton Woods system. The measure did not restore stability to the economy at home, did not restore the U.S. position in the world economy, and did not prevent the further unraveling of the Bretton Woods international monetary system. The rate of price inflation accelerated in 1968 as the economy moved into what would later be recognized as a perverse phenomenon of "stagflation"—mounting inflationary pressures combined with economic stagnation. On the trade front, the overall trade balance fell to a deficit of $2.7 billion in 1968, including a $3 billion deficit on consumer goods and, for the first time in postwar history, an $840 million deficit on automobiles. The United States would never see a trade surplus on manufactured goods again. After 1968 the Bretton Woods edifice was slowly but surely disassembled, culminating with the final separation of the dollar from gold in 1973.

Guns, Butter, and Gold

There can be no doubt that the Johnson's push for a Great Society was driven by a belief within key quarters of his administration, and likely even by Johnson himself, in a social democratic vision for American society. No, it was not a radical vision, but it was the first time that the government had stepped in with an activist fiscal and social agenda at a time when the economy was already growing. The New Deal was about protecting people from the ravages of depression, and the Eisenhower years were about smoothing out the business cycle; but the Great Society, on the other hand, was about recognizing that growth was not enough, that despite the return of general prosperity significant pockets of the country were being left behind.

And yet, for many who have looked back on this moment in American history, the Great Society was a huge disappointment, not a grand success. Daniel Patrick Moynihan captured this feeling when he wrote of "the great failing of the Johnson administration" to create permanent, progressive social change in areas such as full employment and income maintenance "while energies were expended in ways that very probably hastened the end of the period when such options were open."[53] Moynihan's sentiment echoes Hobsbawm's take on the Wilson government. Like Hobsbawm, Moynihan was writing from the frustrating position of having borne witness not only to the birth of a new, social democratic experiment but also to its death after a short life of only four years.

For Moynihan and others who shake their heads and sigh when they think about the Great Society and its short-lived War on Poverty, fault rests with presidential hubris; Johnson was trying to have it all, and in the end he got nothing. The war in Vietnam, the growth of government spending during a time of rapid economic growth—these typical culprits certainly played a role. This chapter has told this familiar story from a very different angle, one that situates the Great Society within a growth program that was deeply embedded in a set of international economic relationships and institutions that were not friendly to these kinds of national policy experiments.

Full employment, antipoverty policies, expansions of the welfare state—these goals were not fused into the normative and ideational DNA of the postwar international monetary order. Moreover, to return again to one of Keynes's most important insights, it was not enough for some people in high positions to want these things; they had to operate within an international institutional environment that would make it easy, or at least possible, for governments to pursue these things. This meant, first and foremost, ready supplies of international credit that, in the 1960s, were not forthcoming.

True, for a very brief moment international economic flows tilted in favor of the United States and allowed the Johnson administration to press ahead with its domestic vision, regardless of international concerns. But, given the nature of the international monetary system as a whole, it could only ever be a brief moment as new imbalances introduced new stresses that, in the end, brought the entire Bretton Woods system down for good.

8 Globalization, Coercion, and the Resiliency of Austerity

FAST-FORWARD THIRTY YEARS FROM THE LATE 1960s, AND IT IS clear that history has come out on the side of economic liberalism. The old orthodoxy of Keynesian demand management and state regulation of the market has given way to a neoliberal orthodoxy that has adapted traditional laissez-faire ideology for the modern world. To be sure, the state remains ever-present in this neoliberal era, but these are states that are now caught up in the "neoliberal dilemma": called on to intervene when markets inevitably fail yet having to craft their interventions as being supportive of, not restrictions on, the workings of the free market. It is in this way that economic management through austerity has been coupled to the larger project of neoliberalism. According to the tenets of economic liberalism, capitalism works best when investors' confidence in markets is high, and nothing makes an investor more confident than a state that walks the "responsible" path of austerity. Public spending to support the poor or create employment and easy access to consumer credit—in the neoliberal paradigm these are the tools-of-the-trade for shortsighted politicians who risk the integrity of free markets to curry political favor.

What is particularly striking about contemporary neoliberalism is that it is an economic paradigm that has not only survived but appears to be flourishing even in spite of the fact that a strong case can be made that the crisis of 2008 was a crisis wrought by neoliberal policies and ways of thinking.

Neoliberalism's resiliency poses difficult questions not just for scholars of politics and policy change but also for those who had hoped that, at the very least, crisis would change how policy makers approached the task of economic management. What has driven this worldwide diffusion of the new economic orthodoxy that is neoliberalism, and how has the ideological core of neoliberalism managed to not just survive but also retain such a powerful hold over policy makers who are shaping the postfinancial crisis future into a landscape of austerity?

One of the central contributions of this book is to show that these linked policy paradigms—economic liberalism and austerity—have deep historical roots that are most consistently tied to the interests of finance, both private and public. Moreover, although economic liberalism and monetary orthodoxy always have adherents and proponents, these policy paradigms exert their strongest influence over economic policy making when the institutions that house these interests grow in power and prestige within national states and within the system of international economic governance. To be sure, these are not the only places where one finds neoliberal ways of thinking. In the postwar period, a strong commitment to economic liberalism and a commitment to austerity shaped the core of Germany's, Italy's, the Netherlands', and Switzerland's growth strategies. Elements of what is now recognized as neoliberal economic thinking could also be found in Walter Heller's "commercial Keynesianism." Even in these cases, however, the commitment to economic liberalism lasted only as long as it was able to satisfy the material needs of the population and keep a lid on political agitation. Chapter 4 showed how, in Italy, the Christian Democrats abandoned economic liberalism in 1962 when it was no longer politically viable. Similarly, in the face of economic crisis in 1966 and 1967, Germany's commitment to economic liberalism was softened by a new policy approach, "global guidance," that made the state responsible for stimulating economic growth through public works projects and fiscal management.[1]

So even though at various times, and in various places, state policy as a whole has been captured by economic liberalism, it is a mistake to attribute the spread of economic liberalism to a particular national interest. Liberalism's and austerity's stronghold has a much more precise location: the institutions of public and private finance. More than any other segment of the broader business community, those whose fortunes are tied to financial investments have the most to lose from not only the monetary and debt crises that follow economic depression but also the price inflation that typically accompanies a booming economy. Public financial institutions—central banks and treasuries—do not operate according to this same logic. They do not seek to maximize profits on financial investments. Yet, as the institutionalized guardians of the value of the currency, both now and in the future, the state's monetary authorities work to preserve an economic climate conducive to finance, an environment where price stability take priority over growth.

The introductory chapter argued that the contemporary resiliency of austerity is tied to the resurgence of finance, specifically the transnationalization of monetary authority whereby state monetary authorities are elevated to the heights of the management of international capitalism. These institutional transformations have been key for restoring and preserving finance's capacity to push national governments back onto the straight and narrow of austerity. In this final, concluding chapter I return to this argument, drawing on the lessons of the historical analysis of the preceding chapters to bring the story of austerity up to the present.

Ideas about Austerity

Mark Blyth has recently argued that, if we want to understand the politics of austerity, we must examine its ideological roots in economic liberalism and the way in which the ideas, norms, and values of economic liberalism have become taken for granted in contemporary policy discussions.[2] Blyth is not alone in this assessment, as several scholars have examined how a neoliberal ideological consensus was forged within the main intergovernmental organizations at the center of the contemporary system of economic governance: the meetings of the G7 finance ministers, the International Monetary Fund, the OECD, and the Bank for International Settlements.[3]

Tracing the origins and manifestations of policy ideas and policy paradigms is clearly necessary for understanding the politics of economic policy making, for without ideas, as Hugh Heclo observed, the complexities of modern economic, political, and social problems would appear as little more than individual data points devoid of meaning or significance.[4] At the same time, complex social problems are open to several interpretations, several ideas about what can and should be done. The postwar era has long been understood to be an era when the ideology of "embedded liberalism" defined international monetary relationships and institutions. Yet, as Chapter 3 shows, the postwar institutions of international monetary management were defined, in large part, by the tension between two competing ideas about international monetary cooperation. On the one hand, embedded liberalism stressed the importance of high rates of economic growth and high levels of employment and also argued that national governments needed flexibility to try a variety of different growth experiments. On the other hand, classical liberals stressed the importance of monetary stability that, in turn, required domestic price stability and a careful monitoring of the international accounts balance.

Moreover, while the OECD gave the goals of growth and stability equal weight in its official policy declarations, in practice classical liberalism's emphasis on monetary stability took precedent. Chapter 4's discussion of the international debates around Italian growth policy in the 1960s shows this most clearly: The international community supported policies for growth when the balance of payments was too much in surplus and supported policies of austerity when the balance shifted to deficit. Growth was not a goal in its own right but a mechanism of domestic economic adjustment to the needs of international monetary stability.

Economic liberalism may have been the intellectual core of the neoliberal consensus of the 1990s, but these ideas were not new. They guided the practices of central bankers during the classical gold standard era, have defined the work of the Bank for International Settlements since its inception in the 1920s, and shaped the debates over domestic adjustment and international monetary stability that took place within the OECD in the late 1950s and 1960s.[5] Understanding the rise, consolidation, and resiliency of neoliberalism and its politics of austerity thus requires more than an investigation into neoliberalism's ideological foundations; it requires an analysis of the way in which institutions support neoliberal ideology over others by increasing the power and influence of social actors who seek to promote neoliberal understandings of economic dynamics.[6] From this perspective, with respect to the contemporary resiliency of neoliberalism and austerity, the question is not so much how neoliberal ideas came to be accepted but rather: How have the actors and institutions that advocate economic liberalism and austerity become able to diffuse the "wisdom" of their own, internal consensus?

The answer is that a combination of international competitive and coercive pressures have led to a deepening of networks of cooperation between national monetary authorities and have propelled this increasingly transnational monetary authority to the heights of the "new international financial architecture." Chapters 5, 6, and 7 show how the international institutional innovations that were an attempt to shore up the Bretton Woods system in the face of accelerating transnational capital flows created new relationships of dependency between national governments and monetary authorities that the latter leveraged to push domestic economic policy into a classically liberal framework.

The global economy has become far more complex and uncertain than it was even during the turbulent years of the late Bretton Woods period, and national governments are even more dependent on the transnational monetary authority to mitigate the effects of this turbulence, especially during times of financial crisis. The elevation of monetary authorities, a process that began in the 1960s, has continued apace since and seems only to proceed further each time global capitalism is confronted with financial crisis. Neoliberalism and austerity remain strong in the face of crisis because the frequent global economic crises that characterize post–Bretton Woods global capitalism have served only to further elevate the monetary authorities' role in the management of global capitalism.

Global Financial Instability and the Consolidation of the Transnational Monetary Authority

The steady removal of controls over transnational capital flows in the 1950s did irreparable damage to the Bretton Woods system and hastened its decline. People like John Maynard Keynes and Harry Dexter White had advocated for strong capital controls because they knew that short-term, speculative capital movements would create wild swings in countries' international accounts, which, in addition to threatening the fixed exchange rate system, would force national governments to sacrifice national growth experiments on the altar of monetary stability. Keynes and White were right to worry about capital flows but not for quite the right reasons. By themselves, accelerating transnational capital flows and the havoc that they wreaked on international accounts did not force national governments to abandon growth for austerity.

What the liberalization of capital did do was elevate monetary authorities' position in the institutions of international economic management. The integrity of Bretton Woods rested on a relative stability of exchange rates, and, in an environment of accelerating capital flows, stabilizing exchange rates increasingly required cooperation between central banks. Chapter 2 documents the institutional innovations that made the monetary authorities central to preserving Bretton Woods: the negotiation of the General Arrangements to Borrow, the establishment of the London Gold Pool, and the ever-growing network of swap arrangements. Through these mechanisms a transnational network of central banks and treasuries conducted day-to-day exchange market interventions to keep currencies stable and, in times of crisis, served as a lender of last resort by arranging emergency balance of payments financing to ward of speculators.

Three significant consequences resulted from these institutional innovations. First, national rivalries among monetary authorities were blunted as these operations increased the frequency and density of international cooperation, bringing about a harmonization of policy views. In the context of these transnational networks, monetary authorities served more as managers of a global monetary system and less as the representatives of their home governments' priorities. Second, as increasingly transnationalized monetary authorities became the de facto managers of the international monetary system, the problem of international economic stability was interpreted through a finance-centric framework, one that believes that stability is best served when national governments prioritize domestic price stability supported by fiscal austerity, monetary orthodoxy, and capital accumulation over wages. Third, national governments' dependency on foreign monetary authorities to mitigate the effects of transnational capital flows was a powerful mechanism of coercion that could be used to push national policy making onto the path of orthodoxy through austerity.

The year 1973 saw the end of the old global regulatory architecture built at Bretton Woods, and the resulting acceleration of economic globalization created a demand for a new kind of international governance of global economic activity.[7] Global trade and capital markets not only survived the turmoil and uncertainty wrought by Bretton Woods's end, they flourished. They also became incredibly unstable. Between 1973 and 1985 there were twenty-five separate banking crises around the world, with nine of them occurring in conjunction with currency crises.[8] Major crises during these years included the failures of the Franklin National Bank in the United States and the Herstatt Bank of Germany in 1974, both of which threatened the stability of the international financial system due to the fact that both banks had large foreign exchange exposures. In 1982, crisis emerged again as the American banking system was ravaged by defaults on loans to developing countries, particularly

Mexico where the largest U.S. banks had nearly half of their total assets tied up. That year, a widespread recession combined with the rising value of the dollar meant that Mexico was both increasingly unable to export goods and saddled with growing interest payments.[9]

As a result of these crises, the monetary authorities of the major capitalist economies have built on the institutional innovations of the 1960s by constructing a "new international financial architecture," a massive international organizational apparatus designed to manage and govern the global economy.[10] It is international in its form and scope and includes both official governmental cooperation and unofficial cooperative efforts from nongovernmental agencies. Just as in the 1960s, when global capital liberalization weakened Bretton Woods institutions and elevated national monetary authorities' role in managing the international monetary system, so too has the dismantling of capital controls in the 1970s combined with the floating of exchange rates raised new problems of international monetary management that has consolidated the monetary authorities' position as the de facto managers of global capitalism.

This further elevation of the transnational monetary authority initially resulted from the pressure that international capital markets were placing on central bankers' ability to manage their currency reserves. Central banks were already having a difficult time dealing with the effects of capital inflows and outflows in the 1960s, and the acceleration of transnational capital flows in the 1970s only made their work more difficult. Attempts to come to agreement on a new system of fixed, or at least stable, exchange rates failed, and there was no serious thought about going back to a period of tighter capital controls. In addition, central banks, even when working together, did not have the financial means to effectively counter the weight of private capital in foreign exchange markets that were both feeding, and feeding off, global financial instability. In this context, the goals of international cooperation among monetary authorities shifted. Rather than try to achieve international monetary stability directly, the monetary authorities began to work—both individually within their own national contexts and collectively within the intergovernmental organizations of economic management—to deal with what they believed were the domestic sources of international economic instability.[11]

First, the monetary authorities aggressively quashed the high rates of inflation that had emerged across North America and Western Europe in the 1970s and, even more important, consolidated their power and autonomy within their national governments to make domestic price stability a central goal of economic policy. Second, they developed a new system of capital regulation that codified the primacy of the global free market for capital. Third, and finally, when these efforts failed to stabilize global financial markets, central banks took on the role of lender of last resort, performing the international emergency financing functions that, in the early Bretton Woods years, had been the domain of the International Monetary Fund. As in the late Bretton Woods period, the deeper significance of these institutional innovations is the way in which they have increased the influence of transnationalized monetary authorities over national governments, which has facilitated the diffusion of neoliberalism and austerity.

Exchange Rate Stability through Price Stability

Maintaining currency stability had always been a challenge during the Bretton Woods years, but those difficulties seem almost trite when compared to the complete disorganization of exchange markets that followed the end of the Bretton Woods fixed-exchange rate system. Between 1971 and 1973, when it was clear that Bretton Woods was coming to a definitive end, the governments of North America, Western Europe, and Japan engaged in a series of discussions over whether currencies should be allowed to float freely in international markets or whether exchange rates needed to be fixed by a new system outside the dollar-gold standard. The same questions about adjustment that had taken place in the 1960s—when and how should it happen and who should bear its costs—were at the heart of these discussions.

The U.S. negotiators wanted a system that self-servingly harkened back to some of Keynes's original ideas. Specifically they wanted mechanisms to compel countries running persistent payments surpluses to grow their economies. In contrast, the Europeans, particularly the French, wanted a system of pegged exchange rates that would force deficit countries to deflate and, in doing so, place limits on the "exorbitant privilege" of the United States. In the end, the finance ministers of France, Germany, Italy, Japan, the United Kingdom, and the United States reached an agreement 1975 at the G8 summit at Rambouillet to legalize floating exchange rates while also agreeing to work together, as Eichengreen describes it, to "promote stable exchange rates by fostering orderly economic conditions."[12] This is one of the most significant consequences of the Rambouillet agreements because it links exchange rate stability to domestic price stability, making national governments responsible for conducting domestic monetary operations with an eye toward maintaining the value of their currency on foreign exchange markets.[13] As Borio and Toniolo observe, this was classical thinking resurgent: "As under the classical gold standard, policymakers become increasingly convinced that the best way of maintaining economic stability was to keep 'one's own house in order.'"[14]

With inflation running rampant across North America and Western Europe, central banks gained a new prestige that they had not enjoyed for quite some time. More than economic stagnation and high rates of unemployment, inflation was roundly perceived to be the most important problem facing the economies of the West. While monetarist and Keynesian economists debated the root causes of, and solutions to, the "great inflation," central bankers generally took a less doctrinaire approach. Money was at the heart of the problem, and managing money is what they did. Initially, many central banks tried to deal with inflation though the practice of "monetary targeting" by establishing some target for the amount of money that should be in circulation at any given time and then conducting monetary operations to achieve this target. By the 1980s, however, this approach had failed to regulate prices or exchange rates. Money was notoriously difficult to measure and the targets almost impossible to hit.[15]

In the 1990s, central banks changed tactics and began to set explicit targets for the rate of inflation as a guide for monetary policy. Economists tend to be enthusiastic about this kind of inflation targeting and credit it with not only breaking the back of the "great inflation" of the 1970s and 1980s but also with keeping inflation, and inflationary expectations, low in the years since.[16] As capital has become ever more mobile, central banks and national governments face greater and greater pressures to maintain the credibility of their financial institutions and practices in the eyes of foreign investors. Because of these pressures, many of the world's central banks have adopted explicit formal commitments to making domestic price stability the primary goal of monetary policy.[17] A survey of eighty-four central banks conducted by the Bank of England found that only four central banks used inflation targeting to guide monetary policy in 1990 but that by the end of the decade fifty more central banks had adopted an explicit inflation-targeting regime. A similar survey of forty-five central banks conducted by the Bank for International Settlements found that in thirty-three cases "price stability—or its equivalent, stability in the domestic purchasing power of the currency—appears as the dominant or one of the dominant legal objectives."[18]

The economic stagnation and high rates of unemployment that have followed in the wake of the global financial crisis of 2008 have not broken this obsession with inflation. The European Central Bank, the Bank of England, and the Bank of Canada all remain firmly anchored to an inflation targeting monetary policy framework. The Federal Reserve Bank made headlines in early 2013 when the Federal Open Market Committee appeared to be ending its long-standing policy of inflation targeting and instead using the rate of unemployment and growth of the real economy as guides for monetary policy. Yet close examination of the wording of these announcements shows that keeping inflation in check is still the Fed's primary concern and that it will pursue other policy objectives only so long as they do not threaten price stability.[19]

Austerity and Inflation Targeting
The significance of the rise and spread of inflation-targeting regimes runs much deeper than the technocratic minutia of the evolution of central bank practice might suggest. It is a key institutional transformation supporting the diffusion and resiliency of neoliberalism and austerity. By linking international financial stability to domestic price stability, central banks and other monetary authorities were able to achieve what classical liberals in the 1960s, who authored documents like the "Code of Good Behavior" and the "Adjustment Process Report" had not been able to: broad acceptance of the idea that national governments had a responsibility to use the tools of domestic economic management to support international monetary stability. Moreover, by forging this link between domestic policy and international monetary stability, central banks and other state monetary agencies became even more directly responsible for managing the post–Bretton Woods global economy, elevating the monetary authorities' position in the institutional nexus of national economic policy making.

Indeed, the assault on inflation has also resulted in significant changes to central banks' relationships to other state agencies. Monetary policy has not only become a more important tool of economic management, central banks have also achieved a great deal of autonomy from other state agencies in conducting monetary policy. This new degree of central bank independence manifests as the central bank having control over appointing its own governor, being able to set monetary policy goals, and as not being beholden to other state agencies or legislatures. Bitterly fought for in the 1950s and 1960s, central bank independence has, like inflation targeting, become the new global norm.[20] These two developments—the shift in central bank practice along inflation targeting lines and the shift in the central bank's relationship to other state agencies—went hand-in-hand. Once committed to inflation targeting, central banks made the case, and economists generally agreed, that only autonomy from political influence could ensure that the bank managers would be able to carry out the necessary operations to ensure that those targets were hit.[21]

Although the political significance of these developments tends to be obscured by the ostensibly neutral, technocratic language in which they are discussed, the elevation of the monetary authorities at both the national and international level helps to explain the rise and consolidation of neoliberal economic paradigms in the 1980s and 1990s and their resiliency in the wake of crisis. John Goodman describes how the ostensible need to follow the gold standard "rules of the game" supported laissez-faire doctrine by providing ideological cover for central banks as they used monetary policy to deflate the economy any time price inflation threatened international banking profits over domestic welfare.[22] Noticing the striking parallel to the past, John Singleton writes in his history of modern central banking that "monetary targeting was in some respects a cover for an old-fashioned policy of deflation implemented by central bankers and a new wave of politicians who took the scourge of inflation more seriously than their predecessors."[23] Inflation targeting serves the same function; it is deflation disguised as rule following.

To be clear, there are important domestic level factors that have shaped central banks and their policies, and there is still a considerable amount of variation in central bank practices and relationships to other state agencies and private financial market actors that cannot be ignored.[24] What also needs to be appreciated, however, is that the diffusion of inflation targeting regimes, with the concomitant rise in central bank independence, is a response to the problems of economic globalization in a post–Bretton Woods world. The transformations in central bank practices and relationships to other state actors that the move to inflation targeting brings about are an inextricable part of the post–Bretton Woods mechanisms of global financial management, mechanisms that bear a striking resemblance to the old international financial architecture of the classical gold standard years without, of course, the gold.

A New Regulatory Framework for Capital

Restrictions on transnational capital movements were relaxed in the 1950s and 1960s and then thoroughly dismantled after the 1970s. Taking capital controls off the global regulatory agenda did not mean, however, that governments were willing or able to leave capital unregulated. In addition to prompting serious discussions about how to best deal with exchange rate stability in an era of flexible exchange rates, global financial crises in 1970s also led to discussions among the monetary authorities over how to keep the liberalization of markets for capital from triggering financial crises that cascaded across the global economy.

These discussions took place within the Bank for International Settlements, which expanded its mission in the early 1970s from mainly addressing problems of international monetary stability to taking on the challenges of European monetary integration and the broader issues of global financial regulation.[25] Like the discussions that took place over the problem of exchange rate volatility, interest in capital regulation was spurred by financial crisis. After the failure of the Franklin National Bank and the Herstatt Bank in 1974, the monetary authorities of the G10 countries formed the Basel Committee on Banking Supervision within the Bank for International Settlements to develop a new system of capital regulation.

As Ethan Kapstein notes, work within the Basel Committee was framed by a belief among central bankers that the global economy needed mechanisms of crisis prevention, not just crisis management, and that preventing domestic bank failures was critical for international financial stability.[26] While bank failures often result from systematic economic dynamics, the Basel Committee adopted a bank-level understanding of bank failure. From this perspective, bank failures occur because individual banks have improperly managed their portfolios: They have too many liabilities that go bad and insufficient assets to cover their losses. One way to reduce the risk of bank failure is to restrict the kind of liabilities and assets that banks can take on, but reaching international agreement on a list of acceptable and unacceptable bank practices was not politically viable and smacked of capital controls. If bank activities cannot be restricted directly, state monetary authorities can limit private banks' activities by limiting their access to credit. This option also proved to not be viable. While a few central banks in centralized, developmentalist states like France and Italy had a long tradition of state control over the credit supply, many other central banks had no experience with this practice. Even more to the point, this would require some kind of world central bank to which all other national central banks were beholden—a prospect that few countries would agree to.

This leaves one final option for monetary authorities seeking to control the activities of their private banks: setting more stringent reserve requirements. If the quantity and quality of bank borrowing and lending activity cannot be controlled directly, then the monetary authority can at least set standards for the amount of capital that banks have to hold in reserve against their liabilities so that, if risky investments go bad, the bank will at least be able to cover its losses.

The central bankers who comprised the membership of the Basel Committee for Bank Supervision adopted this latter approach to deal with bank failures, and after more than five years of steady work the Committee released an international standard for bank reserves called the Basel Capital Accord. By the end of 1990, the central banks of the G10 had all implemented the terms of the Accord, and by 1992 more than 100 countries with significant international banking operations had signed on. Both the World Bank and the International Monetary Fund use the standards set forth in the Accord to assess the strength of potential borrowers' financial institutions.[27]

The basic idea behind reserve requirements is that the level of cash and other liquid assets that banks need to hold in reserve is related not just to the amount of the bank's outstanding loans but also to the risks associated with those loans. What the Basel Accord did was to define a small number of risk categories for all types of bank liabilities and then assign a "risk weight" to those categories. Holding the debt of OECD governments was assumed to be risk-free, and so banks did not need to hold any reserves against those loans. Loans to private firms were deemed to be much more risky and carried a risk weight of 100 percent; for every one dollar of loan, one dollar needed to be held in reserve.[28]

Like the discussions around inflation targeting and exchange rate volatility, the deeper significance of the Basel Accord is obscured by the technocratic minutia of "risk weights" and asset classes. The real significance of the Basel Capital Accord is in the way that it institutionalizes core tenets of economic liberalism into the system of global capital regulation. First, the Basel Accord takes the global free market for capital as given and largely untouchable. Regulation is very much at arm's length, with neither the Basel Committee that designed it, nor any other international body, assuming any direct regulatory powers over individual banks. Rather, the Accord's system of regulation is built on the principle of "home country control": It is the responsibility of national monetary authorities to ensure that their country's banks meet the Accord's terms.[29] The Basel Accord, despite being an international agreement, eschewed any global or international regulation of capital. By building its regulatory apparatus around principle of "home country control," the Basel Accord, like the diffusion of inflation targeting regimes, embodies a core tenet of classical liberalism: International monetary stability is best achieved through domestic adjustment. Rather than attributing financial crisis to the structure of global markets, regulation through reserve requirements puts the onus on individual financial institutions to stand ready to weather the storm.[30]

Second, by opting to regulate banks through their capital reserves, the Basel Accord devolves regulatory authority from the state to private financial actors. Tony Porter recognized this when he noted that "capital standards significantly shift the administrative and financial burden of ensuring that banks are run prudently from supervisory authorities to banks and their shareholders."[31] This feature became even more pronounced after the Basel Accord was revised in the wake of the Asian Financial Crisis of 1997. The "Basel II" framework that emerged from these discussions endorsed an internal ratings–based approach to assessing asset risk, whereby the banks themselves were allowed to use their own calculations of risk to determine how much capital they needed to hold in reserve against their portfolio of assets. To ensure that the banks who adopted the internal rating system were practicing due diligence, the Basel II framework delegated responsibility for monitoring and reviewing the banks' practices to a small number of private credit-rating agencies, like Moody's and Standard and Poor's.[32]

In 2009 the Basel Committee went back to the drawing board to strengthen the Basel II regulatory framework. At the end of 2010 the Committee released a new "Basel III" framework for measuring, monitoring, and supervising bank liquidity risk. Unlike Basel II, which completely overhauled the risk assessment system, Basel III is a much more modest revision to the regulatory framework that has banks hold more liquid assets to be able to better deal with sudden portfolio losses. And yet, for all of the careful, precise language defining and specifying reserve assets and coverage ratios, the core of the Basel regulatory project has not changed.

The evolution of the Basel Accord raises important questions about the regulation, or lack thereof, of the global economy since the collapse of Bretton

Woods. On the one hand it would be a mistake to be dismissive of the Basel Accord as a complete lack of regulation. On the other hand, it would also be a mistake to read into the Basel Accord signs that the neoliberal paradigm may be crumbling.[33] This is regulation shaped by the neoliberal dilemma. The global private market for finance is, from the perspective of the Basel Committee, ungovernable, and the kinds of investment activities that lead to financial fragility are never restricted. All that can be done "is to improve the banking sector's ability to absorb shocks arising from financial and economic stress."[34]

The Lender of Last Resort

Even as the monetary authorities were working to construct a new global regime of financial stability, they were frequently required to deal with the financial crises—some 124 between 1970 and 2007—that seem to be part of the new normal of the post–Bretton Woods years.[35] Just as they had in the 1960s, central banks have served as "lender of last resort" during these times of crisis, using techniques developed in the late Bretton Woods era, like currency swaps and arranging emergency financing, to try to contain the cascading effects of bank failures and restore calm to frantic currency markets.

For example, when the Franklin National Bank failed in the United States in 1974, triggering a global financial panic and a speculative run against the dollar, the finance ministers of the G10 convened at the Bank for International Settlements and agreed to defend the dollar against the speculators. As Eric Helleiner notes, these cooperative efforts were a direct outgrowth of the mechanisms of central bank cooperation that these same finance ministers had developed in the 1960s. Similarly, when Mexico experienced a debt crisis in 1982, Paul Volcker of the Federal Reserve and Gordon Richardson of the Bank of England spearheaded efforts within the Bank for International Settlements to arrange a $1.85 billion loan from the Bank for International Settlements to Mexico. In both of these cases, it was the U.S. Federal Reserve that took the lead in organizing the larger response from foreign central banks, but the United States did not always take the leadership role. When the value of the dollar plummeted in 1985, foreign central banks, led by the Bank of Japan, purchased large volumes of U.S. debt securities to halt the dollar's fall, and when the worlds' stock markets crashed in October of 1987 it was the Bank for International Settlements itself that stepped in to organize the effort among foreign central banks to pump liquidity into the securities markets to keep the crisis from triggering worldwide bank failures. Finally, similar to the way in which the creation of the General Arrangements to Borrow in the 1960s linked International Monetary Fund financing to central bank financing, the Fund's recent stabilization loans have often been "prefinanced" by bridging loans coordinated through the Bank for International Settlements. These examples highlight the emergence of what Helleiner refers to as a "BIS-centered regime" of crisis management, whereby lender of last resort functions have been taken over by collaborative arrangements between central banks and other monetary authorities.[36]

In the wake of the global financial crisis of 2008, central banks have once again stepped in to perform the role of "lender of last resort," arranging loan packages for the debt-laden governments of Western Europe and shoring up currencies through the reactivation of swap lines. Financial assistance to Ireland, Greece, Portugal, and Spain has been arranged by the European Stability Mechanism, an intergovernmental financial organization with a permanent legal status created by the Council of Europe in October of 2010 with seventeen European governments as its shareholders and with a board of directors comprised entirely of the finance ministers of these member governments.[37] Unlike the International Monetary Fund, whose financial resources come directly from its member governments, the European Stability Mechanism raises its funds in private capital markets, issuing top-rated bonds for which investors receive a rate of return that is modest but above the prevailing market rate. In the cases of the financial packages for Ireland, Greece, Portugal, and Spain, the International Monetary Fund has played a subordinate role to the European Stability Mechanism, with the latter providing the lion's share of the financing.[38]

There are two important consequences that follow from this financing structure. The first is that it is yet another way in which the evolving "new international financial architecture" brings together, and elevates, the transnational monetary authority. The European Stability Mechanism is more than just another international organizational site fostering the cooperation and cohesion of European finance ministers; the process of European debt financing has also reinforced transnational financial cooperation between European central banks and the U.S. Federal Reserve. With the euro in crisis, many European central banks have experienced a flight to the dollar and thus have seen their liquid currency reserves plummet. In an effort to stabilize the global market for dollars, the Federal Reserve returned to the playbook of international monetary cooperation in the 1960s and initiated currency swap arrangements with the European Central Bank in 2007, reactivated those swap lines in 2010, and then extended them through 2014.[39]

Second, the ability to support governments in times of financial crisis is now entirely dependent on private investors whose willingness to invest in the European Stability Mechanism's bonds requires assurance that the loans given to debt-addled governments will be repaid. Through these financing mechanisms, the vague specter of "investor confidence" that haunted national governments in decades past has now become much more immediate and much more salient. Thus, as these mechanisms strengthen the ties between public and private finance, the elevation of the transnational monetary authority has brought with it a further concentration of international monetary power into the hands of private transnational capital.[40]

The constraints on national governments that emerge from these financing structures are made clear by the lessons of history. Chapters 5 and 6 showed how similar financing mechanisms were mobilized to push the Kennedy and Wilson governments from their preferred domestic policies and putting them in line with international preferences. The Kennedy administration became increasingly dependent on its network of swap transactions to shore up the dollar in global currency markets in the early 1960s, and the "tight money crowd" at the Bank for International Settlements and the OECD drew explicit attention to this fact as it pushed the Kennedy administration to abandon the monetary pillar of its growth agenda and instead use monetary policy to stem the outward flow of short-term speculative capital. Similarly, the Labour government faced a chorus of voices in the OECD's Working Party 3 that both called on the Wilson administration, time and time again, to improve confidence in the pound sterling by deflating the British economy and also made it very clear that failure to do so would undermine central banks' willingness to support the pound sterling.

The increasing volatility, and fragility of the global financial system that has followed in the wake of the end of the Bretton Woods system has not only elevated the prestige and influence of central banks and other monetary authorities, it has also increased governments' dependency on foreign central banks and private capital markets through a deepening of the lender of last resort functions that they developed in the 1960s. Eleni Tsingou has gone so far as to argue that, in the area of international financial regulation, the distinction between public and private financial power is now obsolete.[41] The result is a sort of anti-Keynesian system of global economic governance, one that seeks not to hold private capital at bay but to welcome private capital with open arms and give it a seat at the table.

The Global Politics of Austerity

The era of neoliberalism and austerity is an era of finance resurgent, not just in the sense that capital flows across the globe with ease or in the sense that economic activity has become increasingly financialized but also in the sense that the new international financial architecture places greater weight on the activities and decisions of central banks and other monetary authorities that prioritize price stability over growth, balanced budgets over employment. The elevation of finance that began in the 1960s, went further still after the collapse of Bretton Woods, and has only been reinforced in the wake of the global financial crisis of 2008 has provided an institutional architecture for the rise, spread, and resiliency of neoliberalism and austerity. Yet, while neoliberal ideology remains secure in its dominance among financial experts and monetary authorities, it has also become the target of a fiercely mobilized public who in recent years have taken to the streets to challenge austerity. How have the *policies* of austerity been able to overcome the *politics* against austerity?

To answer this question, it is useful to once again turn to history and recall Keynes's and White's visions for the postwar international monetary order. Although they differed in important ways, both were premised on a particular understanding of the relationship among democracy, central bank autonomy, and economic policy. Keynes's and White's proposals for an International Clearing Union or some kind of international banking facility emerged, in part, from their belief that shifting responsibility for international monetary and financial issues into a committee of central banks was a minimal requirement for a properly functioning global financial system. Their reasoning was that vesting international monetary management in the hands of a network of central bankers would take monetary power away from private speculators, thus reducing a major impediment to national growth experiments.[42]

However, when Keynes and White were lauding the positive role that central banks could play in international monetary management, they were working at a time when central banks were not independent from the national government. Central banks were not setting the goals of economic policy but were simply carrying out the monetary operations needed to achieve the full

employment goals set by the national government, even if they begrudged doing so. In other words, Keynes and White both believed that central banks
would play a critical role in supporting the project of embedded liberalism,
but their responsibilities would be those of a civil servant, keeping the influence of private capital at bay, which would let the national government experiment with different growth strategies.

In the current era, central banks have taken on the responsibilities of managing the international economy but in a context where they operate with a
great deal of autonomy from national governments and in closer cooperation
with private financial institutions. Central Banks do not follow; they lead.
Moreover, they do not lead as representatives of the people's will but rather as
the guardians of the market, shielding it from an unruly public. This manifests as a complete distrust of democracy. For example, in a speech given in
May, 2010—just one week after Greece agreed to austerity in exchange for
financial assistance from the European Union—a member of the European
Central Bank's executive board discussed "the problems facing modern democracies in making decisions that require citizens to make sort-term sacri-
fices for long-term gains." The statement goes on to suggest that democratic
institutions got in the way of a speedy bailout of Lehman Brothers in the
United States with the consequence being that shortsighted taxpayers and
elected officials now have to contend with a global financial crisis.[43]

Central bankers' concerns with the "problems of democracy" are nothing
new. As Chapter 2 noted, since the end of the classical gold standard, national
governments and the democratic political pressures that they respond to
have often stood in the way of central banks' and other monetary authorities'
ability to structure economic policy around the needs of international credit
markets and price stability. In the gold standard era, the high degree of independence of central banks combined with the need to follow the "rules of the
game" provided monetary authorities with both institutional and discursive
protection from these political forces.

The structure of the new financial architecture appears to be having a
similar effect. Moving regulatory and monetary policy-making authority to
central banks and finance ministries insulates monetary policy making from
mass political pressure. To be sure, these policies are still political in that they
serve as powerful lightning rods of debate, discussion, and social protest, but
voters and protesters do not have a way of directly influencing the officials
who make these policies; the head of a government can be voted out, but not

the head of a central bank.[44] Increasingly technocratic forms of financial market regulation add another layer of insulation from the polity, a case in point being the further development of the Basel Accord. The move to the internal ratings–based approach to setting reserve requirements not only placed more regulatory responsibility into the hands of the banks themselves; it turned the process of financial market regulation into a more deeply technocratic exercise, further divorced from popular understanding.[45]

This is precisely the opposite outcome from that Keynes had in mind when he envisioned the pivotal role that national monetary authorities would play in regulating and stabilizing the international monetary order. After all, Keynes's vision of an international monetary order that would not only protect but privilege full-employment economic policies was premised on his belief that he was witnessing the "euthanasia of the rentiers," a time when plentiful and cheap credit would end "the cumulative oppressive power of the capitalist to exploit the scarcity-value of capital."[46] Clearly Keynes had misread the tea leaves. The rentiers may have been teetering on the brink in the early 1940s, but by the early 1960s they were rejuvenated and today occupy the heights of the new international financial architecture. They are alive and healthier than ever.

Yet, although Keynes may have been a poor prognosticator, he understood that a global capitalism freed of the barbarous logic of orthodoxy required more than a change of hearts and minds; it required robust international institutions that kept the forces of economic liberalism and austerity in check. Finance needed to follow, not write, the economic policy script. Keynes's lesson for today is that breaking the austerity's grip on the contemporary political landscape demands a critical reevaluation of not just the rules themselves, but of the rule makers.

REFERENCE MATTER

Notes

Chapter 1

1. Harvey, *A Brief History of Neoliberalism*, 19.
2. Akard, "Corporate Mobilization and Poltiical Power"; Ferguson and Rogers, *Right Turn*; and Jabko, *Playing the Market*.
3. Fourcade-Gourinchas and Babb, "Rebirth of the Liberal Creed."
4. Krippner, *Capitalizing on Crisis*; see also Krippner, "The Financialization of the American Economy"; Foster and Magdoff, *The Great Financial Crisis*; and Epstein and Jayadev, "The Rise of Rentier Incomes."
5. This was recognized early on by experts working on balance of payments issues. See, for example, Madsen, "Asymmetries between Balance of Payments Surpluses and Deficits," 182–201.
6. For an excellent, recent discussion of the concept of neoliberalism and related scholarship, see Mudge, "What Is Neo-Liberalism?"
7. Bourdieu, "The Essence of Neoliberalism"; and Wacquant, *Punishing the Poor*.
8. Polanyi, *The Great Transformation*.
9. Carruthers, Babb, and Halliday, "Institutionalizing Markets, or the Market for Institutions"; Krippner, "The Making of US Monetary Policy"; and Harvey, *A Brief History of Neoliberalism*, 67–70.
10. Blyth, *Austerity*.
11. Duménil and Lévy, *Capital Resurgent*.
12. See, for example, Prasad, *The Politics of Free Markets*; and Mudge, "What's Left of Leftism?"
13. Simmons, Dobbin, and Garrett, "The Diffusion of Liberalism."
14. Susan Strange, *The Retreat of the State*.

15. Cameron, "The Expansion of the Public Economy."

16. Brady, Seleib-Kaiser, and Beckfield, "Economic Globalization and the Welfare State in Affluent Democracies"; and Cohen and Centenno, "Neoliberalism and Patterns of Economic Performance."

17. Heclo, *Modern Social Politics in Britain and Sweden.*

18. Blyth, "Structures Do Not Come with an Instruction Sheet."

19. Parsons, Abdelal, and Blyth, *Constructing the International Economy*; Goldstein and Keohane, *Ideas and Foreign Policy*; and McNamara, *The Currency of Ideas.*

20. Haas, "Do Regimes Matter?"; and Ikenberry, "A World Economy Restored."

21. Babb, "Embeddedness, Inflation and International Regimes"; Henisz, Zelner, and Guillén, "The Worldwide Diffusion of Market-Oriented Infrastructure Reform"; and Chwieroth, *Capital Ideas.*

22. Meyer et al., "World Society and the Nation-State."

23. Boli and Thomas, "World Culture in the World Polity"; March and Olson, "The Institutional Dynamics of International Political Orders"; and Jepperson, Wendt, and Katzenstein, "Norms, Identity and Culture."

24. Chwieroth, *Capital Ideas.*

25. Beckfield, "The Dual World Polity"; and Chorev, "The Institutional Project of Neo-Liberal Globalization."

26. Dobbin, Simmons, and Garrett, "Global Diffusion of Public Policies," 451–452.

27. Simmons, Dobbin, and Garrett, "The Diffusion of Liberalism," 790–791.

28. Andrews, *International Monetary Power*, 2. See also Kirshner, *Currency and Coercion.*

29. Wendt, *Social Theory of International Politics*; and Schmidt, "Discursive Institutionalism."

30. Eichengreen, *Exorbitant Privilege.*

31. For this argument, see Strange, "The World's Money"; Calleo, "American Domestic Priorities and the Demands of Alliance"; and MacEwan, *Debt and Disorder.*

32. Williamson, "The Strange History of the Washington Consensus"; Gowan, *The Global Gamble*; Pollin, *Contours of Descent*; and Panitch and Ginden, *Global Capitalism and American Empire.*

33. Przeworski and Vreeland, "The Effect of IMF Programs"; Barro and Lee, "IMF Programs"; Barnett and Finnemore, *Rules for the World*, ch. 3; Garritsen de Vries, *Balance of Payments Adjustment, 1945–1986*, ch. 3; Chorev and Babb, "The Crisis of Neoliberalism"; and Simmons and Elkins, "The Globalization of Liberalization."

Chapter 2

1. Keynes to Phillips, 3 August 1942, in *The Collected Writings of John Maynard Keynes* 25 (London: Cambridge University Press, 1980), 159.

2. K. Polanyi-Levitt, "Keynes and Polanyi."

3. Block, *The Origins of International Economic Disorder*, ch. 3.

4. Ruggie, "International Regimes, Transactions and Change."

5. Helleiner, *States and the Reemergence of Global Finance*, 50.

6. O'Riain, "States and Markets in an Era of Globalization."

7. Block, *Origins of International Economic Disorder*, 42–43.

8. Bibow, "Keynes on Central Banking"; and Cartapanis and Herland, "The Reconstruction of the International Financial Architecture."

9. Bloomfield, *Monetary Policy under the International Gold Standard*.

10. Wilkins, "Conduits for Long-Term Foreign Investment."

11. Bordo and Rockoff, "The Gold Standard as 'Good Housekeeping Seal of Approval.'"

12. Verdier, *Moving Money*.

13. Eichengreen, *Golden Fetters*.

14. Polanyi, *The Great Transformation*, 145; and Goodman, *Monetary Sovereignty*.

15. Mouré, "The Bank of France and the Gold Standard"; Germain, *The International Organization of Credit*; Toniolo, *Central Bank Cooperation*, 18–19; and Frieden, "Sectoral Conflict and U.S. Foreign Economic Policy."

16. Berman, *The Social Democratic Moment*; and Przeworski, *Capitalism and Social Democracy*, ch. 3.

17. Burn, *The Re-Emergence of Global Finance*, 56.

18. Flandreau, "Central Bank Cooperation"; and Gallarotti, *Anatomy of an International Regime*, 78–85.

19. Toniolo, *Central Bank Cooperation*, 20–23.

20. Singleton, *Central Banking in the Twentieth Century*, 115.

21. Hall, *The Political Power of Economic Ideas*.

22. Frieden, *Banking on the World*; Cairncross, "The Bank of England"; and Goodman, *Monetary Sovereignty*.

23. Singleton, *Central Banking in the Twentieth Century*, 18 and 32.

24. Epstein, "Monetary Policy, Loan Liquidation."

25. On Switzerland, see Goodhart, *The Evolution of Central Banks*; on Germany, see Singleton, *Central Banking in the Twentieth Century*; on the Bank of England, see Burn, *The Re-Emergence of Global Finance*. On the Netherlands Bank and the Swiss National Bank, see Sayers, *Banking in Western Europe*, chs. 4 and 5; on Belgium, see Buyst et al., *The Bank, the Franc and the Euro*; and on Italy, see Sayers, *Banking in Western Europe*, ch. 3.

26. Greider, *Secrets of the Temple*, ch. 9; and Burn, *The Re-Emergence of Global Finance*, ch. 4.

27. Toniolo, *Central Bank Cooperation*, 323–327; Singleton, *Central Banks in the Twentieth Century*, 95.

28. Crotty, "On Keynes and Capital Flight"; and de Cecco, "Origins of the Post-War Payments System."

29. Block, *Origins of International Economic Disorder*, 56; and Gowan, *The Global Gamble*, ch. 1.

30. Burn, *The Re-Emergence of Global Finance*.

31. Abdelal, *Capital Rules*.

32. Barnett and Finnemore, *Rules for the World*, ch. 3; and Chwieroth, *Capital Ideas*.

33. Hodjera, "Basic Balances, Short-Term Capital Flow."

34. Toniolo, *Central Bank Cooperation*, ch. 11.

35. Horsefield, "Derivation and Significance of the Fund's resources."

36. Chwieroth, *Capital Ideas*.

37. Toniolo, *Central Bank Cooperation*, 363–369.

38. Eichengreen, *Globalizing Capital*.

39. Burn, *The Re-Emergence of Global Finance*.

40. Toniolo, *Central Bank Cooperation*, 399–411.

41. OECD, Economic Policy Committee, Working Party 3, April 16, 1962, meeting minutes, 7.

42. Federal Reserve Bank, Federal Open Market Committee, March 6, 1962 meeting minutes, 61; and meeting minutes, March 27, 1962, 47–51.

43. Federal Reserve Bank, Federal Open Market Committee, May 29, 1962, meeting minutes, 49–62.

44. Newton, "The Two Sterling Crises of 1964"; and Toniolo, *Central Bank Cooperation*, 388–399.

45. Toniolo, *Central Bank Cooperation*, 385–386.

46. Cooper, "Almost a Century of Central Bank Cooperation," 88; Singleton, *Central Banking in the Twentieth Century*, 161; and Helleiner, *States and the Reemergence of Global Finance*.

Chapter 3

1. A few collections of scholarship on the diffusion of Keynesianism make this point nicely. See Hall, *The Political Power of Economic Ideas*; Coats, *The Post-1945 Internationalization of Economics;* and Pasinetti and Schefold, *The Impact of Keynes on Economics*.

2. Bank for International Settlements, *30th Annual Report*, June 13, 1960, Basel, 24.

3. Though he does not use the term "imperial Keynesianism," Fred Block gives a similar interpretation in *The Origins of International Economic Disorder*.

4. Madison, *Monitoring the World Economy*.

5. Nicholls, *Freedom with Responsibility*; Katzenstein, *Policy and Politics in West Germany*; Edelman and Fleming, *The Politics of Wage-Price Decisions*, 223; and Katzenstein, *Corporatism and Change*.

6. Eichengreen, *The European Economy since 1945*, 103.

7. Katzenstein, *Policy and Politics in West Germany*, 94; and Katzenstein, *Corporatism and Change*, 96.

8. Aubrey, *Atlantic Economic Cooperation*.

9. Wolfe, "From Reconstructing Europe to Constructing Globalization"; and Russell, "Transgovernmental Interaction in the International Monetary System."

10. Hall and Soskice, "An Introduction to Varieties of Capitalism." See also Cox and Jacobson, *Approaches to World Order*, ch. 17.

11. Woodward, *The Organization for Economic Co-operation and Development*, ch. 1.

12. OECD, "Resolution of the Council Concerning Further Tasks of Working Party 19 of the Council." May 4, 1959, C(59)71(final), 1–2.

13. OECD, Economic Policy Committee, Working Party 2, "Implementation of the Resolution of the First Ministerial Council." October 11, 1962, CPE/WP2(62)20, 1–23.

14. OECD, Economic Policy Committee, "Proposal by the Group of Economic Experts for a Study of the Problem of Rising Prices." May 11, 1959, CPE(59)3, 1–2.

15. OECD, Economic Policy Committee, "The Current Economic Situation." March 17, 1960, CPE(60)2, 1–21.

16. OECD, Economic Policy Committee, "The Report of the Independent Experts on the Problem of Rising Prices." October 10, 1961, CPE(61)1, 1–5.

17. Hall, *The Political Power of Economic Ideas*.

18. OECD, Economic Policy Committee, Working Party 2, "Growth and Economic Policy." May 6, 1964, CPE/WP2(64)3(1st revision), 6.

19. OECD, Economic Policy Committee, "Meeting of the 25th–26th July, 1960." July 16, 1960, CPE(60)4, 9.

20. OECD, Economic Policy Committee, "Recent Economic Developments and Prospects." February 8, 1962, CPE(62)3, 1–18.

21. Bank for International Settlements, *32nd Annual Report*. June 4, 1962, Basel, 8.

22. Bank for International Settlements, *34th Annual Report*. June 8, 1964, Basel, 5.

23. OECD, Economic Policy Committee, "Second Report on Policies for Price Stability by Working Party No. 4." February 19, 1964, CPE(64)1, 8.

24. OECD, Economic Policy Committee, Working Party 2, "Economic Growth, 1960–1970: A Mid-Term Review of Progress Towards the O.E.C.D. Growth Target." September 27, 1965, CPE/WP2(65)2, 11.

25. OECD, Economic Policy Committee, "Second Report on Policies for Price Stability by Working Party No. 4." February 19, 1964, CPE(64)1, 8.

26. OECD, Economic Policy Committee, "Economic Developments and Short-Term Prospects." June 2, 1964, CPE(64)9, 28.

27. OECD, Economic Policy Committee, "The Report of the Independent Experts on the Problem of Rising Prices." October 16, 1961, CPE(61)3, 1–10.

28. Martin, *Shifting the Burden*.

29. Barnett and Finnemore, *Rules for the World*, ch. 3; and Garritsen de Vries, *Balance of Payments Adjustment*, ch. 3.

30. Clift and Tomlinson, "When Rules Started to Rule."

31. Nicholls, *Freedom with Responsibility*.

32. OECD, Economic Policy Committee, "The Closer Co-Ordination of Economic Policies: Summary of the Suggestions Made by Professor Mueller-Armack." July 2, 1959, CPE(59)4, 1–5.

33. OECD, Economic Policy Committee, "Code of Good Behavior." March 8, 1960, CPE(60)1, 1–9.

34. OECD, Economic Policy Committee, "Report of the Working Party on a Code of Good Behavior." February 11, 1960, CPE(60)6, 1–6.

35. OECD, Economic Policy Committee, "Code of Good Behaviour." November 2, 1960, CPE(60)7, 1–7.

36. Dillon to the Department of State, June 16, 1964. *Foreign Relations of the United States, 1964–1968: Volume 8: International Monetary and Trade Policy*, document 9.

37. OECD, Economic Policy Committee, Working Party 3, "Internal Liquidity and the Balance of Payments: Note by the Delegation of the Netherlands." June 10, 1964, CPE/WP3(64)17, 1–12.

38. OECD, Economic Policy Committee, Working Party 3, meeting minutes. June 17, 1964, 3.

39. Ibid., 3–4.

40. OECD, Economic Policy Committee, Working Party 3, meeting minutes. January 28–29, 1965, 40–41.

41. OECD, Economic Policy Committee, Working Party 3, "The Adjustment Process: Conclusions of the Report." March 25, 1966, CPE/WP3(66)10, 1–16.

42. Otmar Emminger, "Report to the Ministers and Governors by the Group of Deputies." July 7, 1966, Bank for International Settlements, 1–25.

43. Bank for International Settlements, *36th Annual Report*. June 13, 1966, Basel, 23.

Chapter 4

1. Armstrong, Glyn, and Harrison, *Capitalism since 1945*, 20; and Zamagni, *An Economic History of Italy*, 321.

2. Hellman, "Italy," 344–366.

3. Tagliacarne, "Income, Investment and Consumption," 100.

4. Rey, "Italy," 503.

5. Willis, *Italy Chooses Europe*, 18–26; and Barkan, *Visions of Emancipation*, 27–28.

6. Hellman, "Italy," 344, 350–351; and Barkan, *Visions of Emancipation*.

7. Bini and Magliulo, "Keynesianism in Italy"; and de Cecco, "Keynes and Italian Economics."

8. Zamagni, *Economic History of Italy*, 325 and 341; Rey, "Italy," 508; and Armstrong, Glyn, and Harrison, *Capitalism since 1945*, 87.

9. Hellman, "Italy," 339–340; and Maraffi, "State/Economy Relationships."

10. Shonfield, *Modern Capitalism*, 184–192; and Hellman, "Italy," 355–356.

11. Hildebrand, *Growth and Structure*, 48.

12. Allen and Stevenson, *Introduction to the Italian Economy*, 52.

13. Rey, "Italy," 507; and Podbielski, *Italy*, 18.

14. Hildebrand, *Growth and Structure*, 157.

15. OECD, Economic Policy Committee, "Economic Indicators." October 9, 1959, CPE(59)7, 4.

16. OECD, Economic Policy Committee, Working Party 2, "Growth, 1960–1970: A Mid-Term Review of Progress Towards the O.E.C.D. Growth Target." May 5, 1966, CPE/WP2(66)2.

17. Bank for International Settlements, *31st Annual Report*. June 12, 1961, Basel, 18.

18. OECD, Economic Policy Committee, "The Current Economic Position." July 16, 1960, CPE(60)4, 20–21.

19. OECD, Economic Policy Committee, Working Party 3, meeting minutes. February 19–20, 1962, 13.

20. Nicol and Yuill, "Regional Problems and Policy," 417; and Mini, "Foreign Direct Investment in Italy."

21. Greene, "The Communist Parties of Italy and France."

22. Hellman, "Italy," 360.

23. Lange, Ross, and Vannicelli, *Unions, Change and Crisis*, ch. 2.

24. Franzosi, "Strike Data in Search of a Theory"; and Barkan, *Visions of Emancipation*, 56–57.

25. Allen and Stevenson, *Introduction to the Italian Economy*, 114–115.

26. Favretto, *The Long Search for a Third Way*.

27. Hildebrand, *Growth and Structure*, 411.

28. Hansen, *Fiscal Policy in Seven Countries*, 307; and Maes, "The Spread of Keynesian Economics."

29. Bank of Italy, Base Informativa Pubblica, TSCF0060 Households (Financial liabilities—stocks in billions of lire).

30. Rey, "Italy," 512.

31. Hansen, *Fiscal Policy in Seven Countries*, ch. 6.

32. OECD, Economic Policy Committee, "Recent Economic Developments and Prospects." October 23, 1962, CPE(62)10, 5.

33. OECD, Economic Policy Committee, "Recent Economic Developments and Prospects." June 5, 1962, CPE(62)7, 2.

34. Bank for International Settlements, *33rd Annual Report*. June 10, 1963, Basel, 16.

35. OECD, Economic Policy Committee, "Recent Economic Developments and Prospects." June 24, 1963, CPE(63)5, 2 and 7.

36. OECD, Economic Policy Committee, Working Party 3, meeting minutes, November 4, 1963, 1–7.

37. OECD, Economic Policy Committee, "Trends and Problems in 1964." February 17, 1964, CPE(64)4, 4.

38. OECD, Economic Policy Committee, Working Party 3, meeting minutes. February 26, 1964, 5 and 8.

39. Bank for International Settlements, *34th Annual Report*. June 8, 1964, Basel, 12.

40. OECD, Economic Policy Committee, Working Party 3, meeting minutes. June 17, 1964, 2.

41. OECD, Economic Policy Committee, Working Part 3, meeting minutes. October 1–2, 1964, 7–8.

42. Toniolo, *Central Bank Cooperation*, 385–386.

43. Eichengreen, *The European Economy since 1945*, 227.

44. Bank for International Settlements, *36th Annual Report*. June 13, 1966, Basel, 23; and Allen and Stevenson, *Introduction to the Italian Economy*, 76–77.

45. Rey, "Italy," 515.

46. Bank for International Settlements, *35th Annual Report*. June 14, 1965, Basel, 22.

47. OECD, Economic Policy Committee, Working Party 2, "Economic Growth, 1960–1970" (draft outline). September 27, 1965, CPE/WP2(65)2, 26 (emphasis added).

48. OECD, Economic Policy Committee, Working Party 3, "The Italian Balance of Payments (note by the Italian delegation)." October 26, 1965, CPE/WP3(65)17; and OECD, Economic Policy Committee Working Party 3, "The Italian Balance of Payments (note by the secretariat)." October 29, 1965, CPE/WP3(65)18, 1.

49. OECD, Economic Policy Committee, Working Party 3, meeting minutes. November 8–9, 1965, 1–13.

50. OECD, Economic Policy Committee, "Economic Prospects for 1966." February 23, 1966, CPE(66)1, 49.

51. Bank for International Settlements, *37th Annual Report*. June 12, 1967, Basel, 25–26.

52. This point is not only well recognized in the international political economy literature now, but was also clearly understood at the time. For example, see H(st-Madsen, "Asymmetries between Balance of Payments Surpluses and Deficits."

53. OECD, Economic Policy Committee, Working Party 3, meeting minutes. July 26, 1968, 4–17.

54. OECD, Economic Policy Committee, Working Party 3, "Supplementary Note to CPE/WP3(68)23." December 4, 1968, CPE/WP3(68)25, 1; and OECD, Economic Policy Committee, Working Party 3, meeting minutes, December 10–11, 1968, 12.

Chapter 5

1. Hobsbawm, "The Forward March of Labour Halted?" 286.

2. Minkin, "The British Labour Party."

3. Tomlinson, *The Labour Governments*.

4. Minkin, "The British Labour Party."

5. Surrey, "United Kingdom."

6. Pemberton, "Taxation and Labour's Modernization Programme"; and Hall, *Governing the Economy*, ch. 2.

7. Favretto, *The Long Search for a Third Way*, 38–39; and Tomlinson, *The Labour Governments*.

8. Weir, "Ideas and Politics"; and Fourcade, *Economists and Societies*.

9. Armstrong, Glyn, and Harrison, *Capitalism since 1945*; and Hall, *Governing the Economy*.

10. Gourevitch et al., *Unions and Economic Crisis*, ch. 1.

11. Manser, *Britain in Balance*.

12. This latter episode is discussed by Newton, "The Two Sterling Crises," 86–87, drawing on archival documents from the British Treasury.

13. Manser, *Britain in Balance*.

14. Burn, *The Re-Emergence of Global Finance*; and Germain, *The International Organization of Credit*, 44–58.

15. Balogh, "Productive Investment and the Balance of Payments." Balogh's skepticism of economic liberalization manifested as strong attacks against the United Kingdom joining the Common Market. See, for example, his "Postwar Britain and the Common Market."

16. Garritsen de Vries, *Balance of Payments Adjustment*, 51–55 (author's figures, and subsequent figures originally reported in pound sterling converted to dollars at $2.80 per £1).

17. Surrey, "United Kingdom," 531–533.

18. Bank for International Settlements, *32nd Annual Report*. June 4, 1962, Basel, 39–40.

19. OECD, Economic Policy Committee, Working Party 3, July 4, 1961. "Conclusion on the Balance of Payments of the United Kingdom," 1.

20. OECD, Economic Policy Committee, Working Party 3, meeting minutes, January 22–23, 1963, 1–8.

21. Bank for International Settlements, *32nd Annual Report*. June 4, 1962, Basel, 39–40.

22. OECD, Economic Policy Committee, Working Party 2, "Economic Policy Problems Raised by Growth in the 1960s." June 5, 1962, CPE/WP2(62)12, 13.

23. OECD, Economic Policy Committee, Working Party 2, "Implementation of the Resolution of the First Ministerial Council." October 11, 1962, CPE/WP2 (62)20, 18.

24. OECD, Economic Policy Committee, Working Party 3, "Measures and Prospects in the United Kingdom." December 4, 1964, CPE/WP3(64)30, 1.

25. Newton, "The Two Sterling Crises of 1964," 76 and 79.

26. OECD, Economic Policy Committee, Working Party 3, "The Adjustment Process: Memorandum by the United Kingdom." December 29, 1964, CPE/WP3(64)29, 1–10.

27. OECD, Economic Policy Committee, Working Party 3, meeting minutes. December 17–18, 1964, 5.

28. Calculation based on Newton, "The Two Sterling Crises of 1964," figure 2.

29. OECD, Economic Policy Committee, Working Party 3, "Balance of Payments Developments and Prospects for 1965." February 8, 1965, CPE/WP3(65)2, 36.

30. OECD, Economic Policy Committee, "Economic Prospects in 1965." February 1, 1965, CPE(65)3, 3.

31. OECD, Economic Policy Committee, Working Party 3, "United Kingdom Payments Prospects." April 23, 1965, CPE/WP3(65)8, 1–13.

32. Bank for International Settlements, *36th Annual Report*. June 13, 1966, Basel, 7–8.

33. OECD, Economic Policy Committee, "Economic Prospects." June 6, 1965, CPE(65)7, 1–61.

34. OECD, Economic Policy Committee, Working Party 2, "Mid-Term Report on Progress to and Prospects for the Fifty Percent Growth Target, United Kingdom." June 29, 1965, CPE/WP2(65)1/17, 11.

35. OECD, Economic Policy Committee, "Recent Economic Developments." June 5, 1962, CPE/WP2(62)7, 1–20.

36. OECD, Economic Policy Committee, Working Party 3, "Measures and Prospects in the United Kingdom." December 4, 1964, CPE/WP3(64)30, 6 (emphasis added).

37. McGeehan, "Competitiveness," 249.

38. OECD, Economic Policy Committee, Working Party 2, "Economic Growth, 1960–1970." May 12, 1966, CPE/WP2(66)2, 16 and 18.

39. OECD, Economic Policy Committee, "Economic Prospects for 1966." February 23, 1965, CPE(66)1, 12.

40. Ibid., 2 and 4.

41. OECD, Economic Policy Committee, Working Party 3, meeting minutes, January 28–29, 1966, 1–43.

42. Tomlinson, *The Labour Governments*, 53–54.

43. Bank for International Settlements, *37th Annual Report*. June 12, 1967, Basel, 12.

44. Spitzer, "Stand-By Arrangements."

45. OECD, Economic Policy Committee, Working Party 3, meeting minutes. July 16, 1964, 17.

46. Ibid., 18 (emphasis added).

47. Ibid., 18.

48. OECD, Economic Policy Committee, Working Party 3, meeting minutes. October 1–2, 1964, 6.

49. OECD, Economic Policy Committee, Working Party 3, meeting minutes. February 15–16, 1965, 7.

50. Ibid., 10.

51. OECD, Economic Policy Committee, Working Party 3, meeting minutes. May 5–6, 1965, 1.

52. Newton, "The Sterling Devaluation of 1967."

53. OECD, Economic Policy Committee, "Economic Prospects for 1966." February 23, 1965, 65.

54. OECD, Economic Policy Committee, Working Party 3, meeting minutes. July 7–8, 1966, 10.

55. Ibid., 13.

56. OECD, Economic Policy Committee, Working Party 3, "General Balance of Payments Prospects for O.E.C.D. Countries." February 22, 1967, CPE/WP3(67)7, 4 and 33–34; and Bank for International Settlements, *38th Annual Report*. June 10, 1968, Basel.

57. OECD, Economic Policy Committee, Working Party 3, meeting minutes, March 1–3, 1967, 37–38.

58. OECD, Economic Policy Committee, Working Party 3, meeting minutes. July 19–20, 1967, 17.

59. OECD, Economic Policy Committee, Working Party 3, meeting minutes. August 28–29, 1967, 10.

60. Cairncross and Eichengreen, *Sterling in Decline*, 188.

61. Wilson, *The Labour Government*, 453.

62. OECD, Economic Policy Committee, Working Party 3, "The U.K. Situation." November 24, 1967, CPE/WP3(67)27, 1–8.

63. OECD, Economic Policy Committee, Working Party 3, meeting minutes. November 29, 1967, 1–23.

64. OECD, Economic Policy Committee, Working Party 3, meeting minutes. January 22–23, 1968, 2 and 7.

65. Ibid., 6.

66. OECD, Economic Policy Committee, Working Party 3, meeting minutes. March 6–7, 1968.

67. Tomlinson, *The Labour Governments*, 61; and Wilson, *The Labour Government*, 513.

68. OECD, Economic Policy Committee, Working Party 3, meeting minutes. April 23–24, 1968, 24.

Chapter 6

1. On this point, see Strange, "The World's Money"; Calleo, "American Domestic Priorities"; MacEwan, *Debt and Disorder*; and Panitch and Ginden, *Global Capitalism and American Empire*.

2. Fraser and Gerstle, *The Rise and Fall of the New Deal Order.*

3. Sundquist, *Politics and Policy.*

4. Russell, *Economics, Bureaucracy and Race*; Rowan, *The Free Enterprisers*; and Heath, *John F. Kennedy and the Business Community.*

5. Blyth, *Great Transformations*; and Best, "Hollowing Out the Keynesian Norms."

6. A detailed account of these different forms of Keynesianism, and how they manifested in the American context, is found in Collins, *The Business Response to Keynes*; see also Collins, *More.*

7. Solow, "The Kennedy Council in the Long Run"; Akard, "The Return of the Market?"; and Blyth, *Great Transformations.*

8. Salant, "The Spread of Keynesian Doctrines," 49.

9. Coen, "Effects of Tax Policy"; and Pechman, "The Individual Income Tax Provisions."

10. Best, "Hollowing Out the Keynesian Norms"; Martin, *Shifting the Burden*; and McQuaid, *Uneasy Partners.*

11. Heller, *New Dimensions of Political Economy*, 8.

12. Solow, "The Kennedy Council and the Long Run."

13. Brenner, "The Economics of Global Turbulence"; and Webber and Rigby, *The Golden Age Illusion*, ch. 2.

14. Unemployment data from the U.S. Department of Commerce, Bureau of Labor Statistics, Current Population Survey.

15. Block, *Origins of International Economic Disorder*, ch. 6.

16. Kindleberger, "Dominance and Leadership."

17. Board of Governors of the Federal Reserve System, Monetary and Banking Statistics, 1941–1970, Section 12: Money Rates and Security Markets.

18. Tobin, "The Future of the Fed," 26.

19. Heller to JFK, May 27, 1961. Kermit Gordon Papers, Box 38, "Memoranda to the President 1961." John F. Kennedy Presidential Library.

20. Krippner, *Capitalizing on Crisis.*

21. Heller to JFK, July 6, 1962. Kermit Gordon Papers, Box 38, "Memoranda to the President 1962 (2 of 2)." John F. Kennedy Presidential Library.

22. Heller to JFK, 6 July 6, 1963. Kermit Gordon Papers, Box 37, "Memoranda Walter Heller." John F. Kennedy Presidential Library.

23. OECD, Economic Policy Committee, "The Current Economic Situation." April 10, 1961, CPE(61)1.

24. OECD, Economic Policy Committee, "Recent Economic Developments and Prospects." October 23, 1962, CPE(62)10, 7–8.

25. Bank for International Settlements, *32nd Annual Report.* June 4, 1962, Basel, 14.

26. OECD, Economic Policy Committee, Working Party 3, meetings minutes. October 25, 1963, 4.

27. Dillon to JFK, July 12, 1962, POF Box 89, Treasury 7/1/62–7/15/62. John F. Kennedy Presidential Library.

28. Heller to JFK, December 16, 1962, POF Box 63a, Heller, Walter W., 1962. John F. Kennedy Presidential Library.

29. OECD, Economic Policy Committee, Working Party 3, CPE/WP3(61)1, April 26, 1961, 7.

30. OECD, Economic Policy Committee, Working Party 3, meeting minutes. October 26, 1961, 13.

31. OECD, Economic Policy Committee, Working Party 3, "Balance of payments Developments in 1961 and 1962." April 4, 1962, CPE/WP3 (62)13.

32. OECD Economic Policy Committee, Working Party 3, meeting minutes. July 18, 1962, 17.

33. OECD Economic Policy Committee, Working Party 3, meeting minutes. April 17, 1962, 18.

34. Ibid., 19.

35. Bank for International Settlements, *31st Annual Report.* June 12, 1961, Basel, 11.

36. Bank for International Settlements, *32nd Annual Report.* June 4, 1962, Basel, 22.

37. OECD Economic Policy Committee, Working Party 3, meeting minutes, May 29, 1962, 15.

38. OECD Economic Policy Committee, Working Party 3, meeting minutes, October 26, 1961, 16.

39. OECD Economic Policy Committee, Working Party 3, meeting minutes, April 17, 1962, 18.

40. OECD Economic Policy Committee, Working Party 3, meeting minutes, July 18, 1962, 18.

41. Calleo, *The Imperious Economy.*

42. OECD Economic Policy Committee, Working Party 3, meeting minutes, February 27, 1963.

43. OECD Economic Policy Committee, Working Party 3, meeting minutes, April 29, 1963, 5.

44. Heller to JFK, May 5, 1962, "Gold and Domestic Policy." POF, Box 74, "Council of Economic Advisers, 5/1/62–5/5/62," John F. Kennedy Presidential Library (emphasis added).

45. OECD Economic Policy Committee, Working Party 3, meeting minutes, February 27, 1963, 7.

46. Ibid., 12.

47. Ibid., 18.

48. Federal Reserve Bank, Federal Open Market Committee, meeting minute, January 3, 1963, New York, 8–12.

49. Calculated from Bank for International Settlements, *Annual Report*, various years.

50. Bordo, Humpage, and Schwartz, "Bretton Woods, Swap Lines."

51. OECD, Economic Policy Committee, Working Party 3, meeting minutes, December 17, 1963, 7.

52. Federal Reserve Bank, Federal Open Market Committee, meeting minutes, June 19, 1962, New York, 10.

53. Federal Reserve Bank, Federal Open Market Committee, meeting minutes, October 2, 1962, New York, 4.

54. Ibid., 10.

55. Ibid., 31.

56. Federal Reserve Bank, Federal Open Market Committee, meeting minutes, December 18, 1962, New York, 24.

57. Ibid., 52–53.

58. Federal Reserve Bank, Federal Open Market Committee, meeting minutes, March 5, 1963, New York, 43.

59. Federal Reserve Bank, Federal Open Market Committee, meeting minutes, May 7, 1963, New York, 22.

60. Federal Reserve Bank, Federal Open Market Committee, meeting minutes, June 18, 1963, New York, 20.

61. Ibid., 24.

62. Federal Reserve Bank, Federal Open Market Committee, meeting minutes, July 9, 1963, New York, 16.

63. It is also worth noting that committee member Ellis also made this trip to the Bank for International Settlements and reported his impressions to the committee. While starting by saying that he "concurred in many respects with Mr. Robertson's summarization," he then went on to undercut Robertson's entire statement by noting that he felt the Europeans were calling for higher, not lower, interest rates.

64. Federal Reserve Bank, Federal Open Market Committee, meeting minutes, July 9, 1963, New York, 77.

65. MacEwan, *Debt and Disorder*, 37.

66. Strange, "The World's Money," 16.

Chapter 7

1. U.S. Department of Commerce Bureau of Economic Analysis, Table 1.1.1, Percent Change from Preceding Period in Real Gross Domestic Product. Downloaded on December 20, 2006, from www.bea.gov.

2. LBJ to Douglas Dillon, June 16, 1965, NSF Agency File, "Treasury, Department of, vol. 1, 1963–1965," Lyndon Johnson Presidential Library.

3. Krippner, *Capitalizing on Crisis*; and Minsky, *Stabilizing an Unstable Economy*.

4. Heller to LBJ, July 25, 1964, WHCF BE, Box 23, "BE 5 6/12/64–10/31/64," Lyndon Johnson Presidential Library.

5. Dillon, Gordon, and Ackley to LBJ, March 31, 1965, WHCF, Box 23, "BE 5 1/30/65—6/19/65," Lyndon Johnson Presidential Library.

6. Bank for International Settlements, *35th Annual Report*. June 14, 1965, Basel, 5.

7. OECD, Economic Policy Committee, "Economic Prospects for 1965." February 1, 1965, CPE(65)3, 45.

8. OECD, Economic Policy Committee, Working Party 3, meeting minutes, February 15-16, 1965, 11-13.

9. Ackley to LBJ, July 13, 1965, WHCF, Box 17, "IT 59 Organization for Economic Cooperation and Development"; and Eckstein to LBJ, November 1, 1965, WHCF Box 23, "BE 5 National Economy 9/1/65-11/29/65," Lyndon Johnson Presidential Library.

10. Minsky, *Stabilizing an Unstable Economy*; and Krippner, *Capitalizing on Crisis*. See also Wolfson, *Financial Crises*.

11. Board of Governors of the Federal Reserve System, *Banking and Monetary Statistics 1941–1970*, Section 12: Money Rates and Security Markets, Table 12.5 Short-Term Open Market Rates in New York City.

12. For purposes of international comparison, price data comes from OECDstat, Main Economic Indicators. Downloaded on October 10, 2013, from stats.oecd.org.

13. Ackley to LBJ, December 13, 1966, WHCF, FI Box 60, "FI 11-4 10/11/66–12/15/66," Lyndon Johnson Presidential Library.

14. Federal Reserve Bank, Federal Open Market Committee, meeting minutes, April 12, 1966, 33–34.

15. Federal Reserve Bank, Federal Open Market Committee, meeting minutes, June 28, 1966, 17–19.

16. Federal Reserve Bank, Federal Open Market Committee, meeting minutes, September 13, 1966, 20 and 34.

17. Martin to LBJ, December 13, 1966, WHCF, FI Box 60, "FI 11-4 10/11/66–12/15/66," Lyndon Johnson Presidential Library.

18. OECD, Economic Policy Committee, February 23, 1966, CPE(66)1, 73. See also Ackley to LBJ, March 22, 1966, WHCF, IT Box 17, "IT 59 Organization for Economic Cooperation and Development," Lyndon Johnson Presidential Library.

19. OECD, Economic Policy Committee, Working Party 3, meeting minutes, March 4-5, 1966, 13.

20. Ibid., 13.

21. Bank for International Settlements, *36th Annual Report*. June 13, 1966, Basel, 6.

22. Duesenberry, "Report on OECD Meeting," in memo from Ackley to LBJ, July 15, 1966, WHCF, IT Box 17, "IT 59 Organization for Economic Cooperation and Development," Lyndon Johnson Presidential Library (emphasis in original).

23. OECD, Economic Policy Committee, Working Party 3, meeting minutes, July 7-8, 1966, 17.

24. Ibid., 23 and 28.

25. Bank for International Settlements, *37th Annual Report*. June 12, 1967, Basel, 7-8.

26. Ackley to LBJ, November 26, 1966, WHCF, IT Box 17, "IT 59 Organization for Economic Cooperation and Development," Lyndon Johnson Presidential Library.

27. Barr, Schultz, and Ackley to LBJ, December 14, 1966, WHCF, BE Box 25, "BE 5 12/1/66–12/15/66," Lyndon Johnson Presidential Library.

28. President Lyndon B. Johnson's Annual Message to the Congress on the State of the Union, January 10, 1967.

29. Ackley to LBJ, March 29, 1967, WHCF, BE Box 25, "WE 6 12/1/66–7/31/67," Lyndon Johnson Presidential Library.

30. Cohen to LBJ, July 14, 1967, WHCF, LE Box 164, "LE/WE 6 11/22/63–8/31/67," Lyndon Johnson Presidential Library.

31. This brief summary was adapted from a very useful paper on balance of payments accounting by Pippenger, "Balance-of-Payments-Deficits."

32. This gap became the subject of balance of payments discussions at the meetings of the Federal Open Market Committee in 1966 (Federal Reserve Bank, Federal Open Market Committee, meeting minutes, September 13, 1966, 22–23).

33. Federal Reserve Board, Federal Open Market Committee, meeting minutes, November 1, 1966, 5.

34. Burn, *The Re-Emergence of Global Finance*; and Versluysen, *The Political Economy of International Finance*.

35. Bordo, Humpage, and Schwartz, "Bretton Woods, Swap Lines," 16.

36. OECD, Economic Policy Committee, Working Party 3, meeting minutes, July 6–7, 1965, 3.

37. Federal Reserve, Federal Open Market Committee, meeting minutes, September 13, 1966, 23.

38. Ackley to LBJ, May 26, 1967, WHCF, FI Box 51, "FI 8 10/23/66–8/8/67," Lyndon Johnson Presidential Library.

39. Ackley to LBJ, July 1, 1967, WHCF, FI Box 2, "FI Finance 1/25/67–7/15/67," Lyndon Johnson Presidential Library.

40. Memo, Henry Fowler to LBJ, July 19, 1967, WHCF FI Box 2, FI Finance 7/16/67–, Lyndon Johnson Presidential Library.

41. Memo, Walter Heller to LBJ, July 11, 1967, WHCF FI Box 2, FI Finance 1/25/67–7/15/67, Lyndon Johnson Presidential Library.

42. Block, *The Origins of International Economic Disorder*, 145.

43. Collins, "The Economic Crisis of 1968."

44. Cohen to LBJ, October 17, 1967, WHCF, LE Box 164, "LE/WE 6 9/1/67"; and Cohen to LBJ, October 17, 1967, WHCF, WE Box 15, "WE 6 8/1/67–12/31/67," Lyndon Johnson Presidential Library.

45. Cohen to LBJ, November 2, 1967, and Cohen to LBJ, December 3, 1967, WHCF, LE Box 164, "LE/WE 6 9/1/67," Lyndon Johnson Presidential Library.

46. Draft Report to the President, Fowler to LBJ, December 18, 1967, National Security File, Subject File, Box 3, "Balance of Payments Vol. 4, January 1967 [2 of 2]," Lyndon Johnson Presidential Library.

47. Read to Rostow, February 23, 1968, National Security File, Subject File, Box 3, "Balance of Payments, Vol. 5 [2 of 2]," Lyndon Johnson Presidential Library.

48. Rostow to LBJ, March 12, 1968, National Security File, Subject File, Box 3, "Balance of Payments, Vol. 5 [1 of 2]," Lyndon Johnson Presidential Library.

49. Fowler to LBJ, March 16, 1968, National Security File, Agency File, Box 65, "Treasury, Department of 4/67–1/69 Vol. 3 [1 of 2]," Lyndon Johnson Presidential Library.

50. Collins, "The Economic Crisis of 1968."

51. Okun to LBJ, May 21, 1968, WHCF, FI Box 2, "FI Finance 7/16/67," Lyndon Johnson Presidential Library.

52. Johnson, "Address to the Nation."

53. Moynihan, *Maximum Feasible Misunderstanding*, 193.

Chapter 8

1. Katzenstein, *Policy and Politics in West Germany*, 90–92.

2. Blyth, *Austerity*.

3. Baker, *The Group of Seven*; Chwieroth, *Capital Ideas*; and Abdelal, *Capital Rules*.

4. Heclo, *Modern Social Politics in Britain and Sweden*.

5. Baker, *The Group of Seven*, ch. 4; and Borio and Toniolo, "One Hundred and Thirty Years."

6. Chorev, "Institutional Project of Neo-Liberal Globalism."

7. Evans, "Fighting Marginalization."

8. Laeven and Valencia, "Systemic Banking Crises," table 3.

9. Helleiner, *States and the Re-Emergence of Global Finance*; and Wolfson, *Financial Crises*.

10. Eichengreen, *Toward a New International Financial Architecture*; and Kenen, *The International Financial Architecture*.

11. Eichengreen, *Globalizing Capital*, ch. 5.

12. Ibid., 138.

13. Baker, *The Group of Seven*.

14. Borio and Toniolo, "One Hundred and Thirty Years," 54.

15. Singleton, *Central Banking in the Twentieth Century*, ch. 11.

16. Bernanke and Mishkin, "Inflation Targeting"; and Mishkin, "From Monetary Targeting to Inflation Targeting."

17. Polillo and Guillén, "Globalization Pressures and the State"; Hall, *Central Banking as Global Governance*; and Maxfield, *Gatekeepers of Growth*.

18. Mahadeva and Sterne, *Monetary Policy Frameworks*; and Bank for International Settlements, "Issues in the Governance of Central Banks." Report from the Central Bank Governance Group (May 18, 2009), 21.

19. See, for example, Board of Governors of the Federal Reserve System, Press Release, May 1, 2013; available at www.federalreserve.gov/newsevents/press/monetary/20130501a.htm.

20. Polillo and Guillén, "Globalization Pressures and the State." For quantitative measures of central bank independence, see Arnone, Laurens, and Segalotto, "Measures of Central Bank Autonomy."

21. Bernanke and Mishkin, "Inflation Targeting."

22. Goodman, *Monetary Sovereignty*.

23. Singleton, *Central Banking in the Twentieth Century*, 197.

24. For a good review of the domestic political economy of monetary institutions, see Bernhard, Broz, and Clark, "The Political Economy of Monetary Institutions."

25. Toniolo, *Central Bank Cooperation*, 438.

26. Kapstein, *Governing the Global Economy*, ch. 5.

27. Alexander, Dhumale, and Eatwell, *The Global Governance of Financial Systems*; and Tarullo, *Banking on Basel*.

28. The details of the Basel Accord can be found in Basel Committee, *International Convergence of Capital Measurements*.

29. Kapstein, *Governing the Global Economy*, ch. 5.

30. Germain, *The International Organization of Credit*, 146.

31. Porter, *States, Markets and Regimes*, 62.

32. Basel Committee, *International Convergence of Capital Measurement*; and Tarullo, *Banking on Basel*.

33. Cartapanis and Herland, "The Reconstruction of the International Financial Architecture"; and Widmaier, "Constructing Monetary Crises."

34. Basel Committee, "Basel III," 1.

35. Laeven and Valencia, "Systemic Banking Crises."

36. Helleiner, *States and the Reemergence of Global Finance*, 171–172, 183–184, 188; Glyn, *Capitalism Unleashed*, 81; and Borio and Toniolo, "One Hundred and Thirty Years," 60.

37. The European Stability Mechanism (ESM) was preceded by the temporary European Financial Stability Facility (EFSF), which was established in May of 2010. Both the EFSF and the ESM operated concurrently through the middle of 2013, at which point any remaining financial obligations held by the EFSF were taken over by the ESM. For purposes of simplicity and clarity, I refer only to the ESM in this chapter, even though some of the operations being discussed were technically those of the EFSF.

38. Information on the activities of the ESM can be found at www.esm.europa.eu/index.htm and www.efsf.europa.eu/about/index.htm.

39. See www.federalreserve.gov/newsevents/press/monetary/20121213a.htm.

40. Underhill, "Keeping Governments Out of Politics."

41. Tsingou, "Regulatory Reactions to the Global Credit Crisis."

42. Cartapanis and Herland, "The Reconstruction of the International Financial Architecture"; and Bibow, "Keynes on Central Banking."

43. Bini Smaghi, "Lessons of the Crisis: Ethics, Markets, Democracy," May 13, 2010. Unione Cristina Imprenditori Dirigenti, Milan. Available at www.ecb.europa .eu/press/key/date/2010/html/sp100513.en.html.

44. Carruthers, Babb and Halliday, "Institutionalizing Markets"; and Maman and Rosenhek, "The Contested Institutionalization of Policy Paradigm Shifts."

45. Porter, "Risk Models and Transnational Governance."

46. Keynes, *The General Theory*, 376.

Bibliography

Abdelal, Rawi. *Capital Rules: The Construction of Global Finance*. Cambridge, MA: Harvard University Press, 2007.

Akard, Patrick. "The Return of the Market? Reflections on the Real 'Conservative Tradition' in U.S. Policy Discourse." *Sociological Inquiry*, 65, no. 3–4 (1995): 286–308.

———. "Corporate Mobilization and Political Power." *American Sociological Review* 57, no. 5 (1992): 597–615.

Alexander, Kern, Rahul Dhumale, and John Eatwell (2006). *The Global Governance of Financial Systems*. New York: Oxford University Press, 2006.

Allen, Kevin and Andrew Stevenson. *An Introduction to the Italian Economy*. London: Martin & Robinson Company, 1974.

Andrews, David. *International Monetary Power*. Ithaca, NY: Cornell University Press, 2006.

Armstrong, Philip, Andrew Glyn, and John Harrison. *Capitalism since 1945*. London: Basil Blackwell, 1991.

Arnone, Marco, Bernard J. Laurens, and Jean-François Segalotto. "Measures of Central Bank Autonomy: Empirical Evidence for OECD, Developing, and Emerging Market Economies." IMF Working Paper #WP/06/228 (October, 2006): 1–38.

Baker, Andrew. *The Group of Seven: Finance Ministers, Central Banks and Global Financial Governance*. New York: Routledge, 2006.

Aubrey, Henry G. *Atlantic Economic Cooperation: The Case of the OECD*. New York: Frederick A. Praeger, 1967.

Babb, Sarah. "Embeddedness, Inflation and International Regimes." *American Journal of Sociology* 113, no. 1 (2007): 128–164.

Balogh, Thomas. "Postwar Britain and the Common Market." *New Left Review* I/16 (July–August, 1962), 21–30.

———. "Productive Investment and the Balance of Payments: The British Case." *The Review of Economics and Statistics* 39, no. 1 (1957): 84–88.

Barkan, Joanne. *Visions of Emancipation: The Italian Workers' Movement since 1945.* New York: Praeger, 1984.

Barnett, Michael, and Martha Finnemore. *Rules for the World: International Organizations in Global Politics.* Ithaca, NY: Cornell University Press, 2004.

Barro, Robert J., and Jong-Wha Lee. "IMF Programs: Who Are Chosen and What Are the Effects?" *Journal of Monetary Economics* 52, no. 7 (2005): 1245–1269.

Basel Committee on Banking Supervision. "Basel III: International Framework for Liquidity Risk Measurement, Standards and Monitoring" (December, 2012). Basel, Switzerland: Bank for International Settlements.

———. "International Convergence of Capital Measurement and Capital Standards: a Revised Framework" (June, 2006). Basel, Switzerland: Bank for International Settlements.

Beckfield, Jason. "The Dual World Polity: Fragmentation and Integration in the Network of Intergovernmental Organizations." *Social Problems* 55, no. 3 (2008): 419–442.

Berman, Sheri. *The Social Democratic Moment: Ideas and Politics in the Making of Interwar Europe.* Cambridge, MA: Harvard University Press, 1998.

Bernanke, Ben, and Frederic Mishkin. "Inflation Targeting: A New Framework for Monetary Policy?" *Journal of Economic Perspectives* 11, no. 2 (Spring, 1997): 97–116.

Bernhard, William, J. Lawrence Broz, and William R. Clark. "The Political Economy of Monetary Institutions." *International Organization* 56, no. 4 (Autumn, 2002): 693–723.

Best, Jacqueline. "Hollowing Out the Keynesian Norms: How the Search for a Technical Fix Undermined the Bretton Woods Regime." *Review of International Studies* 30, no. 3 (2004): 383–404.

Bibow, Jorg. "Keynes on Central Banking and the Structure of Monetary Policy." *History of Political Economy* 34, no. 4 (2002): 749–787.

Bini, Piero, and Antonio Magliulo, "Keynesianism in Italy: Before and after the *General Theory.*" In *The Impact of Keynes on Economics in the Twentieth Century,* edited by Luigi Pasinetti and Bertram Schefold, 131–152. Northampton, MA: Edward Elgar, 1999.

Block, Fred. *The Origins of International Economic Disorder.* Berkeley: University of California Press, 1977.

Bloomfield, Arthur. *Monetary Policy under the International Gold Standard, 1880–1914.* New York: Federal Reserve Bank of New York, 1959.

Blyth, Mark. *Austerity: The History of a Dangerous Idea.* New York: Oxford University Press, 2013.

———. "Structures Do Not Come with an Instruction Sheet." *Perspectives on Politics* 1, no. 4 (2003): 697–706.

———. *Great Transformations: Economic Ideas and Institutional Change in the Twentieth Century.* New York: Cambridge University Press, 2002.

Boli, John, and George Thomas. "World Culture in the World Polity." *American Sociological Review* 62, no. 2 (1997): 171–190.

Bordo, Michael, Owen Humpage, and Anna Schwartz, "Bretton Woods, Swap Lines and the Federal Reserve's Return to Intervention." Federal Reserve Bank of Cleveland, Working Paper #12-32 (2012): 1–35.

Bordo, Michael D., and Hugh Rockoff. "The Gold Standard as 'Good Housekeeping Seal of Approval.'" *Journal of Economic History* 56, no. 2 (1996): 389–428.

Borio, Claudio, and Gianni Toniolo, "One Hundred and Thirty Years of Central Bank Cooperation: A BIS perspective." In *Past and Future of Central Bank Cooperation*, edited by Claudio Borio, Gianni Toniolo, and Piet Clement, 16–57. New York: Cambridge University Press, 2008.

Bourdieu, Pierre. "The Essence of Neoliberalism." *Le Monde Diplomatique*, (December, 1998). Available at http://mondediplo.com/1998/12/08bourdieu.

Brady, David, Martin Seleib-Kaiser, and Jason Beckfield. "Economic Globalization and the Welfare State in Affluent Democracies, 1975–2001." *American Sociological Review* 70, no. 6 (2005): 921–948.

Brenner, Robert. "The Economics of Global Turbulence." *New Left Review* 229 (1998): 1–265.

Burn, Gary. *The Re-Emergence of Global Finance.* New York: Palgrave-MacMillan, 2006.

Buyst, Erik, Ivo Maes, Walter Pluym, and Marianne Danneel. *The Bank, the Franc and the Euro: A History of the National Bank of Belgium.* Tielt, Belgium: Lannoo Publishers, 2005.

Cairncross, Alec. "The Bank of England: Relationships with the Government, the Civil Service, and Parliament." In *Central Banks' Independence in Historical Perspective*, edited by Gianni Toniolo, 39–72. New York: Walter de Gruyter, 1988.

Cairncross, Alec, and Barry Eichengreen. *Sterling in Decline.* Oxford, UK: Basil Blackwell, 1983.

Calleo, David. "American Domestic Priorities and the Demands of Alliance." *Political Science Quarterly* 98, no. 1 (1983): 1–15.

———. *The Imperious Economy.* Cambridge, MA: Harvard University Press, 1982.

Cameron, David R. "The Expansion of the Public Economy: A Comparative Analysis." *The American Political Science Review* 72, no. 4 (1978): 1243–1261.

Carruthers, Bruce, Sarah Babb, and Terence Halliday. "Institutionalizing Markets, or the Market for Institutions." In *The Rise of Neoliberalism and Institutional Analysis*, edited by John Campbell and Ove Pedersen, 94–126. Princeton, NJ: Princeton University Press, 2001.

Cartapanis, André, and Michel Herland. "The Reconstruction of the International Financial Architecture." *Review of International Political Economy* 9, no. 2 (2002): 271–297.

Chorev, Nitsan. "The Institutional Project of Neo-Liberal Globalism: The Case of the WTO." *Theory and Society*, 34, no. 3 (2005): 317–355.

Chorev, Nitsan, and Sarah Babb. "The Crisis of Neoliberalism and the Future of International Institutions: A Comparison of the IMF and the WTO." *Theory and Society* 38, no. 2 (2009): 459–484.

Chwieroth, Jeffrey. *Capital Ideas: The IMF and the Rise of Financial Liberalization.* Princeton, NJ: Princeton University Press.

Clift, Ben, and Jim Tomlinson. "When Rules Started to Rule: The IMF, Neo-Liberal Economic Ideas, and Economic Policy Change in Britain." *Review of International Political Economy* 19, no. 3 (2012): 477–500.

Coats, A. W. *The Post-1945 Internationalization of Economics.* Durham, NC: Duke University Press, 1997.

Coen, Robert. "Effects of Tax Policy on Investment in Manufacturing." *The American Economic Review* 58, no. 2 (1968): 200–211.

Cohen, Joseph N., and Miguel A. Centenno. "Neoliberalism and Patterns of Economic Performance, 1980–2000." *Annals of the American Academy of Political and Social Sciences* 606 (2006): 32–67.

Collins, Robert M. *More: the Politics of Economic Growth in Postwar America.* New York: Oxford University Press, 2000.

———. "The Economic Crisis of 1968 and the Waning of the 'American Century.'" *American Historical Review* 101, no. 2 (1996): 396–422.

———. *The Business Response to Keynes, 1929–1964.* New York: Columbia University Press, 1982.

Cooper, Richard N. "Almost a Century of Central Bank Cooperation." In *Past and Future of Central Bank Cooperation*, edited by Claudio Borio, Gianni Toniolo, and Piet Clement, 76–112. New York: Cambridge University Press, 2008.

Cox, Robert, and Harold Jacobson. *Approaches to World Order.* New York: Cambridge University Press, 1996.

Crotty, James. "On Keynes and Capital Flight." *Journal of Economic Literature* 21 no. 1 (1983): 59–65.

de Cecco, Marcello. "Keynes and Italian Economics." In *The Political Power of Economic Ideas*, edited by Peter A. Hall, 195_230. Princeton, NJ: Princeton University Press.

———. "The Origins of the Post-War Payments System." *Cambridge Journal of Economics* 3 (1979): 49–61.

Dobbin, Frank, Beth Simmons, and Geoffrey Garrett. "The Global Diffusion of Public Policies: Social Construction, Coercion, Competition, or Learning?" *Annual Review of Sociology* 33 (2007): 449–472.

Duménil, Gérard, and Dominique Lévy. *Capital Resurgent: the Roots of the Neoliberal Revolution.* Cambridge, MA: Harvard University Press, 2004.

Edelman, Murray, and R. W. Fleming. *The Politics of Wage-Price Decisions: A Four Country Analysis.* Urbana: University of Illinois Press, 1965.

Eichengreen, Barry. *Exorbitant Privilege: The Rise and Fall of the Dollar and the Future of the International Monetary System*. New York: Oxford University Press, 2011.

———. *Globalizing Capital: A History of the International Monetary System*. Princeton, NJ: Princeton University Press, 2008.

———. *The European Economy since 1945*. Princeton, NJ: Princeton University Press, 2007.

———. *Toward a New International Financial Architecture*. Washington, DC: Institute for International Economics, 1999.

———. *Golden Fetters: The Gold Standard and the Great Depression, 1919–1939*. New York: Oxford University Press, 1995.

Epstein, Gerald. "Monetary Policy, Loan Liquidation, and Industrial Conflict." *Journal of Economic History* 44, no. 4 (1984): 957–983.

Epstein, Gerald, and Arjun Jayadev. "The Rise of Rentier Incomes in OECD Countries: Financialization, Central Bank Policy and Labor Solidarity." In *Financialization and the World Economy*, edited by Gerald Epstein, 46–74. Northampton, MA: Edward Elgar Press, 2005.

Evans, Peter. "Fighting Marginalization with Transnational Networks." *Contemporary Sociology* 29, no. 1 (2000): 230–241.

Favretto, Ilaria. *The Long Search for a Third Way: The British Labour Party and the Italian Left since 1945*. New York: Palgrave MacMillan, 2003.

Ferguson, Thomas and Joel Rogers. *Right Turn: The Decline of the Democrats and the Future of American Politics*. New York: Hill & Wang, 1987.

Flandreau, Marc. "Central Bank Cooperation in Historical Perspective." *Economic History Review* 50, no. 4 (1997): 735–763.

Foster, John, and Harry Magdoff. *The Great Financial Crisis: Causes and Consequences*. New York: Monthly Review Press, 2009.

Fourcade, Marion. *Economists and Societies: Discipline and Profession in the United States, Britain and France*. Princeton, NJ: Princeton University Press, 2009.

Fourcade-Gourinchas, Marion, and Sarah Babb. "Rebirth of the Liberal Creed: Paths to Neoliberalism in Four Countries." *American Journal of Sociology* 108, no. 3 (2002): 533–579.

Fraser, Steve, and Gary Gerstle. *The Rise and Fall of the New Deal Order, 1930–1980*. Princeton, NJ: Princeton University Press, 1990.

Franzosi, Roberto. "Strike Data in Search of a Theory: The Italian Case in the Postwar Period." *Politics and Society* 17, no. 4 (1989): 453–483

Frieden, Jeffrey. "Sectoral Conflict and U.S. Foreign Economic Policy." *International Organization* 42, no. 1 (1988): 59–90.

———. *Banking on the World: The Politics of American International Finance*. New York: Harper & Row, 1987.

Gallarotti, Guilio. *The Anatomy of an International Regime: the Classical Gold Standard, 1880–1914*. New York: Oxford University Press, 1995.

Garritsen de Vries, Margaret. *Balance of Payments Adjustment, 1945–1986*. Washington, DC: International Monetary Fund, 1987.

Germain, Randall. *The International Organization of Credit: States and Global Finance in the World-Economy.* New York: Cambridge University Press, 1997.

Glyn, Andrew. *Capitalism Unleashed: Finance, Globalization and Welfare.* New York: Oxford University Press, 2006.

Goldstein, Judith, and Robert Koehane. *Ideas and Foreign Policy: Beliefs, Institutions and Political Change.* Ithaca, NY: Cornell University Press, 1993.

Goodhart, Charles. *The Evolution of Central Banks.* Cambridge, MA: MIT Press, 1988.

Goodman, John B. *Monetary Sovereignty: The Politics of Central Banking in Western Europe.* Ithaca, NY: Cornell University Press, 1992.

Gourevitch, Peter, Andrew Martin, George Ross, Stephen Bornstein, Andrei Markovits, and Christopher Allen. *Unions and Economic Crisis: Britain West Germany and Sweden.* London: George Allen & Unwin, 1984.

Gowan, Peter. *The Global Gamble: Washington's Faustian Bid for Global Dominance.* London: Verso Press, 2003.

Greene, Thomas H. "The Communist Parties of Italy and France: A Study of Comparative Communism." *World Politics* 21, no. 1 (1968): 1–38.

Greider, William. *Secrets of the Temple: How the Federal Reserve Runs the Country.* New York: Simon & Schuster, 1987.

Haas, Peter. "Do Regimes Matter? Epistemic Communities and Mediterranean Pollution Control." *International Organization* 43, no. 3 (1992): 377–403.

Hall, Peter. *The Political Power of Economic Ideas: Keynesianism across Nations.* Princeton, NJ: Princeton University Press, 1989.

———. *Governing the Economy: The Politics of State Intervention in Britain and France.* New York: Oxford University Press, 1986.

Hall, Peter, and David Soskice, "An Introduction to Varieties of Capitalism." In *Varieties of Capitalism,* edited by Peter Hall and David Soskice, 1–68. New York: Oxford University Press, 2001.

Hall, Rodney Bruce. *Central Banking as Global Governance: Constructing Financial Credibility.* New York: Cambridge University Press, 2008.

Harvey, David. *A Brief History of Neoliberalism.* New York: Oxford University Press, 2005.

Hansen, Bent. *Fiscal Policy in Seven Countries.* OECD: Paris, 1969.

Heath, Jim. *John F. Kennedy and the Business Community.* Chicago: University of Chicago Press, 1969.

Heclo, Hugh. *Modern Social Politics in Britain and Sweden.* New Haven, CT: Yale University Press, 1976.

Helleiner, Eric. *States and the Reemergence of Global Finance: From Bretton Woods to the 1990s.* Ithaca, NY: Cornell University Press, 1994.

Heller, Walter. *New Dimensions of Political Economy.* Cambridge, MA: Harvard University Press, 1966.

Hellman, Stephen. "Italy." In *European Politics in Transition,* edited by Christopher Allen, Joan Debardeleban, Stephen Hellman, and Jonas Pontuson, 319–450. Lexington, MA: D. C. Heath and Company, 1987.

Henisz, Witold, Bennet A. Zelner, and Mauro F. Guillén. "The Worldwide Diffusion of Market-Oriented Infrastructure Reform, 1977–1999." *American Sociological Review* 70, no. 5 (2005): 871–897.

Hildebrand, George M. *Growth and Structure of the Modern Italian Economy.* Cambridge, MA: Harvard University Press, 1965.

Hobsbawm, Eric. "The Forward March of Labour Halted?" *Marxism Today* (September, 1978): 279–286.

Hodjera, Zoran. "Basic Balances, Short-Term Capital Flow, and International Reserves of Industrial Countries." *Staff Papers of the International Monetary Fund* 16, no. 3 (1969): 582–612.

Horsefield, J. Keith. "Derivation and Significance of the Fund's Resources." In *The International Monetary Fund 1945–1965, Volume II*, edited by Margaret de Vries Garritsen and J. Keith Horsefield, 349–380. Washington, DC: IMF, 1969.

H(st-Madsen, Poul. "Asymmetries between Balance of Payments Surpluses and Deficits." *Staff Papers of the International Monetary Fund* 9 (1999): 182–201.

Ikenberry, G. John. "A World Economy Restored: Expert Consensus and the Anglo-American Postwar Settlement." *International Organization* 46, no. 1 (1992): 289–321.

Jabko, Nicholas. *Playing the Market: A Political Strategy for Uniting Europe, 1985–2005.* Ithaca, NY: Cornell University Press, 2006.

Jepperson, Ronald, Alexander Wendt, and Peter Katzenstein. "Norms, Identity, and Culture in National Security," in *The Culture of National Security*, edited by Peter Katzenstein, 33–75. New York: Columbia University Press, 1996.

Johnson, Lyndon Baines. "Address to the Nation Announcing Steps to Limit the War in Vietnam and Reporting His Decision Not to Seek Reelection," March 31, 1968, *Public Papers of the Presidents of the United States: Lyndon B. Johnson, 1968–69*, volume I, entry 170, 469–476. Washington, DC: Government Printing Office, 1970.

Kapstein, Ethan. *Governing the Global Economy: International Finance and the State.* Cambridge, MA: Harvard University Press, 1994.

Katzenstein, Peter. *Policy and Politics in West Germany: The Growth of a Semi-Sovereign State.* Philadelphia: Temple University Press, 1989.

———. *Corporatism and Change: Austria, Switzerland and the Politics of Industry.* Ithaca, NY: Cornell University Press, 1984.

Kenen, Peter B. *The International Financial Architecture.* Washington, DC: Institute for International Economics, 2001.

Keynes, John Maynard. *The General Theory of Employment Interest and Money.* New York: Harcourt and Brace, 1936.

———. *The Collected Writings of John Maynard Keynes* 25. London: Cambridge University Press, 1980.

Kindleberger, Charles. "Dominance and Leadership in the International Economy: Exploitation, Public Goods, and Free Rides." *International Studies Quarterly* 25, no. 2 (1980): 242–254.

Kirshner, Jonathan. *Currency and Coercion: The Political Economy of International Monetary Power*. Princeton, NJ: Princeton University Press, 1995.

Krippner, Gretta. *Capitalizing on Crisis: The Political Origins of the Rise of Finance*. Cambridge, MA: Harvard University Press, 2011.

———. "The Making of US Monetary Policy: Central Bank Transparency and the Neoliberal Dilemma." *Theory and Society* 36, no. 6 (2007): 477–513.

———. "The Financialization of the American Economy." *Socio-Economic Review* 3, no. 2 (2005): 173–208.

Laeven, Luc, and Fabian Valencia. "Systemic Banking Crises." IMF Working Paper #WP/08/224 (September, 2008): 1–80.

Lange, Peter, George Ross, and Maurizio Vannicelli. *Unions, Change and Crisis: French and Italian Union Strategy and the Political Economy, 1945–1980*. Boston: George Allen & Unwin, 1982.

MacEwan, Arthur. *Debt and Disorder: International Economic Instability and U.S. Imperial Power*. New York: Monthly Review Press, 1993.

Madison, Angus. *Monitoring the World Economy, 1820–1992*. Paris: Organization for Economic Cooperation and Development, 1995.

Maes, Ivo. "The Spread of Keynesian Economics: A Comparison of the Belgian and Italian Experiences." National Bank of Belgium, Working Paper #113 (April, 2007): 1–27.

Mahadeva, Lavan, and Gabriel Sterne. *Monetary Policy Frameworks in a Global Context*. New York: Routledge, 2000.

Maman, Daniel, and Zeev Rosenhek. "The Contested Institutionalization of Policy Paradigm Shifts." *Socio-Economic Review* 7, no. 2 (2009): 217–244.

Manser, W. A. P. *Britain in Balance*. London: Longman Group, 1971.

Maraffi, Marco. "State/Economy Relationships: The Case of Italian Public Enterprise." *British Journal of Sociology* 31, no. 4 (1980): 507–524.

March, James G., and Johan P. Olson. "The Institutional Dynamics of International Political Orders." *International Organization* 52, no. 4 (1998): 943–969.

Martin, Cathie Jo. *Shifting the Burden: The Struggle over Growth and Corporate Taxation*. Chicago: University of Chicago Press, 1991.

Maxfield, Sylvia. *Gatekeepers of Growth: The International Political Economy of Central Banking in Developing Countries*. Princeton, NJ: Princeton University Press, 1997.

McGeehan, Joy M. "Competitiveness: a Survey of Recent Literature." *The Economic Journal* 78, no. 310 (1968): 243–262.

McNamara, Kathleen. *The Currency of Ideas: Monetary Politics in European Union*. Ithaca, NY: Cornell University Press, 1999.

McQuaid, Kim. *Uneasy Partners: Big Business in American Politics, 1945–1990*. Baltimore: Johns Hopkins University Press, 1994.

Meyer, John W., John Boli, George M. Thomas, and Francisco O. Ramirez. "World Society and the Nation-State." *American Journal of Sociology* 103, no. 1 (1997): 144–181.

Minkin, Lewis. "The British Labour Party and the Trade Unions." *Industrial and Labor Relations Review* 28, no. 1 (1974): 7–37.

Mini, Peter V. "Foreign Direct Investment in Italy, 1956–1963: Some Developmental Aspects." *American Journal of Economics and Sociology* 27, no. 1 (1968): 77–87.

Minsky, Hyman. *Stabilizing an Unstable Economy*. New Haven, CT: Yale University Press, 1986.

Mishkin, Frederic. "From Monetary Targeting to Inflation Targeting." World Bank Financial Sector Strategy and Policy Department, Policy Research Working Paper #2684 (2001): 1–42.

Mouré, Kenneth. "The Bank of France and the Gold Standard, 1914–1928." In *International Financial History in the Twentieth Century: System and Anarchy*, edited by Marc Flandreau, Carl-Ludwig Holtfrerich, and Harold James, 95–124. Cambridge, UK: Cambridge University Press, 2003.

Moynihan, Daniel Patrick. *Maximum Feasible Misunderstanding: Community Action in the War on Poverty*. New York: The Free Press, 1972.

Mudge, Stephanie Lee. "What's Left of Leftism? Neoliberal Politics in Western Party Systems." *Social Science History* 35, no. 3 (2011): 337–381.

———. "What Is Neo-Liberalism?" *Socio-Economic Review* 6, no. 4 (2008): 703–731.

Newton, Scott. "The Sterling Devaluation of 1967, the International Economy and Post-War Social Democracy." *English Historical Review* 75, no. 515 (2010): 912–945.

———. "The Two Sterling Crises of 1964 and the Decision Not to Devalue." *Economic History Review* 62, no. 1 (2009): 73–98.

Nicol, William, and Douglas Yuill. "Regional Problems and Policy." In *The European Economy: Growth and Crisis*, edited by Andrea Boltho, 409–445. New York: Oxford University Press, 1991.

Nicholls, A. J. *Freedom with Responsibility: The Social Market economy in Germany, 1918–1963*. Oxford, UK: Clarendon Press, 1994.

O'Riain, Sean. "States and Markets in an Era of Globalization." *Annual Review of Sociology* 26 (2000): 187–213.

Panitch, Leo, and Sam Gindin. *Global Capitalism and American Empire*. London: Merlin Press, 2004.

Parsons, Craig, Rawi Abdelal, and Mark Blyth. *Constructing the International Economy*. Ithaca, NY: Cornell University Press, 2010.

Pasinetti, Luigi, and Bertram Schefold. *The Impact of Keynes on Economics in the 20th Century*. Northhampton, MA: Edward Elgar, 1999.

Pechman, Joseph A. "The Individual Income Tax Provisions of the Revenue Act of 1964." *The Journal of Finance* 20, no. 2 (1965): 246–272.

Pemberton, Hugh. "Taxation and Labour's Modernization Programme." *Contemporary British History* 20, no. 3 (2006): 423–440.

Pippenger, John. "Balance-of-Payments-Deficits: Measurement and Interpretation." Federal Reserve Bank of St. Louis (November, 1973), 6–14.

Podbielski, Gisele. *Italy: Development and Crisis in the Postwar Economy*. New York: Oxford University Press, 1974.

Polanyi, Karl. *The Great Transformation: The Political and Economic Origins of Our Time*. Boston: Beacon Press, 1957.

Polanyi-Levitt, Kari. "Keynes and Polanyi: the 1920s and the 1990s." *Review of International Political Economy* 13, no. 1 (2006): 152-177.

Polillo, Simone, and Mauro F. Guillén, "Globalization Pressures and the State." *American Journal of Sociology* 110, no. 6 (2005): 1764-1802.

Pollin, Robert. *Contours of Descent: U.S. Economic Fractures and the Landscape of Global Austerity*. London: Verso, 203.

Porter, Tony. "Risk Models and Transnational Governance in the Global Financial Crisis." In *Global Finance in Crisis*, edited by Eric Helleiner, Stefano Pagliari, and Hubert Zimmerman, 56-73. New York: Routledge, 2010.

———. *States, Markets and Regimes in Global Finance*. New York: St. Martin's Press, 1993.

Prasad, Monica. *The Politics of Free Markets: The Rise of Neoliberal Economic Policies in Britain, France, Germany and the United States*. Chicago: University of Chicago Press, 2006.

Przeworski, Adam. *Capitalism and Social Democracy*. New York: Cambridge University Press, 1985.

Przeworski, Adam, and James Vreeland. "The Effect of IMF Programs on Economic Growth." *Journal of Development Economics* 62 (2000): 385-421.

Rey, Guido. "Italy." In *The European Economy: Growth and Crisis*, edited by Andrea Bothlo, 502-527. New York: Oxford University Press, 1991.

Rowan, Hobart. *The Free Enterprisers: Kennedy, Johnson and the Business Establishment*. New York: G. P. Putnam and Sons, 1964.

Ruggie, John G. "International Regimes, Transactions and Change." *International Organization* 36, no. 2 (1982): 379-415.

Russell, Judith. *Economics, Bureaucracy and Race: How Keynesianism Misguided the War on Poverty*. New York: Columbia University Press, 2004.

Russell, Robert W. "Transgovernmental Interaction in the International Monetary System, 1960-1972." *International Organization* 27, no. 4 (1973): 431-464.

Salant, Walter S. "The Spread of Keynesian Doctrines and Practices in the United States." In *The Political Power of Economic Ideas*, edited by Peter Hall, 27-52. Princeton, NJ: Princeton University Press, 1989.

Sayers, R.S. *Banking in Western Europe*. Oxford: Clarendon Press, 1962.

Schmidt, Vivien. "Discursive Institutionalism: the Explanatory Power of Ideas and Discourse." *Annual Review of Political Science* 11 (2008): 208-236.

Shonfield, Andrew. *Modern Capitalism: The Changing Balance of Public and Private Power*. New York: Oxford University Press, 1965.

Simmons, Beth A., Frank Dobbin, and Geoffrey Garrett. "The Diffusion of Liberalism." *International Organization* 60, no. 4 (2006): 781-810.

Simmons, Beth A., and Jeremy Elkins. "The Globalization of Liberalization: Policy Diffusion in the International Political Economy." *American Political Science Review* 98, no. 1 (2004): 171-189.

Singleton, John. *Central Banking in the Twentieth Century.* New York: Cambridge University Press, 2011.

Solow, Robert M. "The Kennedy Council in the Long Run." In *Economic Events, Ideas and Policies,* edited by George L. Perry and James Tobin, 111–135. Washington DC: Brookings Institution, 2000.

Spitzer, Emil G. "Stand-By Arrangements." In *The International Monetary Fund* (vol. 2), edited by Margaret Garritsen de Vries and J. Keith Horsefield, 468–491. Washington, DC: International Monetary Fund, 1976.

Strange, Susan. *The Retreat of the State: The Diffusion of Power in the World Economy.* New York: Cambridge University Press, 1996.

———. "The World's Money: Expanding the Agenda for Research." *International Journal* 36 (1981): 691–712.

Sundquist, James. *Politics and Policy: The Eisenhower, Kennedy and Johnson Years.* Washington, DC: The Brookings Institution, 1968.

Surrey, Michael. "United Kingdom." In *The European Economy: Growth & Crisis,* edited by Andrea Boltho, 528–553. New York: Oxford University Press, 1991.

Tagliacarne, Guiglilmo. "Income, Investment and Consumption." In *Review of the Economic Conditions of Italy: Ten Years of Italian Economy, 1947–1956.* Edited by Banco di Roma, 97–116. Banco di Roma: Rome, 1956.

Tarullo, Daniel K. *Banking on Basel: The Future of International Financial Regulation.* Washington, DC: Peterson Institute for International Economics, 2008.

Tobin, James. "The Future of the Fed." *Challenge* 9, no. 4 (1961): 24–28.

Tomlinson, Jim. *The Labour Governments 1964–1970, Volume 3.* Manchester, UK: Manchester University Press, 2004.

Toniolo, Gianni. *Central Bank Cooperation at the Bank for International Settlements, 1930–1973.* New York: Cambridge University Press, 2005.

Tsingou, Eleni. "Regulatory Reactions to the Global Credit Crisis." In *Global Finance in Crisis,* edited by Eric Helleiner, Stefano Pagliari, and Hubert Zimmerman, 21–36. New York: Routledge, 2010.

Underhill, Geoffrey. "Keeping Governments Out of Politics." *Review of International Studies* 21, no. 3 (1995): 251–278.

Verdier, Daniel. *Moving Money: Banking and Finance in the Industrialized World.* New York: Cambridge University Press, 2002.

Versluysen, Eugene. *The Political Economy of International Finance.* New York: St. Martin's Press, 1981.

Wacquant, Loic. *Punishing the Poor: The Neoliberal Government of Social Insecurity.* Durham, NC: Duke University Press, 2009.

Webber, Michael J., and David L. Rigby. *The Golden Age Illusion: Rethinking Postwar Capitalism.* New York: Guilford Press, 1996.

Weir, Margaret. "Ideas and Politics: the Acceptance of Keynesianism in Britain and the United States." In *The Political Power of Economic Ideas,* edited by Peter Hall, 53–86. Princeton, NJ: Princeton University Press, 1989.

Wendt, Alexander. *Social Theory of International Politics*. New York: Cambridge University Press, 1999.

Widmaier, Wesley. "Constructing Monetary Crises: New Keynesian Understandings and Monetary Cooperation in the 1990s." *Review of International Studies* 29, no. 1 (2003): 61–77.

Wilkins, Mara. "Conduits for Long-Term Foreign Investment in the Gold Standard Era." In *International Financial History in the Twentieth Century: System and Anarchy*, edited by Marc Flandreau, Carl-Ludwig Holtfrerich, and Harold James, 51–76. Cambridge, UK: Cambridge University Press, 2003.

Williamson, John. "The Strange History of the Washington Consensus." *Journal of Post Keynesian Economics* 27, no. 2 (2004): 195–206.

Willis, F. Roy. *Italy Chooses Europe*. New York: Oxford University Press, 1971.

Wilson, Harold. *The Labour Government, 1964–1970: A Personal Record*. London: Weidenfeld, 1971.

Wolfe, Richard. "From Reconstructing Europe to Constructing Globalization: The OECD in Historical Perspective." In *The OECD and Transnational Governance*, edited by Rianna Mahon and Stephen McBride, 25–42. Vancouver: University of British Columbia Press, 2008.

Wolfson, Martin. *Financial Crises: Understanding the Postwar U.S. Experience*. London: M. E. Sharpe, 1994.

Woodward, Richard. *The Organization for Economic Co-operation and Development (OECD)*. New York: Routledge, 2009.

Zamagni, Vera. *An Economic History of Italy, 1860–1990*. New York: Oxford University Press, 1993.

Index